P9-DJL-326

Tarrant Trains Gun Dogs

Tarrant Trains Gun Dogs

Humane Way to Get Top Results

Bill Tarrant

Photographs by Bill Tarrant with special credit to Foster Bailey, Butch Goodwin, Harry Schraeder, and Dee Tarrant

Stackpole Books

Published by
STACKPOLE BOOKS
5067 Ritter Road
Mechanicsburg, PA 17055

Printed in the United States of America

10 9 8 7 6

First Edition

Also by Bill Tarrant

Best Way to Train Your Gun Dog
Hey Pup, Fetch It Up!
Bill Tarrant's Gun Dog Book: A Treasury of Happy Tails

Library of Congress Cataloging-in-Publication Data

Tarrant, Bill.
Tarrant trains gun dogs : humane way to get top results / Bill Tarrant : photographs by Bill Tarrant.
p. cm.
Includes index.
ISBN 0-8117-1723-2
1. Hunting dogs. 2. Hunting dogs – Training. I. Title.
SF428.5.T382 1989
636.7′5 – dc19 88-26774
CIP

This book is dedicated to my friend
BILL BERLAT
and to all dogs who have been—in the name of training—shot, shocked, beat, stomped, cursed, kicked, and otherwise brutalized by man's inhumanity to life.

Contents

Introduction

IT'S A DOG'S world. But we forget this. If we ever granted it. For we're humans. Humans divorced from nature. And we take one of nature's inhabitants, the dog, take him out of his natural world and bring him into ours, and tell him to point or fetch or sit or heel. We don't ask the dog. We tell the dog. And we tell the dog in human terms.

For who thinks of the dog? More to the point, who *thinks* dog? I don't mean think human about dogs, but think as dogs about dogs.

Plus, who can read a dog? The dog is constantly telling us something, but are we tuned in? No. The dog is a foreign language. And how does an American function in a foreign country? A frustrated American! Know what he usually does when he loses control? He shouts. And the greater his frustration (for he can't make himself understood), the louder he shouts. Notice any similarity between this behavior and the way some of us train dogs?

Know why we can't read dogs? Because we view them as little humans in fur coats. We keep looking for human responses, not dog responses. Or worse, some of us don't think the dog has any thoughtful responses at all.

Think not? I'll give you an example. A dog in stress will resist you. But let's say you're training dumb, so you bear down. Finally the dog gives in. Know when? When he sighs. That's the way with all animal life. When you finally accept your fate, you sigh.

But how does a dog sigh? Like us? Hardly. But that's what we're looking for, isn't it? For the dog to throw up its arms and take a deep breath. But a dog sighs by relaxing his shoulders and upper leg muscles. If you're watching, you'll see it.

Yet, if you miss this, the dog also will tell you he's sighing by swallowing–taking a big gulp. For a dog to swallow is for a dog to sigh. A horse sighs by alternately wetting and smacking his lips. But beware. If the horse just smacks dry lips, he's mighty mad. He's not about to give in; he's about to take you on.

Now, dog or horse, when they've encountered stress on three straight occasions–and sighed–they're yours. That's the end of their resistance.

And, I'm quick to tell you, possibly the end of the animal's spirit. Seldom should a dog or horse be placed in such a training situation. *Ideally they should be positioned to self-train, or be trained by other animals, and they should always be brought along so anything bad that might happen to them will never be associated with a human being.*

Now, I don't mean an older dog should train a pup. This seldom works out–the pup learns the bad as well as the good. I mean dogs should be placed in controlled situations where they train each other–and don't know they're doing it.

The Litter-Box Check Cord

An example would be the litter-box check cord.

When pups open their eyes (by three weeks), outfit each with a trailing hank of ⅜- or ¼-inch nylon cord tied about their necks. This can be done so the rig won't slip by placing an overhand knot in the end of a twenty-four-inch cord, looping the cord about Pup's neck, then tying another overhand knot part way down the cord–leaving it open–through which you insert the knotted end and butt it tight to the second knot.

Now cinch it all up. The nylon collar should just be tight enough around Pup's neck so you can insert two fingers to their first knuckles between cord and fur.

Check the knot often. Pups grow fast.

Why the cord? Well, watch what happens. One of these little guys rises and ambles off. His trailing cord serpentines about the nest. Another pup sees the moving cord. He slaps it with a paw. But the cord slips away. He grabs it in his toothless mouth. The cord keeps moving.

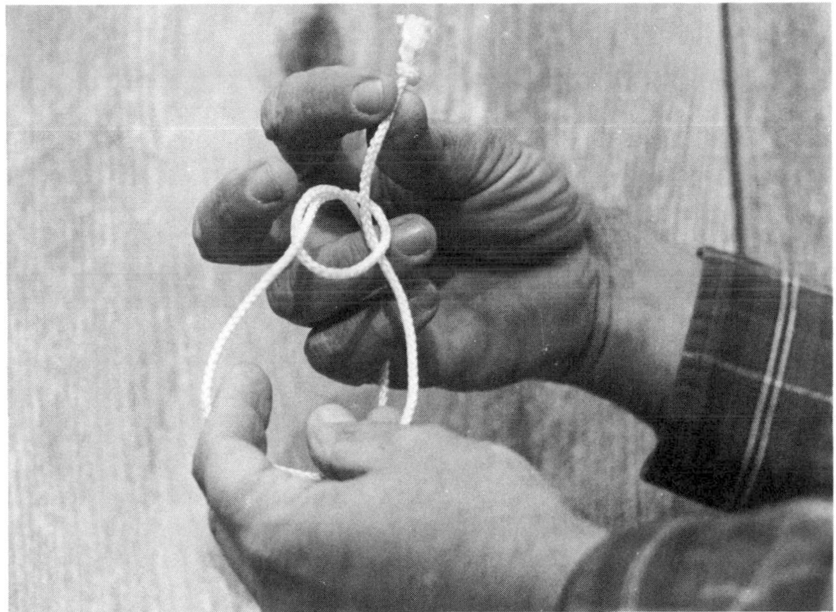

A slip-proof knot is used for the litter-box check cord. Pup's neck fits through large opening; the small opening is cinched up tight against the tied-off end.

He bites down hard and rears back. And suddenly, on the other end of that cord, a pup is jerked down for the first time in his life—and he panics. He squeals, he lunges, he squirms, he drools, he goes bug-eyed, leaps, and breaks loose.

Later, this pup that broke free grabs some other pup's trailing check cord. And so it goes, day after day. To this end: all pups learn to give to the lead. They learn that contraption about their neck isn't going to hurt them. Plus, their necks become sensitized to go with the tug—it becomes second nature.

Now this is important, for how does a man control a dog? With a collar about his neck. Now all we need to do is walk into the nest, reach down and take a cord, pick it up, give it a tug, and heel a pup away. A happy pup. A grudgeless pup. A pup that heels naturally, for all his fight against the lead has been vented on his own kind.

But to have put a collar on Pup for the first time, snapped a leash, and stepped off saying, "Heel," would have seen Pup drop his anchor, sit flat on his rump, rear back, brace his front legs, and look straight at you—dogs know where the hurt comes from—with terrified eyes. Now you're the culprit. You're the enemy. You're the thing that must be fought. And this is how you and Pup are going to start life together?

Is there any comparison between the two methods? Of course not. One is training with your head. The other is training with a heavy hand. One is thinking dog, the other is thinking human. One is psyching pups along, the other is muscling them.

But man's not to blame if he doesn't know how to train a dog. Holed up in our concrete caves, what do we know about nature? Our world is automatic tellers, off-ramps, laser-beam checkout counters, drive-through hamburger stands. And who do we cope with day after day? Dogs? Hardly. We cope with people.

And how do we work? Are we animal trainers for a circus? Do we tend lions at the zoo? Hardly. We work in shops, factories, and offices – places we never take a dog. Never meet a dog.

We live in a man-made world, not the world God made. The Garden of Eden was a mighty fine place for a dog. Madison Square Garden is something else. What's more, as man divorced himself from nature he simply became unnatural. Yesterday's paper told me the

Pointer pup on left is teaching pup on right to give to the lead – no grudge, all play.

National Park Service at the El Tovar hotel on the lip of the Grand Canyon just placed mice on the protected species list. Mice along with deer, elk, bear, and mountain lions can't be killed there. If you want to know the truth, man in the unnatural world might just be getting senseless. A job may open one day at the El Tovar hotel for a game warden to arrest poaching cats.

Considering what we are, and Heaven help us, what we may become, how are we to know what a dog is telling us? How are we to retain enough nature in us to know how to psych a dog?

Momma Dog

Well, I'll give you a tip. Watch the greatest dog trainer who ever lived. The trainer who had the job thousands of years before man ever brought the dog to his cave. Look at momma dog.

She brings her pups along with a balance of mock malice and love.

Momma dog is the greatest trainer of them all.

When her pups are out of line she stands above them, snarling, her eyes but slits, her white canines flashing. She leans forward, breathing hot and hard, she's tense, she's menacing. And that's that! It's all mock malice. It's all an act, never an action. Momma dog never lifts a paw.

And how does she reward? She drops prone, rolls over on her back, bares her vital parts, and closes her eyes: Momma dog sheds herself of all defenses. Momma dog becomes the least of them. The Bible tells man to become the least of them if he wants to lead. Interesting, isn't it?

Okay, what's momma dog showing us? Just this: The best way to train a pup is all bark and no bite. Also, she's showing us a trainer just needs to put in his bluff so good he's never challenged. If he's never challenged, he's never tested. Never tested, never bested. Never bested, never feared. And never feared, he doesn't need to shift from bark to bite. You can train with love when you're not feared. For never was a man so strong as when he was gentle. I offer Jesus and Gandhi as examples: Their gentleness moved worlds.

So let's do what momma dog showed us. Lie on the floor with a bunch of pups and see what they do. You're overrun, right? All licked in the face, and snuggled up to, and the great mystery of you is explored down to the hole in your ear. Now you are no longer menacing. You are something Pup can accept. Something he won't fear coming to when called.

Remember. You are a mystery to a pup. An awesome mystery. Consider your size. For you to encounter something as big to you as you are to Pup, the thing would have to be eighteen feet tall, and a grown elephant only stands eleven feet at the shoulder.

How would you act before something eighteen feet tall?

But, how would you act if this thing lay down and let you crawl all over it? If it let you assume mastery over it—even to sticking your finger in its ear?

That's going to build confidence, isn't it?

If this monster wants you to come to him, let's say, will he have to get out a whip to force you to comply? I'd think not. He just has to call, and you're on your way. And to make you come even faster, all the monster has to do is lower himself: assume but part of the defenseless position.

But somehow the monster has hurt you, and you don't want to go to him, for he may hurt again. So he calls you, but you want to run away. Now does he come running after you with a whip? Maybe. If he's a thoughtless monster.

But this monster thinks of you. He drops to one knee, or he bends

A child on the floor is the greatest humanizer Pup can have.

over at the waist – postures he takes to scratch your ears or lower your feed pan – so you're more inclined to stop running away and go back to him.

Or the monster turns completely around and starts walking the other way. What's this? He doesn't care? He really doesn't want me? Well, nothing in life can stand rejection. So you run to him, in a sense your action yelling, "Hey, don't forget me!"

Momma dog teaches us all this. All we have to do is watch her. And we have to think in dog terms, not as humans.

Now, if we lived with our dogs, we'd learn all these things. It's just doggy sense. We'd learn what we're really saying when we note, "It takes a child to bring a pup along." The child is not eighteen feet tall, he lies on the floor for a licking, and he thinks in puppy terms, for he's not yet grown to be a human.

But there's more.

Work Makes the Dog

Listen to Jack Knox, a Scotsman who now trains sheep dogs in America. Jack, who has won both the American and Canadian championships with his border collies, tells us, "When I was a lad of fifteen, I took to work as a shepherd in the Highlands. I didn't have a dog because I wanted to train it and sell it [which he now does], and I didn't have a dog because I wanted to train it and go have fun with it [which he now does]. I needed that dog to do my work.

"But in America, so much sheep dog work is for trials . . . it's a game we play. And people who have the dogs usually have no sheep, and people who have sheep usually have no dogs.

"So we have to make work for the dog here . . . but in Scotland as a boy . . . *the work made the dog.*"

This is akin to modern man who no longer does manual labor, so he makes work by jogging. My dad, who worked seventy-two hours per week during the Depression, didn't belong to a health club.

Now come with me to the Sonoran desert country. It was a hot, brittle-dry morning, typical of early spring. I was perched on some corral poles near Litchfield Park, Arizona. A lean, hard, handsome kid was overseeing a shipment of sheep to market. Assisting him was a nondescript mongrel pup, a ten-month-old bitch.

I sat spellbound. In ten months this gyp had learned sheep, corrals, men, dogs, terrain, fencing, eighteen-wheelers, and her trainer. The kid would yell at her, "Get on up," or "Come here," or "Don't let it get away," and the little gyp turned his words to deeds.

When the sheep were loaded, I sidled up to the boy and said, "What an amazing job you've done with that pup . . . you're really a dog trainer."

He laughed and said, "Me? A dog trainer? Hardly. I just take her everywhere I go in the back of the pickup."

And that, my friends, is as powerful, as provocative, and as revealing a statement as the one uttered by Jack Knox. He said, "The work made the dog." And the Arizona shepherd said, "I just take her in the back of my pickup."

So here's what we have. Men with work for their dogs train them in the natural course of making their daily rounds. And men who live with their dogs build a rapport without the pressure of training sessions—it all comes naturally, just like pups jerking each other with the litter-box cords.

And all this is denied to most of us anymore. We don't have work for dogs, and we don't do our daily work with dogs. So we must improvise. And this means two things: First, we must take our dogs into our homes and into our lives. They can't be abandoned, or exiled, in kennels out back. We must also travel with them. We must always have them with us. Matter of fact, there are some of us who even let them share our bed.

Second, we must train our dogs outside training situations. Consider a typical scene: the man works in a factory all week, grabs his dog Sunday morning, drives out to the country, releases the dog, and orders, "Find a bird," or "Fetch a bird."

The training session is contrived: the trainer is probably tense, hurried, impatient; the dog is totally unprepared, and anxious about the doom he smells on the man (see next chapter).

How much better it would be if the man spent fifteen minutes a day with his dog: training five minutes before work, five minutes when he got home, and five minutes before going to bed. Such training sessions would soon become natural, easygoing. The pup, expecting them, would look forward to them. The man, knowing if the dog goofs, it makes no difference. "We'll try it tomorrow."

Plus, when man lives with his dogs he begins to learn their nature, their way of saying things (oh, yes they do), their needs, their capabilities, their moods. And by the same token, the dog learns all these things about man.

When man moved to town and left the land, the dog was not the beneficiary. The terriers that once earned their keep catching rats in coal mines must now justify their lives by sitting pretty on quilted sofas. The poodles that retrieved waterfowl now sit beneath dryers at beauty parlors. And pointers who lived to put birds on the table now more often than not vie for silver to enhance the fireplace mantel.

What's necessary now is for man to understand—and to grant—who he is and what he is and where he is and to sensitize himself to the nature and needs of his dog. In a sense, the man and his dog are like frogs we used to keep in glass jars for high-school biology. The frogs always died. Man and dog, alike, now live in an unnatural world.

For man to stay alive and keep his dog with him, he's going to have to improvise. He's going to have to be more thoughtful. He's going to have to turn to his dog and say, "What's that? I missed it. Would you mind telling me one more time?"

And when the dog answers, the man must listen.

1

Talk to the Animals

SINCE CHILDHOOD WE'VE been told, "What you don't know won't hurt you." True? Hardly.

Many of us who live closely with our dogs begin to notice some very strange things. Things, if you will, "We don't know."

Let me explain. For many years I had an uncanny $2 dog-pound dog that shadowed my daily life. A mongrel, she was. A bit of fluff and later fat, a gun-shy creature, a laugh-off to whoever saw her. Her coat was grizzled, her nose bent to the right, her feet were feathered with fur, and her tail belonged to someone else. But bright! I think, near as I can tell, she had a 300-word vocabulary. And she could talk back. I'll never forget the day she leaped from our walk to land in the street. A motorist slid sideways after hitting his brakes. He laid on his horn in anger.

The little dog, her name was Poo, walked to the driver's door, looked up at the irate motorist, raised her head to clear her throat, and told him in no uncertain terms, "Woo, woo, woo, woo." Poo was my kind of gal.

Her favorite place, and favorite pastime, was to sleep beneath my typing table while I worked. She'd sleep so sound she'd snore. And I'd stand to go get a book or a cup of tea or visit the john, and Poo wouldn't move. But just let me stand with the thought of going out into the back yard, and Poo would beat me to the screen door.

How did she know? There are dog theorists who say dogs are telepathic—a big word that means communication outside normal sensory channels. That may well be the case. But I also began to wonder if my thoughts triggered different chemical odors to be released from my body. Or, could it be I was physically doing something different when I was going to leave the house? Something obvious like clearing my throat or shuffling my shoe soles? I monitored myself, but I could find no discernible clue I was giving the little dog.

For years this went on. I'd be sitting there trying to share some thought with you about dogs—while all the time I was admitting, when it came to the ultimate in dog behavior, I was totally stupid. It was Poo who should be writing the books, not me!

Then I began questioning others. And the stories started accumulating. I asked Jim Pettijohn, a seasoned big-jet, trans-Atlantic pilot and long-ago competitor on the retriever field trial circuit, about dogs reading our minds, or cuing off our scents, and he said, "Or cuing off even more than that."

"Take Chief," he said, "my Lab field champion. I could fly out and be gone for days. The schedule was never the same. No set routine. And yet, that day I was coming home Chief would take his place at the front door.

"He'd do it early in the morning. He'd wait all day. He'd know. And he wouldn't do it any other day. Chief just knew."

"Surely Chief had a clue," I said. "Your wife, Gloria. Maybe she knew, and something about her behavior, or her scent, or whatever, told Chief you were coming home." But Jim smiled and said, "Gloria didn't always know. I'd surprise her. But not Chief. Chief always knew."

Mind Readers?

I was recently looking for a pup as a gift for my wife. She loves Lhasa Apsos, and I was going through the nearby metro-center newspaper, calling one Lhasa classified ad after another. Eventually I talked to a delightful lady who mentioned she had, ". . . something less than sixteen dogs in the house." (The reason for her hazy recall is that this city has a limit on dogs per household.)

We talked further, all quite openly, and the lady said she could be bathing her lot of ". . . nearly sixteen Lhasas," and be standing there at the sink deciding which one she'd bathe next. But when she made up her mind to get one particular female dog—we'll call her Lucy—then Lucy would have left. Lucy would be hidden under a bed.

The lady went on to explain that after she noticed this phenomenal behavior she began to check. She'd purposely walk toward Lucy as though her bath was next–but it was all a ruse–and lo and behold, Lucy would lie there. But when the lady really had decided Lucy was next, the dog would have disappeared.

All of which means Lucy could read the lady's mind, right? If not, then what? That's the question. How do dogs know? And it's not all dogs, I'll admit that. And maybe, it's not all people.

A fellow dog man recently told me a certain person was going to put down two Chesapeake Bay retrievers. The Chesie man had to leave immediately for another city to take a job, and he could not keep the dogs. Worse yet, his efforts at advertising the dogs proved futile. So far as he figured, there was nothing else for him to do but destroy the dogs. Or maybe the man just pulled a bluff, saying he would kill the dogs on the hunch some soft-heart would bail him out.

Whatever the reason, I was appalled. These fine dogs could not die. So I went with my fellow dog man and fetched the dogs home, intending to place them with the humane society until suitable families could be found for them.

Well, the large male was very disturbed at being wrested from his master and home. He was large, he was powerful, and he was confused. Not mean. Confused. My dog friend reached for his leash–to take him from his departing master–and the Chesie just missed putting a canine hole in my friend's hand as though it had been shot through with a .22.

I then told the master to put the Chesies in my Blazer and leave. And to let the Chesies see him leave. Then I backed out of the man's drive and headed home. The huge male Chesie (ninety pounds at twenty months) would not sit. He stood with his front legs up against the back of my driver's seat, his five-gallon head reaching nearly to the windshield. It was testy. I felt like an airline captain in the Near East with this shaggy behemoth holding a gun to my head.

But just a second. Why did I tell the master to leave? By turning his back on his dogs, he was telling them it was all right to go with me. So long as he stood there looking at the dogs they were predisposed to side with him. But having him put the dogs in the car and having him walk away told the dogs that this was his will. He wanted them to go with me. And that turned the trick. For I was thinking dog.

When we arrived home, I flipped open the back gate and handled the two Chesies to the ground. The male responded to my wishes, the female was not a factor. I led the male to a fence post and snubbed him off until the humane society would open. But my dog friend made the mistake of approaching the big Chesie; you would have sworn a grizzly bear had cut loose. Never have I heard such a dog threat. The teeth snapped in the cold air: clear and brittle and ominous.

Why? This other man was not part of the dog deal. The master did not scold the dogs when the man took their leash at the house and the male snapped. No. The dogs knew the master entrusted the dogs to me. I oversaw loading them, I drove, and I let them out. They knew this. They knew I was their substitute master.

I walked over to the Chesie after he bit at my friend and talked to him in what I figured was soothing dog talk. He didn't know about it, though. His whiskey-colored eyes told of the promise he'd just made to me and my kind. But then the dog lowered his head for just an instant. The eyes averted for but a second. And that breaking of the stare told me of a breaking in the dog's commitment. The breaking of the stare told me the dog would accept me. I walked down his long curly back, dangling my hand, then I sat on the ground, and he muzzled me and kissed me like a pup.

Here was feigned death turned to putty. What had the dog read about me that he did not read on my friend? Or on others? That's right. Other dog men came that early morning, and I warned them, "Stay away from that big Chesie." They laughed and walked directly to him – only to face an explosion of wheat-colored fur, the great snapping of teeth, and the bared and sickly pale gums.

I can honestly say the big Chesie and I understood each other. But then I can't. He understood me, and I lucked out with him. I have no more idea of what I was doing right than the man in the moon. Why was this confused dog tolerating me? What was I doing different? And was it my actions, voice, posture, facial expressions, or touch? Was it my scent? What was it that told this dog to let me through his guard, but keep all others away? I can come up with no other answer than this: I live with dogs. I eat, sleep, drink dogs. They're in my house, my bed, my car, my vacations, my holidays, my hunts, my walks. They're buried in my yard, pictured on my walls, sneaked into the hospital when I'm ailing, taken to parties. The word is, if you don't want his dogs, don't invite Tarrant.

The Dog in Me

So right or wrong, I think the big Chesie accepted the dog in me. Not the human, but the dog. I've been around dogs so long I've become like them. And dogs read this. The other day I went to sleep in a dental chair. The dentist remarked, "That's the first time that's happened."

I laughed and told him, "It's easy . . . I learned it from the dogs. If there ain't anything going on, go to sleep."

I like the dog in me. It's made me a better human. The way I figure it, God gave dogs all the virtues He said man should have and generally doesn't: things like loyalty, love, devotion, selflessness, patience, forgiveness, and on and on. Gene Hill, the acclaimed outdoor writer, once observed, "Tarrant is so doggy I'll bet he circles three times before he lays down to sleep."

For some time I kept a pair of coyotes: Bonnie and Clyde. I mated them and trained their beget. It was all an experiment. I wondered if I could find something man had missed when he domesticated the dog: something that would help us train our dogs better, more easily, more effectively. The value of the litter-box check cord was proven, for example, with these coyote pups.

Bonnie and Clyde never liked me. But they tolerated me. Why? And what were their feelings toward me? Respect? Resentment? Grudge? Resignation? Who knows, but I could work with them. I could collar and leash them and heel them and tell them to sit and stay and all that, and we'd have a tolerable training session.

But just let me leave town. Just let me leave a kennel boy to shovel out their runs, and invariably Bonnie would nip the kennel boy in the rump. Always the same place. Just let the kid turn his back, and Bonnie would have him.

My question then and now was this: Why didn't Bonnie bite the kennel boy when I was across the creek at the house? How did she know I was out of town? And why bite the kennel boy and never me?

Well, my reason in relaying all of this is simple. If we knew what we were observing in dogs (and in humans) we'd be light-years ahead in our training techniques and philosophy. It doesn't do a bit of good to say the dog reads our mind. If so, how? And how can we measure it? That's what's important. And it doesn't do any good to say such a man or woman has a way with animals. If they have a way, then what is that way? Why is it? How is it? How do you get it?

These are questions that, hopefully, will one day be answered. For as long as we see dogs that seemingly understand the impossible and men who seem to have a special way with animals, we in truth don't know what we're looking at.

And worse yet, no one's really studying any of this. Oh, there are some who say they are animal behaviorists, but quite frankly they don't know any more than you or I do. If so, let them explain this uncanny behavior I see all the time with animals—especially dogs. And explain it without all that Pavlovian dribble: the bell rings, the

Author and Lab stop to "talk" while Happy Timing. *They've used this tree stump for years to let the other know what they're thinking.*

dog salivates. Or any of that talk about, "A dog is a pack animal and therefore. . . ." That answers nothing.

Sense of Place

Another phenomenon of dogs is that they have a precise sense of place. As I've told readers for years, never take a dog back to any place he's been hurt. He'll associate the place with the pain. And the stories are all too common about the dog being given away – being driven 500 miles away – and breaking loose and finding his way home. Watch your own dog. Take him 200 miles to hunt. When you near home does he not stand up in his crate, or in the car? Does he not suddenly show you he knows where he is and that place is home? Do dogs then, like pigeons, have a homing device? Do they respond to magnetic forces? Or like geese, do they navigate by the light of the sun and moon and stars? Again, who's studying this?

Also, dogs are critical listeners. Most I've met can differentiate their master's car engine a block away. If they can discriminate such sound, then what do they hear in our voice?

And until we know these things, we don't know nothing.

That's the ultimate thing we must puzzle out. And only a child's song hints at it. Something about "talking to the animals." And I ask you, who among us can call himself an animal trainer until we know what we're "talking" about?

Well, let's turn to the next chapter, and I'll offer a hunch or two on what I think's happening: Why we see this uncanny behavior in our dogs. And we'll zero in on the dog's scenting ability.

To a human being, seeing is believing, but to a dog his nose knows. Think not? Have your wife toss the dogs in your bed while you're lying there. Doesn't the dog immediately come to smell you? Makes you wonder who else has been there.

But the fact is the dog can even see you get in bed and he'll still come to smell. Which means, reality to a dog is scent, and that's where we'll turn now.

2

Scent Makes Sense

WE'RE IN THE topsy-turvy town of Nogales, Arizona, a border-patrol check station where during the fresh-produce season 200 eighteen-wheelers – snorting and belching, brakes squealing – may come through each day: the rumble of it all, the mass and the mess of it all. A semi-truck pulls in among all the others. It's loaded with nine tons of onions. Nine tons of fresh, green onions. A dog named Lobo walks up, takes a sniff, and tells his handler, "It's here."

Customs Officer Douglas Toenjes digs down through the pungent cargo and finds ten grams of cocaine: that's 0.353 ounces (approximately one-third the weight of a copper penny). Found in nine tons of onions.

Man has no sense comparable to a dog's sense of smell. It is miraculous. So, until something's smelled in a dog's world, it ain't identified. Dogs even taste with their nose. Think not? Offer Pup a tidbit (now, I'm not talking about a kennel-starved dog that'll glomp and swallow a wagon wheel if you toss it to him). Offer Pup something he's not had before. Go ahead. Call him in and do it. Before he takes the morsel I'll bet he smells it, right? Matter of fact, dogs don't chew most of their food. So I would think if they're going to taste it, they do so by smell before ever taking it to mouth.

Tomorrow night when you come home and Pup meets you at the door, see if he doesn't smell you. Oh, he may be leaping and carrying on, but still he'll probably sniff you out. Only then are you certified.

So let's examine the dog's nose. It is a miraculous device composed of chambers and receptors and all sorts of moisteners and backup cells and brain connectors that we'll simply lump into the one term: "smell cells." I'm no expert on the matter, but it is said man has about five million of these smell cells. Dogs on the other hand, depending on the canine olfactory expert you're talking to, can have from 125 to 1,000 million of them.

Dogs have adapted smell cells, which are extremely sensitive to odors that relate to peril, food gathering, perpetuation of the species – anything that means life or death. Of importance to us (as we'll see later) is the dog's phenomenal discrimination of butyric acid found in sweat. Tests have shown that dogs smell sweat one million times better than we do. And it's stunning to learn the average adult sweats a quart a day. Without exaggeration, then, we can say we do give a dog a snootful.

But that's not all. The dog also discriminates smells given off by our natural skin oils and a complex of gaseous components created by what we eat and what we wear – everything from soap to smoke.

But let's move on. If you keep your dog(s) in a distant kennel (and you're sure working against yourself if you do, for he/they feel abandoned), then do this. Go out your back door and walk toward your dogs. But instead of walking normal, I want you to limp. This should prompt a pandemonium of barks and growls. As you near, the dogs should be barreling to the back of their kennel runs, ducking into their dog houses – all the time growling at you. Why? Because they see differently than we do.

I'm not an eye doctor. I only know what I'm told. The retina of the eye is made up (in part) of rods and cones. Rods are sensitive to low intensities of light. Cones are also light sensitive, but they register color as well. It so happens dogs have more rods in relation to cones than we do. Which means dogs are better adapted for dusk and dawn. Plus, they have a light-reflecting layer in the eye (the tapetum lucidum), which intensifies vision with minimal illumination. This layer is what gives you the picture of a dog with yellow eyes when photographed with a flash camera.

I first discovered the dog's superior night vision by falling over him: flat on my face. That's right. I'd get up at night to go to the john, couldn't see a thing in the dark, and fall over one of several sleeping dogs in my bedroom. Why didn't they move from my path? They figured I could see in the dark as well as they could. I soon learned to shuffle my feet to the john.

Also unique to a dog's vision is this: it is more discriminating of movement and less of detail. A rabbit knows to freeze before the beagle. Consequently, here you come toward the kennel limping! You've presented the kennel dog(s) with a different movement, and they go bonkers.

For, I repeat, they can see your movement, but can make out no detail as to your clothes, hair, or face.

Consider also that dogs have 250 to 270 degrees of vision, whereas we have 180. Dogs have phenomenal peripheral vision (which becomes very important to us when teaching whoa, as we'll see later). But the dog pays for this by having less binocular power than we do. Plus, the dog sees things poorly immediately before him. They have no need for close-up sight. Their enemy and their food has appeared for eons several yards before them.

Finally, as soon as you draw near enough to the kennel, the dog(s) will get a whiff of who you are and will come wagging and leaping. Scent makes sense.

Miraculous Behavior

With these things in mind, then, let's turn back to our concern of the last chapter. There we wondered how dogs seemingly perform miraculous behavior. It seems, if you will, that dogs read our minds. And some theorists might say our dogs have extrasensory perception. I wonder. It seems more likely to me that one of two things is happening. Either dogs interpret our thought through scent, or they learn us so well they can predict our thoughts and resultant moves through (to us) imperceptible stimuli. At any rate, if a dog wants to interpret your mood, it's a sure bet he'll smell it more than see it. We got a quart of sweat a day to prove that.

Therefore, if dogs are going to "read our minds," I submit they do so with their nose. That's my hunch, anyway. And unbeknownst to us, some thoughts we have may emit odors. *When we think, we stink.* Simple as that. And some dogs may smell better than others, and some people may emit odor more than others. Possibly that's why we have people who just don't have a way with animals, as well as others who make their living training them. And I admit, nothing I propose has scientific research to back it up. So you don't need to agree with me. But here's the catch: disprove what I'm saying, okay?

Scent

I now ask you to consider Joe Simpson's dogs. Joe's the miracle dog trainer of Danville, California, who coached dogs to sniff out boiled glass ash trays buried in beach sand and washed and rewashed by the tide. Incidentally, disturbed earth has a strong smell to a dog. But a backhoe dug a continuous trench for the ash trays: the whole course was disturbed earth.

Joe walked his dogs on course, and the dogs alerted on the no-scent ash trays. Both Duke University and Stanford Research Center oversaw the tests for the Department of Defense. Joe tells me the experiment resulted in Stanford saying the dogs smelled the boiled glass ash trays while Duke said, "No, the dogs knew the ash trays were there through extrasensory perception." When both research groups asked Joe how his dog did it, he told them, "Hell, I don't know." And you can't say the dogs cued off Joe: he didn't plant the ash trays; he didn't know where they were.

So if Joe Simpson's dogs could smell scentless, boiled, buried-with-rubber-gloves, tide-washed, glass ash trays, then surely they could smell any nuance our body emits as a result of thought stimulation—especially if we're emotionally aroused. But those dogs couldn't read Joe's mind: he didn't plant the ash trays. The dogs had to smell them. And that's why I submit we emit odor(s) when we think. Decisions become smells. And sensitive dogs perceive these smells, classify them, and respond to them.

That's not to say dogs don't also react to other stimuli. They hear well. In a closed house they can hear a dog pass down the street. Or do they smell them? I live by a forest service road, and my dogs can hear a Jeep coming three minutes before I can make it out.

So what of the dog's hearing? Humans, depending on their age, have a hearing range up to 30,000 cycles. Dogs have an upper limit that some researchers say reaches 100,000 cycles. In other words, the dog hears ultrasonic sound. Which certainly helps him locate rodents and other small and squeaking prey. Consider the coyote: his primary diet is the field mouse.

Dogs also respond to touch. It's been theorized they pick up static electricity to foretell an approaching storm. If they can do that, they can certainly respond to the hand of man or the cold nose of another dog.

So let's put all we've learned into focus. When we pull up in a farmer's yard and get out of the pickup to ask permission to hunt his land and eight assorted farm dogs come milling and displaying around us, one man makes it to the door and the next man ends up on a tree limb. I feel the would-be hunter emits an odor the dogs interpret. And if there's a dog in that pack that's a bully, then the man goes airborne should he emit the odor of doubt or malice. But let the man emit confidence and he can make it to the porch. It's that simple. And that complicated.

We've heard it said, "A horse can tell if you're afraid of him." So can dogs. They read it in your sweat. So doing, a dog will try to put his bluff on you so you will become his subordinate. That's why you can't coddle a dog to performance. You must be firm. And too many people think this means being physical, even brutal. Never. It just means you let the dog smell your ease about him, your assurance you can control him, and that's what he lets you do.

Some of you will remember Freeman Lloyd. I hope you do. He was Gun Dog Editor of *Field & Stream* for over forty years. One time in South Africa he was on the docks when a rope broke, a crate dropped, and a lioness jumped from her captivity. Freeman roared at the beast, "Kennel, Katrina," and the lioness jumped back into her splintered crate. How else would a dog man react? What else would he say? The cat was loose and needed to get back in her box. However, you must know Freeman helped capture the lion and had named her Katrina. Katrina knew Freeman. So now I figure Katrina was stunned by the man's audacity, by the man's self-assurance. By God, the man told the cat to kennel up and the cat did. It's also possible the cat smelled the fact Freeman Lloyd (like most dog men) was a little nuts. That cat got back in her crate for safety.

J.A. Hunter, one of the few immortal white hunters of Africa, tells us in his book, *Hunter*, that eye contact is critical when facing a lion, Cape Buffalo, elephant—whatever has yet to decide whether or not to charge and kill you. Break eye contact and the animal is on you.

Beryl Markham tells us the same thing in her book, *West With the Night*. She relates the encounter of herself and two Masai warriors with a lion standing over a dead meal in the grass. One Masai told her, "Observe his eyes, he thinks very hard of many things." Later the warrior stood up and walked with indifference past the lion. Beryl says, "I do not know how he knew that that particular instant was the right instant or how he knew that the lion would accept a truce." I will answer Beryl. The lion read it all in the warrior's eyes. Had eye contact been broken, Beryl would probably never have lived to write her book. You must read these two books by J.A. Hunter and Beryl Markham, plus a third big-game book by Hunter Wells entitled, *They Call Me Hunter*. These three hunter-authors lived as intimately with wild game as I have with dogs. And the four of us have come to the same conclusion: *there is nothing more critical than eye contact in holding a beast at bay or a dog at compliance*.

We've heard it said, "You can't fool a dog." Tradition has it that dogs are good judges of men's character. If your dog don't like the guy, you better be leery of him as well. Women have similar intuition. *Webster's New World Dictionary* tells us intuition is the "ability to perceive or know things without conscious reasoning." And that may be the case with women – they've always been a mystery to me – but not with dogs. I'm certain dogs smell a man's character. The evil or crafty man emits this fact through his pores – and in his eyes.

Yet everything I've just proposed must be taken with a grain of salt, for dog behavior may be determined by routine. Dogs have uncanny clocks in them. They're also extremely sensitive in cuing to commonplace things. I have a West Highland white terrier male who knows the tune at the end of the ten o'clock news. That means he'll be let outside. If I had that tune to play all day, could I get him to go out with a record player?

Another house dog of mine – this one sleeps against my left shoulder every night – awakens me at exactly six o'clock each morning. Never a moment earlier or later. And this is in all seasons with both winter and summer sun. The little dog knows the time of day without light.

It goes on and on. The stories are legion – you have your own. And I tell them not for their quaintness, but to press home this one fact. Dogs are extremely sensitive. They cue to microseconds, minute snatches of scent, routine, place, sound, and what all else. And for a trainer to beat them and kick them and shout at them is barbaric and stupid and useless.

I've said time and time again, if you're going to train a gun dog, you've got to be smarter than the dog. And what human being doesn't rear up and blurt, "Well, I sure as hell am smarter than some dog."

Well, are we? Really? If the dog can "read" our thoughts, then how bright are we when we don't have the foggiest notion of what the dog's thinking? And if we don't know that, how are we going to train him?

Communications

All training is communications. And all communications is transmitted messages through mediums. Thoughtful trainers know how to code their messages and what channels to send them on. They may even know how to manipulate their body scent – and not even realize they're doing it. As we're prone to say, "Just God's gift." Or others will dismiss it by saying, "He just has a talent for it."

Marshall McLuhan, the late and profound professor of communications who spent the latter part of his life studying TV, said, "The medium is the message." By that he meant the TV, itself, became more important in molding our society than any information it carried. And that may be the precise way our body scent is interpreted by dogs. The medium is the message. The medium is us. And not what we say.

So pay attention to your dog. Watch his behavior. For his behavior is his reaction to you. Anything that doesn't seem right, puzzle it out in terms of what we've said here. Take mood. I'm sure dogs smell our moods as well as see their outward signs. And that's why I've told my *Field & Stream* readers so many times that when you don't feel well don't take Pup to field. Frustration, fright, and worry all have to be strong emotions that issue body scents. And if so, they are undoubtedly negative scents.

I'll never forget a lad I knew thirty years ago who wanted so very much to make a field trial champion. And he had a good dog. But every time the boy took the dog to trial the dog folded. Why? I think I now know. The boy gave off the scent of his doubt and his concern. The dog was whipped before the breakaway. Yet in training sessions, when there was no pressure on the boy, the dog was a crackerjack.

Now, regarding all the above, I don't say I have all the answers. It may well be I have no answer at all. But I know dogs are uncanny creatures with capabilities far beyond our knowledge. And in the last analysis it may be an extreme sensitivity that cues them to our thoughts—like a human couple married sixty years who know what each other is thinking. I so wish the keys to all this could be found in my lifetime, for I know such keys exist. I just don't know where to get them or how to use them.

I hope my hunches prompt others more competent than myself to unravel the mystery of the intuitive dog. Yet, I'll still advise them to concentrate on the dog's nose. Especially when we realize a dog can be sprayed by a skunk right out of the car and yet point every available covey during a day's hunt. Anything that discriminating bears a ton of investigation.

Until now, unlike our dogs, we're the ones who've been skunked in every way we've tried to understand this miraculous creature.

3

You Ought to See Him Use a Whip

THE DEPRESSION WAS at the bottom of the bucket in Wellington, Kansas: a rusted-out bucket. On a Sunday afternoon in August, a guy stopped along the curb before our house, tooted his horn, and yelled at my dad, "Hey, Bill . . . want'a come along? I'm going to buy a bird dog pup."

Dad jumped in the front seat, I got in the back. The car was a 1928 Chrysler with mohair seats, and it was 110 degrees in the shade. I wore short pants and that mohair pricked like a scrub brush. The hot wind torched me through the open windows. I was wishing I hadn't come along when I heard this guy yell over to my dad, "Boy, can this guy train a dog . . . you ought to see him use a whip."

Dad nodded his head. He could appreciate this. He, too, usually had thunderstorms in his own head, that flash of lightning, the great tornado of his charge, and he'd beat me with his belt, yelling, "I'm going to teach you something, Billy, if I have to kill you."

Teach me? What was I learning? That the only benefit of the belt and my rump was to release my dad's uncontrolled rage! No longer hot, I was seized by cold shivers in that back seat. And the fantasies came: I'd tear the whip from the dog trainer's hands and make him eat it, I'd spring the latch on his pens and let all the dogs bolt free. And I'd run with them, laughing and playing in the tall yellow grass, sleeping under the heavy-crowned cottonwoods down along the river, and waiting in the back yard for the garbage men to take their noon break – with all the dogs and me sharing their lunch pails or picking through the tidbits in the truck bed while the flies whirled, seepage leaked, and the stench bore skyward.

That afternoon Dad also bought a pup. He brought him home, named him Ted, and now there were two of us to beat. After a year Dad declared to mother, "That damned dog ain't ever goin'a learn anything . . . I'm goin'a take him out in the country and dump him."

So he did. And my mother's in the front seat biting a handkerchief and my sister's bawling in the back and I'm riding along detached, somewhere in black space, my jaw set, my lips drawn to a thin seam. Ted had been the best friend I'd ever had. He slept with me on the living room sofa, and when he'd yawn at night and stretch those long legs out he'd dump me to the hardwood floor. I'd stand him up, his legs to the ceiling like he was cast in bronze, and wedge back in. Then he'd pass gas and my eyes would water.

Mother couldn't afford to feed Ted, but she let me pilfer an egg, a slice of bread. Then, when Ted was hit a glancing blow by a car or looked like he had distemper or mange, he'd crawl under the front porch, and mom would mix white gravy and sneak it to me to wiggle before me under the porch and pet old Ted while he ate and I cried.

Well, Ted had survived it all, but not this. He was to be dumped and I'd never see him again. My best friend tossed out like a hobo in a train yard.

Dad opened the door, dragged Ted to him, took off the collar (for that cost money), and kicked Ted in the butt. We left him standing in the ditch in a cloud of dust.

I'll never remember the drive home, it was interminable. All I could see was Ted, bewildered, looking from side to side, watching as the car roared away.

Into the drive we whomped (there was no drive, just a curb to jump so's to park the car in the front yard), and Dad was making a lot in his whining voice about having to waste his Sunday afternoon on a worthless dog.

But wait. What's this? There's Ted. Standing on the front porch, laughing. His tail's beating, his mouth's open: *laughing!*

Dad never recovered from this. "How in the hell did he get here?" he kept asking over and over. He capitulated and went into the house, slamming the screen door.

Ted and I had many years together. Ted standing on that front porch that Sunday afternoon taught me *victory*. And with no whip involved. That was the most important lesson I ever learned.

If you're ready to learn, too, then come with me. We'll go get you a pup.

4

If Pup Did the Picking, Would He Pick You?

SO YOU'RE READY for a pup! Pooch-bellied, perk-eared, curled in a cardboard box, running sideways on chunky and uncertain legs, teetering headlong into his milk bowl, stumbling back to stare into the unknown with hazy blue eyes.

It's a good thing you're after. Him grown one day – you see it now – the tailfeathers of a neon pheasant angling from your gamebag, a brace of snub-nosed bobwhites weighting your hand, a tuxedo-clad pintail laid in the grass. And the pup-grown-to-dog has found all this and fetched all this, and without him you'd be minus bird and buddy.

So you're ready for a pup. But are you?

Pups are like a bucket; you can only pour out what you've poured in. If you've neither got the need nor inclination to put a lot of time and thought and effort into Pup, then let him pass. Otherwise, I can predict, you'll just end up kicking the bucket.

Consequently, before you take on a pup you need seven things.

When picking a pup the average guy or gal wonders, "Does this one have the stuff? Will he do a good job for me?" These are the questions you should ask yourself.

Bill Berlat, to whom this book is dedicated, sits in a puppy pen hefting a pair of pups, hoping he'll choose the right one.

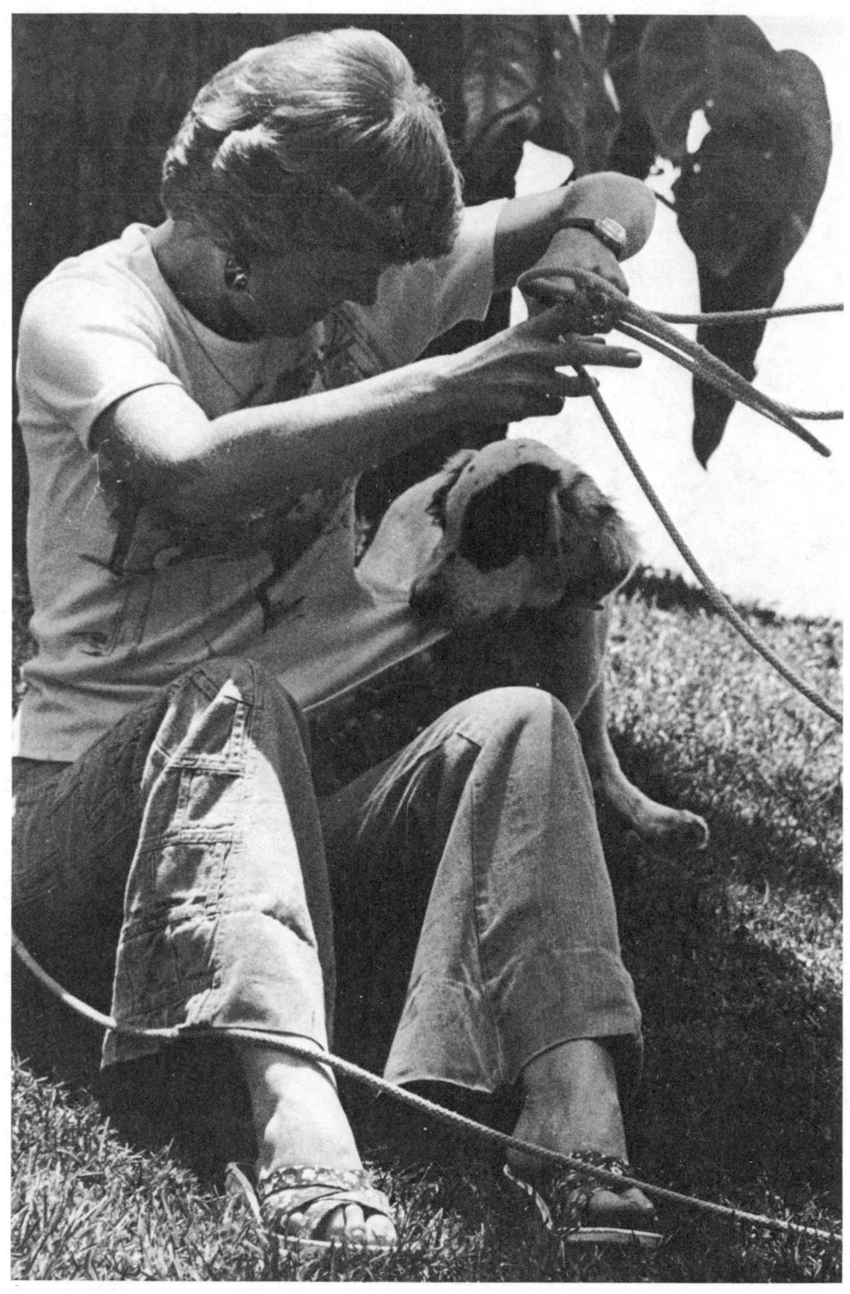

Setter pup tells author's wife, "Okay you pulled me . . . now let me pull you." Dee wears pup-proof clothes.

Temperament

What's your nature? Are you easygoing, soft-spoken, slow-to-anger, patient, and reflective? If so, you're ready for Pup. If not, let Pup pass. A short temper and a heavy hand never made a gun dog.

Now let me digress. Most gun dog books are based on professional notions and practices. They are entirely different from yours. The poor pro generally takes what's handed him: could be a two-year-old, hard-headed, half-wild maverick. Plus, the guy who owns him demands, "I want him ready for bird season in three weeks." Ha! What's the poor pro to do? Bear down, that's what. And that's where the old dog-training term comes from: breaking him! The dog is broke, not nurtured. It's not the pro's fault. Nor the dog's. It's the owner's fault: his interest is birds, not dogs. His interest is miracles for the lowest buck.

Now to the pro's defense. Ninety-five percent of all dog-training breakthroughs come from the pros. And always will. If given the time, they can develop a class gun dog by never laying a hand on him. Plus, it's easier to train thirty dogs than it is one. And, the pro has the facilities and the birds. Remember, when talking of bird dogs, bird's half the name: the first half.

So there is no condemnation of the pro in this book. There is only the condemnation of dog owners who don't know which way's up and don't care and never will.

Now back to picking a pup.

Sufficient Time

There are few men whose lives don't grant them time to train a pup, bring him along, humanize him, sensitize him, and turn him into a gun dog.

The bare minimum is, say, five minutes of yard work in the morning, then scratch Pup's belly, rub his ears, and freshen his water.

When you get home from work at night, have another session. After supper, spend another five minutes playing or training. Just before going to bed, spend five more minutes on what you're trying to teach. That's twenty minutes, split into four segments, and that's more than ample to start a pup.

But that's only one kind of time. That's the time a pilot, for example, is actually taking off or landing the plane. What about all the cruise time?

While reading your paper you can dangle an arm and scratch Pup's ears. Put a bare foot on him while you're having supper – sure, he's under the table and you've kicked off a shoe! Take time during TV commercials to get a tidbit and tell Pup, "Sit." When he's complied, give him the reward; tell him, "Good boy," and go back to the tube.

Snatch-a-minute training is great for several reasons. One, Pup has a very short attention span. Five minutes is more than ample for training sessions until Pup is six months old. Two, let's hope the trainer doesn't get frustrated in five minutes. Three, Pup's not going to be a stellar performer each time out. If he's off his game, put him away.

Four, training different times of day gives Pup a different perspective. The shadows change. The earth dries up. The wind starts to blow. But at night . . . that's when you and Pup can have fun. You stand in the light and cast Pup into the dark. Launching into the black unknown will help Pup build confidence. He'll also learn he has a nose.

Five, all gun dogs are working dogs, the instinct being bred into them as sure as God put horns on antelope. Training sessions are work substitutes. Sure, we know they're play sessions. But in Pup's mind, work is play.

If you can't find work for a working dog, then don't put him on relief in your back yard. An idle dog that's bred for work is nervous misery. Such a dog eats metal buckets, he eats his own feces, he chews down the dog house, he fence fights, he digs great holes, and he sulks and gives you mean looks; he also runs a half-mile straight out of a kennel gate when finally released for the sheer joy of feeling his muscles move.

So have a heart. Turn time on your hands, or time on your rump, into a gun dog. Work him, or never put him on the payroll.

Pup's Place

If you're worried about the carpet or the sofa or the doodads, and you turn purple and scream and run like you had the scours every time Pup walks through, stands up, or squats down, you don't have a home for Pup. You have a mine field.

All that *pick pick pick* will wear Pup spiritless. And one maniacal act will destroy him forever. That's right. One heavy hand is identical to one atom bomb. You will destroy the enemy, but there'll be nothing left to rebuild.

So pick a room for Pup that has no carpet. Something that's hardwood, linoleum, or tile. Now if a buddy misses the spittoon or a pup doesn't get you to the back door in time – you can mop it all up. Whatever's adangle, store it. Whatever's breakable, put it away. Whatever's chewable, move it to another room. Pup-proof the place; remove all temptations, all attractions that will cause Pup to displease you. Pup will hear, "No," too often in his life. Reserve your "No," to bring him along, not to protect your property. Build a room where seldom a discouraging word is heard.

Why? Because this is the most important place, at the most important time, in Pup's whole life. Here's where Pup learns every nuance of your voice, your facial expressions, your body movements – every quirk in the beast that is you, the man – and you learn the same about Pup.

Here you tune your psyches to each other, in whisper, in gentleness, in cool reflection. No hassle. No boisterousness. For remember, a hunter and a gun dog are a team. The closer the team members, the better the performance.

A Private Yard

You can't do Pup justice without a parcel of land outside your back door. Private land. Your land. Having a small yard outside your back door gives Pup, one, a place to upchuck or stool on a moment's notice; two, a kindergarten where he'll learn the basics; three, a playground where he can chase sparrows, bury bones, tear up old tennis shoes; and four, a retreat where he can sit alone and think.

This yard must be pup-proofed, same as your house. No need putting Pup someplace it's inevitable he'll be yelled at. If you've got exotic plants out there you don't want eaten or dragged out by the roots or tinkled on or rolled in – then move 'em.

This yard is also Pup's toilet. If you can't grant him that, and if you can't handle the shovel, then forget about taking on Pup.

Also, if you don't want to rake up chewed twigs, bits of garden hose, or canvas seats out of your deck chairs, then do Pup a favor. Never bring him home.

One more thing. This yard is where Pup barks. His kingdom. His territory. He's king of the mountain and will permit no encroachment. There are ways we can keep the noise down, but not the feeling of territoriality. Pup may want to put the meter reader on the roof. Or keep the neighbors awake. Be prepared.

It goes without saying this yard must be escape-proof. Not only to keep Pup from climbing out or digging under, but to keep other dogs from getting in. Dogs will actually climb a fence paw-over-paw to greet a bitch in heat. Where I live, coyotes will storm a wall to eat a pet. And gates must be padlocked. Repairmen, delivery men, and kids can leave a gate ajar, letting Pup run away.

Pup's Wheels

If you own some velvet-upholstered gobble-up eight, then forget about Pup. Pup needs transportation fit for a dog. An old pickup with faded paint and crumpled fenders, where wind whips about the cab and tickles Pup's nose. Or an old station wagon with the ceiling ripped out and the floor mats muddied. For this rig takes you and Pup training. And your mind's on Pup, not wheels.

Once again, you must keep Pup in a fussless environment. When Pup gets to be a dog things can be different. You can kennel him on the floorboards of your Mercedes and take him to the bank. But while Pup's a baby he requires a world where you never have to say, "No." This is a good time to consider a kennel crate for Pup. There are many good ones on the market. It will provide a safe way to train Pup.

Some Old Clothes for Yourself

Pup can't tell the difference between your tattered, canvas field pants and your green tux with the leopard lapels. I can't tell you how many times I've seen hunters entice their gun dogs to leap up for a pat of love only to go into the motel, change into their see-me duds, then knock Pup's head off because he leaps to greet when he's taken from the car to dump.

A Stretch of Country

You can't shoot guns within city limits and Pup's a gun dog. You must find some country. Pup needs a place where he can meet and learn to manage varmints, ditches, ice, puddles, sticks, toads, stink birds, gullies, cactus, bluffs, logs, sandburs, butterflies, skunks, hedge balls, fallen apples, cows, box turtles – Pup must learn the territory. He must assure himself there's nothing out there that's going to hurt him. Plus, he must learn to handle land and water, timber tangles and running briar, row crops and stone walls, and barbed wire.

You can have a lot of fun, a lot of memorable moments for both yourself and Pup in the parlor or out the door in your back yard. But the country is where Pup will have the time of his life. Especially if he has another pup, or pups, to lead him on. That's the ideal. Pup'll break cover because he's being pulled on by one of his own kind rather than being pushed by you. He'll take to water to be part of the gang, not to be launched alone and fearful into the deep and unknown. Remember, I said it's easier to train thirty dogs than one.

This is where it helps to join a dog club where you can go with others of like interest and dogs of similar capability to romper-room the day. But one word of caution. You're there for training Pup, not for club politics. It's easy to get the two confused.

If you're not close to a dog club, you can gather up the neighbor's pups. Note, I didn't say dogs. Dogs can intimidate and give wrong examples. Make it pups. Or make it kids. Nothing can lead a dog like a kid.

Pup will need this free reign to knock holes in the skyline. It may be for three months, six, nine, or twelve. How long depends on Pup. When nothing in the field is a distraction, Pup can then concentrate on you and your training. But his Happy Timing has no instructions afield, just hide and go seek, touch and go, bump and run.

So these are the imperatives, the seven musts: temperament, time, yard, country, clothes, care, and a place in your home Pup can call his own. These are the things Pup would look for if he were picking you.

5

Picking Pup: The Other Side of the Coin

MANY PEOPLE HAVE strange notions in their head put there by a faulty press, by purists, by tradition, and by people who want dogs for beauty contests.

I've got a relative who's deep into family genealogy. He recently told me I descended from royalty on my granddad's side, and on my grandmother's side I can boast of the first settler in the New World who planted wheat.

So, like pedigreed gun dogs, I'm a blue blood. But I ask you, seen any classified ads lately seeking a prince to plant wheat?

So the breeder tells you this pup comes from a long line of champions. And sure enough, there it is, a pedigree unfurled nine feet long. At the far end you'll see Pup's twenty-times remote granddaddy was a field champion. Well, that pup is as far removed from that dog as I am from the Queen of England.

Plus, who's to say that granddaddy was prepotent? Did he throw true? And besides, I'm sure that 60, 70, 80 percent of a dog's performance comes from the dam. So we get real silly about pedigrees. Why? Because there's big money in it. There's money in registering litters and pups for the kennel club. And there's money for the breeder and for holding field trials and dog shows. And in America, where the money goes, so goes the heart. Consider, there ain't no stud book nor any dog publication honoring the mongrel, right?

Yet, among the finest hunting dogs I've taken to field a high portion have been mixed bloods. Remember, most pure-bred dogs were created through selective breeding. They were all "mongrels" to start with. And that would still be the case today, if the registering kennel clubs hadn't closed their books. (They have in America, but not in England: you can still get an authorized outcross there.) And in America there will be rare exceptions – the Field Dog Stud Book permitted an Irish setter outcross to an English setter during this century and registered the beget as a red setter, a breed that's proving mighty capable under the gun.

So I plead with you, right off, when going to find a pup to make into a gun dog, don't read pedigrees as a guide. There will be some exceptions: you see the name ELHEW on an English pointer's pedigree and you know you've got something. Bob Wehle is the greatest dog breeder who ever lived. Nevertheless, ask to see the sire and dam hunt. Look at action, not paper.

Another thing, don't go buy a book on the breed you're considering and read the standard. A standard is a description of what the dog should look like and how he should be built.

But I've never seen a standard yet (except those I've written) that deals with what you want to find in a hunting dog. For no standard deals with functional conformation. Most standards are concerned with what a dog should look like, where the only standards that interest you and me are those that relate to performance afield.

Also, most standards will explain the dog's traits, saying, for example, "This breed is great with kids," or "This breed is happy-go-lucky," etc. . . .

Bosh! The truth is there's more difference between dogs of the same species than there is between species.

The greatest problem with standards is they assume one-to-one duplication through reproduction. And they don't take into account biological variances, or just as important, the impact environment plays on the developing pup/dog.

So what you want to check in picking a pup is functional conformation, plus performance of sire and dam. Environmental factors also are important if the pup has any age on it. Most important, go to the kennel and ask to see both parents work game. Watch them run. See them get into birds. If you like what you see, and approve of the appearance of the kennels (beware of filth), then look hard at functional conformation.

Functional Conformation

Most of us have been guilty. "Hey Hank," we've boasted, "I'm dating the Downtown Merchants Annual Pageant beauty queen."

And the reply comes, "Yeah . . . can she cook?"

"Cook?" we stammer, "What's that got to do with anything?"

Dog men have not been immune. Many of us love a beauty contest. It matters not if the dog can smell a turkey in his kennel run: to look good is to be good.

I've been re-reading a rare volume off my book shelf, *The Setter*, written by Edward Laverack, London, 1872. English setter men (and women) will recognize this as one of two Titan names in the breed. The other being Purcell Llewellin, to whom, incidentally, Laverack dedicated his book.

Mike Gould displays magnificent Lab as he points out functional conformation.

Laverack loved the English setter and dedicated his life to improving the breed for the gun. Yet I want you to browse with me as Laverack lists points of conformation a bona fide gun dog must have. I don't ask you to accompany me to poke fun at Laverack. Far from it. I want, instead, for you to recognize what people are saying when they talk of gun dogs—or more to the point, what *they're not saying*. And what they're not saying is really what the hunter must hear.

Head

"I will commence with the head," writes Laverack, "which should be long and rather light, though not too much so. I do not like a heavy headed or deep flewed dog, it indicates sluggishness." Oh, come now Laverack, like narrow eyes indicate a con artist? The head is merely the box that holds the computer called a brain. That brain is programmed in the womb (though it is modified by the environment). It's known a hard head throws hard heads. Biters make biters. We don't look at the shape of a dog's head to predict behavior. We look at what the mommy and daddy do and realize the percentages go with the beget doing likewise.

For a while I went along with this big-headed assumption that more brains would be stored in a warehouse than a john. But then along came Poo, my two-dollar dog-pound dog with a head the size of an apple, and I verified a 300-word vocabulary for her before she died. When I was working on my doctorate at Michigan State in the 1950's, we had a research computer called Mystic. The thing was so large it could have overlapped a baseball diamond. Now we have computers that'll do more than Mystic did, and we hold them in our hand.

Another thing, Laverack's heavy-headed dog was assumed to be sluggish. Butte's Blue Moon, the immortal Lab national champ, had a head the size of his water bucket. But when you lined Moon for a bird he hadn't seen fall, you had to be prepared to stop him in the area or he'd overrun it four miles. Sluggish? Lord Bomar was another one. At twelve years of age he whipped me good at a Dallas field trial. He ran like a puppy. He hit a log, I recall, right before the casting line and rolled it over. So much for big-headed sluggishness.

Nose

Laverack continues, "Nose large, moist, cold, and shining, slightly depressed in the centre [English spelling], and expanded at the nostrils." Now what's all this got to do with anything? Can the dog smell?

That's the question. And does he have the biddability to learn how to use his nose. For you can teach a dog to use his nose, but you can't improve it. We have a town dog named Bandit who's reputed to have traveled twelve miles to a love tryst. I've had sons of national champs who couldn't smell their feed pan. You can check the sire and dam for nose and hope for the best. But at no time is the luck of the draw more prevalent than getting a dog with a good nose.

Eyes

Laverack then explains, "Eyes bright, large, full, mild, and intelligent, and free from rheum or discharge, in color dark hazel. . . ." Laverack didn't know it, but he hit upon something here. Dark eyes are the result of pigmentation. And there is a direct relationship between eye color and eyelid color in dogs: matter of fact, geneticists aren't yet sure if these colors are determined by one or two sets of genes. Anyway, we want a dark eyelid to protect the dog from skin sensitivity to the sun and possible cancer.

And we want a dark eye to better handle a glaring sun. You see, a bird dog looks for objectives, runs there, then shifts to nose to discern scent cones given off by birds. All bird dogs are initially sight hunters – they have to be.

Bone balconies should protrude above the eyes to knock away field cover and protect the eyes from foreign matter. And what we want most of all is a dog with deep-set eyes. Pop-eyed dogs must quit the hunt in tears due to dust and abrasion and sun glare.

Ears

Laverack says, ". . . ears [must] be set low on the head, and flat to the cheeks: they should be rather long than otherwise, not too pointed, and thin in the leather. A prick-eared dog is unsightly; it gives him a bad appearance. . . ." Well, we're back to the beauty pageant. Did you check out your wife's ears before you married her? All that matters to a hunter about ears is this: thick, heavy-furred, long-eared dogs are subject to heat in the ear canal, which can become an irritant or even a haven for bacteria. Now short-eared dogs do have some problems, but not connected with beauty. English pointers and Labrador retrievers, for example, don't have enough hair on their ears to insulate against fly bites – especially in the crease where the ear flops over. So you've got a kennel maintenance chore: forever putting gunk on the ears to ward off flies and heal the mess caused by them.

Plus there is this. A long, thin ear will split on you. There's tremendous force generated when a dog shakes his head, enough to split the edge. These can be near impossible to heal during hunting season. And finally, Ben Lilly, the immortal master of hounds for bear and mountain lions, observed that long-eared dogs have comparably long toe nails that easily lame a dog and make him unsuitable for hard hunting.

Neck

"The neck," says Laverack, "should be muscular and lean, slightly arched at the crest, and clean cut where it joins the head. . . ." The hunter's primary concern with a dog's neck is this: does it hold the dog's head high enough to avoid cover? A high head keeps debris from invading eyes and mouth, it lofts the nose above inhaled irritants, and it lets the dog's sighting be high enough so he can spot likely objectives. It also allows the dog, after wing and shot, to see the deadfall to the ground for the fetch.

Shoulders

Laverack then writes, "The shoulders I consider one of the most important parts of the setter." He then goes on to say why: in terms of beauty. (Incidentally, skin any gun dog out and lay his carcass on the table and, except for those with docked tails, you'd be hard put to tell the difference in species. Therefore, Laverack's setter is all our gun dogs.) Laverack makes the point the dog's back should be short. Which is totally wrong. The longer the spine in a dog (or horse), the more it can reach with its legs: it's got a longer wheelbase.

A short-coupled dog cannot extend its race. Its effort is up and down—not great reach and long pull.

What Laverack should have concerned himself with shoulders (and hips) was a deep, over-canopied acetabular angle where the femoral head enters and sets. In other words, a deep-cupped receptor for the upper leg bone's rounded head. The shoulders and hips are the dog's shock absorbers and axles. A dog is a running machine. A pounding, running machine. Once that cup/ball fails, the dog is finished. I know, I write this sitting here with two steel hips. And I recall my days on the circuit when pros would shoot cortisone into dogs with hip dysplasia to get one more race out of them. How I wish those pros could have hobbled with knives sticking in them the way those dogs and I have. Not for a month and a year. I'm not that way. But just for fifteen minutes. They would have retired the dog.

Chest

Now Laverack hits the mark when he tells us, "Chest rather wide, and deep in the brisket; with good, round, widely sprung ribs: a narrow-chested dog can never last. . . ." He finally said something. You want a deep heart girth in the hunting dog so when he heats up he has room for his lungs and heart to expand within the rib cage. Laverack's right. A pigeon-chested dog will quit you. He has to. Either that or pass out.

The dog is an oxygen-consuming machine. When the mountain railroads replaced the old steam locomotives with diesel they had to triple the horsepower. Diesel just required three times the oxygen needed by a steam engine. So we don't want diesel dogs, we want steam-engine dogs. Follow me?

Let me digress. I doubt if in the history of man there have been ten gun dog books written that could teach us something. And the worst of the lot are those generally sold in book stores: the shopping-center library. The handful of bona fide classics can usually be found only in gun dog supply stores. Which is not to say they don't carry a lot of pulp, too. And there is this about some gun dog writers. Many "forget" to give a reference. So a lot of books are "duplicates" of some original thinking. Learn your dog literature. Go to the primary source.

And do I say this to protect my royalties? God, no. I say it because those bad books have ruined more gun dogs than the good books have been able to make. My heart is with the dog. I don't want him in the hands of an idiot. I want him to have every chance he can have.

Among the really great classics is Jack Harper's *Bird Dogs and Field Trials*. Read it. Jack talks of heart girth as I do above and says in jest those skinny dogs have both legs coming out of the same hole. The point being, if you see a dog, or a pup, looking like that, avoid it like the plague.

Hips

Laverack now works his way back to the dog's hips and tells us they should be, ". . . well bent and ragged, the more bent the better; here is the propelling power." This "bent" aspect is most apparent in English pointers because they have little hair to hide their skeletal structure. What Laverack either did not note or failed to mention is the fact the higher we move the hunting dog's tail forward, the longer we extend the loin, hip, and thigh muscles: drivers of the pelvic limbs. Said another way, if through selective breeding we raise the sacrum then we will lengthen the gluteus medius muscle. When we get that muscle lengthened, then we build it up, like 4-H kids make lambs stand to eat. We elevate Pup's dog house, for example, and make him jump all day long.

A high-tailed structure permits the back feet to reach farther and trail longer, making a greater arc of the wheel. We note this when we say, "He's a roller."

Finally, you can liken all this rear-end construction to a fender on a car running in mud. A low fender (low tail) is going to hinder the motion of the wheel. Lift that tail (lift the fender) though, and you give freedom to a great arc of muscle, free-wheeling to a greater diameter of wheel.

Forearm

Laverack then says the forearm should be, ". . . big, very muscular; the elbow well let down. . . ." But he offers no reason for such anatomy. What we need is a strong foreleg with all joints straight and sound. They are the shock absorbers and the hinges. If they're misaligned, they'll sore up and the dog will have to quit the hunt. But more than that, the professor of hunting dogs, Delmar Smith, of Edmond, Oklahoma, tells us in a book I wrote titled, *Best Way to Train Your Gun Dog*, "We don't want no leg sticking out like the elbow in a chicken's wing. That dog will sore up on ya, can't work the next day.

"Nor do we want a bench-legged dog, or one that's spraddly legged. Bench-legged back legs step on the front . . . so the dog shortens his gait or he'll trip himself. With a straddle-legged dog the legs are winging . . . coming up on the outside of the fore elbows. Takes that dog an acre to turn.

"Me? I want a little bit cow-hocked dog. When they reach up there and hit that ground, they straighten out."

Especially important, cow-hocked hind legs place both feet near the same spot for takeoff. That gives spring and distance and balance. Think. Do you jump straddle-legged?

Then too, the cow-hocked legs straighten on push. This action gives the leg the spring of a released bow. And that's most of a dog's running: the push with the back. It's like a motorcycle with the chain to the back wheel. The back has all the power, the front's just for steering. And also like a motorcycle, when a dog runs cow-hocked, with feet to a center line, he's highly maneuverable. That's the dog you find twisted to pretzel on emergency brake points.

If a dog can reach but can't push, he's a prancer. We've seen that. If he can push but can't reach, he runs over himself. We've seen that, too.

But if he can both reach and push, he's a runner. And that's what we all want to see.

Feet

Laverack then mentions the feet, saying they should be, "very close and compact. The foot I prefer is the hare, or spoon-shaped one, which enables him to have free action on the pad or ball of the foot instead of the toes. . . ."

Sorry Laverack, we want just the opposite. A dog's got to have a good, tight, sound foot—that's for sure. But sprinters run on ball and toes. A dog running flat-footed is akin to us running in wooden clogs. Besides, a hunting dog's toes are his knobbys. They dig and hold and push off.

Splayed toes are easily broken, snagged, and/or sprained. For the toes to spread is to expose the recesses and invite stones and thorns and awns to lodge in the crevices. Consequently, Laverack should have said we want a high-toed foot.

A loose foot—as Laverack says to avoid, but does not say why—splats on impact, does not bounce, and therefore relays all force to ankles, knees, and hips (or shoulders). Dogs with such feet don't want to get out of the crate for the second day's hunt.

High toenails will help the foot take a glancing blow on rock and will help keep a nail from splitting.

Now let's pause. I ask you, "Ever seen high toenails published in a standard?" No. Nor any of the things we're considering. Yet these are the vital things to note when looking for a gun dog pup.

And know this. Many dogs achieving field championships today are not necessarily the ones you want a pup from. Too many judges are testing dogs for the wrong things. For this very reason I created an entirely new hunting-retriever testing format in America to replace the classic retriever field trial that was asking the dog to trip over his own instincts in order to win. And when he wouldn't trip, too often he was brutalized into performance contrary to his nature.

This book was written for the sole and express purpose of attacking brutality in dog training. Yet here we have a field trial concept among retrievers that is being perpetuated to this very day. Not only that, some people are trying in earnest to have the new hunting-retriever notions I conceived and others implemented (notions, mind you, that did away with any need for brutality in training) enveloped and suffocated so their non-dog-caring game can continue. And what do I mean by non-dog-caring? I mean any time a dog must be beat, kicked, burnt, electrically shocked, shot, cursed, or mauled in order to get him compliant enough to pass some unnatural field test. That's not caring.

But you must know this. These people are not training gun dogs. How could they be? They won't even allow the handler to fire a gun! Enough said.

But I will add this. The humane groups used to come to the field trials and object to live ducks being thrown to earth. Right they should. Then these do-gooders thought they'd accomplished something. Ha! They were looking at dogs retrieving these ducks that had been electrocuted, beaten with BB-loaded whips, dragged by chains through ponds—the do-gooders watched the result of atrocities and never knew they occurred.

Back Yard Breeding

Let's move on. I don't have a chapter in this book on breeding (see Harper's book for the best information), so I will mention this. Some of the best gun dogs I've ever had, or have ever seen, came from back yard breedings. They were what I call Happy Accidents. Take my great Lab, AFC Renegade Pepe, and his sister, Jim Culbertson's FC, AFC Keg of Black Powder. These littermates both became immortal to my way of thinking. But get this, five repeated breedings of the same sire and dam never produced a pup worth taking to field.

Such realities have prompted me to say many times, "Don't spend your time pickin' a pup, spend your time prayin'." For the Lord sends down a miracle pup only once in a million. It's no different with us humans. How many of us are on this planet—four or five billion? And within this mass, how many will compete in the Olympics? Will it not boil down to—what is it?—eight, ten, twelve men running the hundred meters? I don't know track, just dogs, so forgive my ignorance, but get my point. If you were going to pick these eight, ten, or twelve men who run the hundred meters, where would you have looked for their parents eighteen years ago?

Plus there's this: are you going to predict their offspring will run the hundred meters at the Olympics twenty years from now? Well, if you only considered functional conformation, then they should. So I confess that even the best system is faulty. But nevertheless it's the best means we have today of selecting a gun dog.

Tail

When Laverack arrives at the dog's tail he says, "The tail should be set high, in a line with the back: medium length, not curled or ropey, to be slightly curved or scimitar-shaped, but with no tendency to turn upwards; the flag or feather hanging in long pendant flakes." Laverack wants in a tail what a show girl wants in a feather boa. Flash.

While hunting in England I've been told the dog's tail should be quarter past nine. In other words, as Laverack notes, straight out. Why? In Labs we know the otter tail is extended in water for a rudder. But the setter? Oh, he does use it to help turn, to be certain. But German shorthairs turn and they have a tail–that's what–six inches long?

But Laverack's not finished with the tail. He adds, "The feather should not commence at the root but slightly below, and increase in length to the middle, then gradually taper off toward the end. . . ." To which I ask, how many dog tails ever pointed a bird, or fetched it up? In other words, what difference does a tail make? Unless it's to slap away a fly or beat in a rhapsody of love for bird and handler.

But alas, the world is based on folly. If the dog running before judges does not have a tail set that meets the fad of the day, he'll not be watched. That's why I implore you, never take to the trial trail. Make birds on the table more necessary to your life than silver on a mantel. You and that dog and bird are the hunting world. Except for the new hunting retriever clubs, the shoot-to-kill or foot-hunting bird dog clubs, or shoot-to-retrieve boys, there's little about field trials that apply to a day's shoot. Field trials are a game. Hunting is life. The two won't be confused if you're a bona fide hunter.

Well, Laverack waxed poetically about a picture in his head. But it's a bird in hand we want. So we wonder why the man never mentioned the fact we want tight testicles on a dog so they won't sore up from rubbing stubble and briar all day, which lessens his performance. Same goes for a bitch: consider the discomfort of a big-titted bitch trying to hunt. All that abrasion. I just passed up a good gun-dog prospect for this very reason: she had extraordinarily long teats.

High Pain Threshold

We also need a high pain threshold in our gun dog. A dog that's just less sensitive to pain. Like those people who never take the needle before having their teeth filled. We want a dog who won't honor sandburs or briar or sharp gravel. What we want is a dog that can take it. Heart and drive have a lot to do with this–as does the dog's central nervous system. I once had a pointer, demented to the hunt, that ran full-force into a strip of galvanized roofing stuck in the ground and cut himself from shoulder to shoulder. I threw him on the tailgate of the pickup, sewed him up, and off he went. I don't recommend this MASH procedure for all of you. Dr. Dick Royse, whom you'll meet in the next chapter, had run me through a crash vet's course. I carried a small dispensary in my dog truck.

Bite

We also check the sire and dam's bite. The dog's fuel is his food. If he has a bad bite, he may not eat properly. This can lead to digestive problems that'll put him off his game. Or he may have his teeth go bad before his time and deny you several good years of field service. But mostly we want good bite in the bitch. She has to chew the umbilical cord during whelping, and if her teeth don't match she can tear the pup's navel—which will hemorrhage, and the pup can die.

Skin

Neither did Laverack mention a dog's skin: it must be loose. If the dog gets hung up on barbed wire, let's say, the skin will roll and release. But should the skin be tight, it can likely tear. Also, it's interesting to note a black-footed dog will be less likely to lose a pad than a white-footed one. Dark pigment just builds a stronger skin.

But when you've got all the above you ain't got nothing—unless the dog has that nature required for trainability, a good brain for learning and remembering, a disposition for compromising, and the guts to do the job when the going's tough. I remember Pepe winning a Colorado Springs trial because he was the only dog who would retrieve a planted duck from atop a beaver's dam: the whole thing pointed sticks, sharp and lethal. And we were running in ice and the sticks were slick and no way could he get purchase.

You can check the parents for these traits, but really, they seem to be magical qualities unique to each individual. Plus the environment starts to work on Pup's behavior: in a way, modifying the genetics of the animal. Dogologists even surmise a pup's place in the uterus can affect his behavior. It's all too mystical to contemplate: I stick to praying.

But don't do what most people do and overlook the importance of the dam when picking a pup. That puppy's been living inside her sixty-three days, and has been dependent on her in the whelping bin until you pick it up. And folks, a majority of the determinants in that pup's life have already come about before you ever show up.

It's been done almost beyond the human eye or human knowledge. But it's been done. Whether or not that pup will be shy has largely been determined by mom: its boldness, its sensitivity to pain, its desire to please, and yes, its self-appraisal. And the breeder's had his hand in all this, too. Is he harsh-voiced? Does he move abruptly (remember dogs see motion)? Is he impatient? All that sort of stuff. And the other pups have made their imprint, as well as the other dogs in the kennel.

The only other time we make a pick in our life that's equally chancy and baffling is getting married. The good marriages are made in Heaven, I believe, and so is the pup you want to take home. Heaven help us.

Finally, I don't jump Laverack because he's not here to defend himself. To the contrary, I hold the man in high esteem. He pioneered where I now flounder. And let's hope 100 years from now a wiser dog writer takes me equally to task. My interest is you. Your decision is no better than the information on which it is based. You need facts, not poetry, to find a gun dog. And you need reasons, not adjectives, to make the pick.

But get all the above and have it sick, then you ain't got nothin' at all. So let's call in an expert. When picking the pup you look for more than functional conformation.

6

Picking a Healthy Pup

DR. DICK ROYSE, the premier Wichita, Kansas, vet, can diagnose a dog better over the telephone than most vets can with the animal on their table. He tells us, "These people come into my clinic because they've gone to look for a pup, and they've been taken in by this sad-waif-looking little thing that's either the runt, or undernourished, or has some type of impairment, or was sitting off in the corner of the pen all by itself, and appeared lonely. And it's a pitiful sight.

"So out of compassion . . . and young people between eighteen and twenty-eight seem most susceptible to this, as though that lonely castoff pup reflects something in their own lives . . . and feeling sorry for the pup say, 'Oh, gee, that's the one I want,' and take it home.

"And what you see is what you get. . . ."

Doc puffs on his pipe, gets only air, looks into the black innards of the thing and says, "It's nice people are so compassionate. No quarrel with that. But it's unfortunate, due to the end result. People must be more objective when picking a pup. Compassion can just get them a very sick pup and a lot of problems and the grief that comes when the pup dies."

He's got the pipe stoked now and under a billow of smoke he continues, "The first thing a pup prospect should look for is cleanliness. Is the place clean, tidy, well-kept, bright-looking, happy-looking,

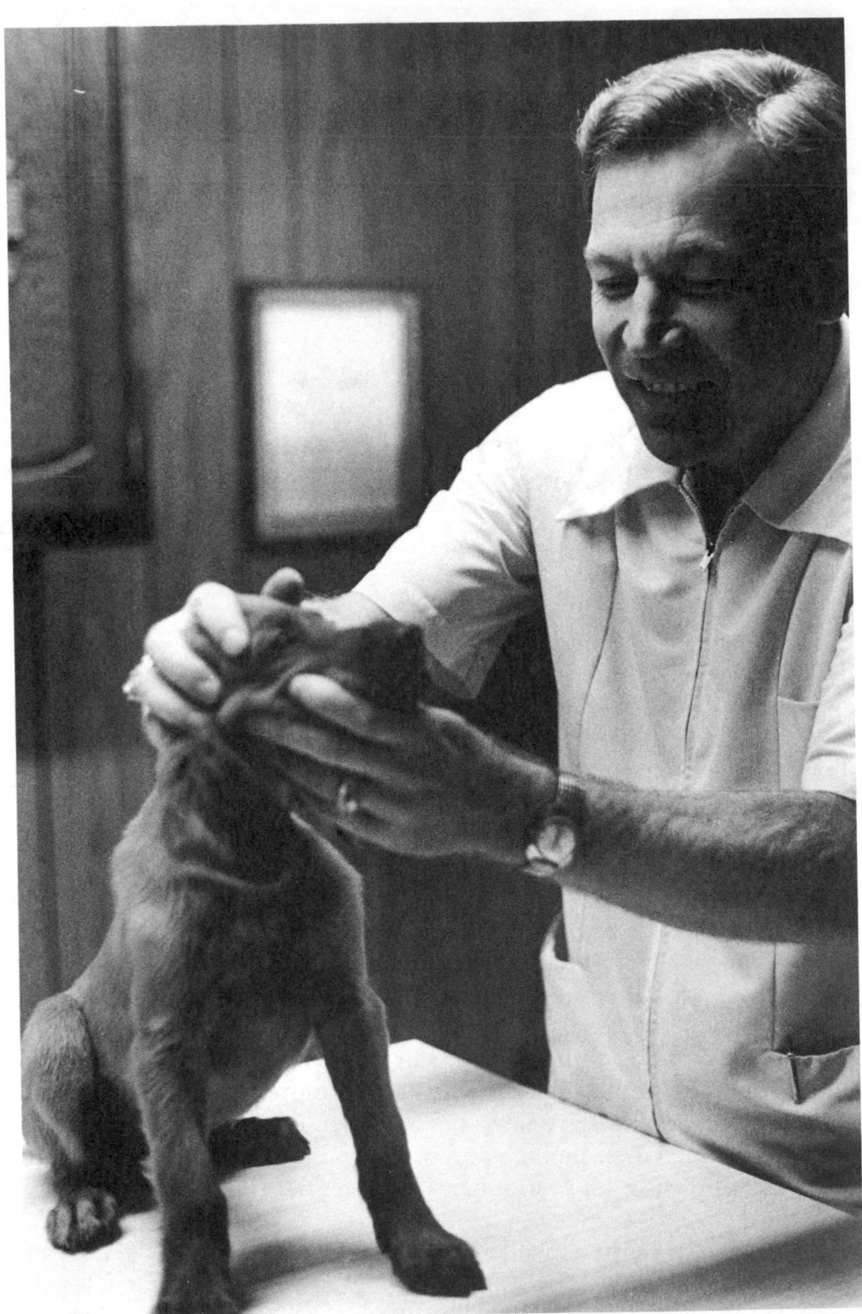

Dr. Dick Royse inspects Irish setter pup for prospective buyer.

free of flies and debris? Does it smell to high heaven? Are ten pups crowded into one crate? It's difficult to get a healthy pup from ill-kept premises.

"Then look at the pups. First, look at them in the litter. Which ones appear stronger, more active, more dominant? Which ones strut, up on their toes, perky-eared, bright-eyed? Which ones hold their ground? Which ones try to take the ground from you, or their littermates?

"When you've picked one that appeals to you (remember, you're looking at fifteen years with this guy), get him off by himself. Now what's his response? Is he still active, eager, peppy? Granted, different people want different things in a dog. The go-getter wants a dog that'll go get 'em. I guess a junk-yard man wants a junk-yard dog. Such people seek traits of dominance, aggression, and all that. Fine. They get what they want, plus a hard-going pup is probably feeling good, probably healthy.

"But this doesn't mean he's any more healthy than the shy pup. Nor does it mean a shy dog is undesirable as a gun dog. Maybe the owner wants something he can handle, something gentle. Maybe a considerate owner knows the dog will spend most of its life in the back yard, and a pup with fire will eventually burn a hole in the fence or fold from boredom.

"So what I'm saying is this, bold or shy, the pup should be active both in and out of the litter. He should have a spring in his step, curiosity, a happy face.

"Consequently, how do you tell whether the pups are sick or well? Lots of ways. Here's what we look for."

Appearance

"That pup has to have bright, clear eyes. A smooth, slick hair coat. A clean muzzle and nose. Beware of the pup that has a discharge from the nose or one that's drooling around the mouth.

"The pup should stand erect on his feet, not splayed out, not 'coon-footed' as we call it. He should be clean. I mean physically clean. He shouldn't have feces all over him. He shouldn't be messy. He shouldn't stink."

Doc presses his pipe stem against the bridge of his spectacles to push them up his nose and says, "Take the pup and turn him over. Look at his tummy. He shouldn't have any red spots, skin eruptions, or pustules [pimples]. That tummy should be very smooth . . . and most puppies at the age they're picked, at weaning age, should have slightly pink tummies.

"Now if there's a discharge from the male dog's penis, you may or may not have to worry about it. The prepuce [foreskin] on a male pup is like a dirt scoop. It's forward and it's got a slit in it, and every time that pup lies down on the ground or runs through the grass, he can pick up a little dirt or pollen or whatever in the prepuce opening. And it's just common bacteria that will develop in there.

"The puppy should be in good flesh. You shouldn't see his ribs sticking out. He should be solid in your hand, the more dense the better. Observe all over the skin closely for any eruptions under the hair. Run the hand against the lay of the hair. Look for sores or scaliness. Observe if this puppy, or these puppies, sit around and scratch a lot, dig at their ears.

"If this pup has a pot belly, try to see if it's in perspective. Sure, you get to the kennel ten minutes after feeding and all the pups look bloated. But if you've got a puppy that is all tummy, yet his ribs are sticking out and his backbone shows, be suspicious; he may be heavily parasitized [got worms]. Because a premier sign of worms is false fat in a pot belly.

"If feces are smeared on the underside of the tail, below the rectum, and below the haunches, that puppy has to have diarrhea. Or he's had diarrhea. Could be worms. Because there are about three or four types of the main parasites that do cause diarrhea in pups.

"Check the color of the pup's mucous membranes. Lift up his lip and pull down his lower eyelid; that skin should be a bright, healthy pink. But on dark-skinned dogs these membranes can be pigmented toward liver, and that's all right. But if either the gums or the conjunctiva [eyelid liner] are blanched out white, beware of anemia.

"What I'm saying is if that pup shows a pot belly, anemia, or diarrhea, then you're looking at three good indications he's got worms.

"Now, with that pup still turned over, look for an umbilical hernia, indicated by a little cleft or bubble at the belly button. Such a hernia is not necessarily harmful, depending on the dog's size, its sex, and its intended use. A very small umbilical hernia on a dog is probably of no consequence. But if it's a very large one on a bitch that's going to be bred, that bubble may herniate when she's pregnant and cause problems.

"As for bite . . . check the occlusion of that pup's incisors and front teeth. If he's parrot-mouthed – so he can't scoop feed out of a pan – you've got troubles."

Doc jams a fingertip into the pipe gone cold. This smoking is a Sunday pastime. I never see the pipe at his clinic. So he gets it going again and makes a lot of it, puffing nothing, and says, "On joints it's hard to say anything about a pup. They're all awkward. Obviously a pup shouldn't limp, obviously he should track well [back feet follow the front]. He should not be weak in his hindquarters nor fall from one side to the other. But beware of extremely enlarged joints. If the puppy looks like he's knobby at his carpals, wrists, elbows, or hocks . . . that may mean he has rickets.

"However, you should ask the breeder if both sire and dam have OFA [Orthopedic Foundation for Animals] certification that attests to an absence of hip dysplasia. It's imperative you ask this for a gun dog. They've got the weight to aggravate weak hips into a real problem.

"But the most important question for the breeder is whether or not he's wormed the pups. If he says, 'Yes,' and you ask, 'How many times?' and he says, 'Once,' then be suspicious. Those pups may be clean of parasites, but with no more worming than that you'll need to work with your vet to check for and to combat worms.

"Also check the breeder's heartworm-prevention program. If the dam is presently a carrier of immature heartworms, these can cross the placenta membrane and infest the pups in the embryo. The mature heartworm will not develop in the pup for nine to twelve months.

"Also ask the breeder what type shots he's given for distemper, hepatitis, parvo, and leptospirosis. Many pups have died because a breeder said, 'Oh, they got their shots.' And he was telling the truth. But the buyer didn't understand that the pup needs a follow-up booster. Be sure at what time and how many shots the pup has had."

Clean Bill of Health

"Then before the deal is made," says Doc, pointing at me now with the pipe's stem, "the breeder must be told the sale is dependent on a clean bill of health from a vet. If the breeder hedges or says, 'No,' then go. If he says, 'Sure, take the pup and look him over,' then get to a vet and do just that. A reputable breeder will want to know the results. A reputable breeder is aware things can crop up in his kennels that he's not even suspecting . . . even if he's conscientious. By taking the pup to a vet you're doing the breeder a favor. The reputable breeder will thank you for it."

Doc sighs and says, "But who gets to talk to the breeder anymore? There's too many of these doggy-in-the-window impulse purchases. Heck, people pick up a pup on a whim somewhere between a shopping-center purchase and their way to the parking lot. It's the old thing of getting home with a goldfish and finding you don't have a bowl."

He sighs again and says with a great release of voice, "Oh well . . .

let's get back to worms. Why am I so hard-nosed about 'em? Well, not only will they kill a pup, but let's say you take a pup home that's got hookworms. Got any other pets around? Know what? Now they've all got hookworms. These worms are lightning contagious.

"Same with external parasites. Take home fleas and your other pets have fleas. Fleas and ticks carry disease. So, once again, when you've got that pup turned over and you're looking at his belly, see if any fleas take off. You can see 'em running on the bare spots of the tummy and under the legs. Anybody can find a tick. Just rub the hair the wrong way, feel around. Little ticks are the size of a match head and look like tiny hard-shelled crabs. Big ones may be the size of a piece of hominy.

"And ear mites? They'll spread, too. Just look in the ear for dirt: waxy debris. Take a sniff. Mites cause a stink.

"And what else do you take home besides internal and external parasites? How about mange? If a pup sits around scratching a lot and you're thinking fleas but can't find 'em, maybe the pup's got a subtle mange. That's one thing. But what if the pup's got sarcoptic mange? Carry him on to your place and all your other pets can have it, too.

"And distemper's something else you can take home. People look for this, but they usually don't know the symptoms. They lift a pup and he upchucks. 'Distemper,' they say. Hardly. Pups vomit easily, what with their scavenging habits and their voracious eating. They upchuck like a baby, bingo!

"So everyone should know distemper's symptoms: lethargy, runny pussy eyes, snotty nose, quite often a dry, short, hacking cough, usually a loss of body weight, and a poor appetite or no appetite at all.

"But how are you going to judge things like appetite by just looking at a bunch of pups running around in a pen? You're not. So it's imperative – that pup must go directly from the breeder to the vet. There's no other way. Or else you may not be buying pleasure at all. You may be paying money for a pup's pain, your pain, and a fistful of problems . . . all of which you could have avoided. If you want a sick pup, that means you want to be a sick pup nurse.

"And that's not what people want," says Doc as he knocks out the pipe on an ash tray and pokes the pipe in his breast pocket. "They want a buddy, not a bed case."

7

Caring for the New Pup

THE ESSENTIALS FOR happiness in our lives are something to hope for, something to do, and something to love. In other words, all those good things that happen when you get a new pup.

With each new pup comes the hope he'll be the gun dog of your life. You'll have lots to do bringing him along. And what's easier to love than a pup?

Now hope and love come easy. It's all that "doing something" that can be a chore.

So let's make the job easier by discussing some imperatives in bringing a new pup into the home. First off, it's much easier, but less gratifying, to raise Pup in a kennel. For most of the day you've placed a kenneled pup in a penalty box: cut off from you and your doings. His life is a chain-link fence, a concrete pad, a water bucket, and maybe an automatic feeder. Pup can live out there with hardly a human contact. He turns, then, to the other dogs for guidance and amusement. If no other dogs exist, he turns to nothing. From such a sterile environment many a field champion has been raised, and some mighty fine hunters. But a friend? Someone who knows your every mood, who can read your slightest cues? Who knows the subtleties of your voice, your facial expressions, your stance? Hardly.

To have a complete gun dog, the dog must share your complete life. Which means he must be raised in your house.

There are pitfalls to avoid in bringing Pup inside. He must be brought alone. Oh, how many of us have succumbed to the temptation of picking out Pup, but then lingering to also buy a littermate? And now you've got two pups in the house, but more than twice the trouble and less than half a chance of training either.

These two pups have been companions from the womb. They'll continue to share the world through common eyes. The most important reference in their lives will be each other, not you! And that destroys all we try to do by bringing Pup inside. You must be Pup's total life. This cannot be shared with another pup. Pup must become totally dependent upon you. Not only in being bedded down and fed, but in play, love, and care – everything.

It's miraculous what a pup can learn the first six weeks he's in your home. He'll learn "No," "Let's go outside," "Come on," "Let's eat," "Quit it," "Go on." He'll also learn his name as well as the names of the other dogs, and the times to feed and sleep and walk and bark. Not only will he recognize praise, such as "That's a good boy (or girl)," when he does his business in the fenced-in back yard, but he'll also begin searching for the praise – and doing things to earn that praise. Now we're raising a tractable dog. A dog that values our good will. Oh, the kennel dog may work for you out of training or routine, but the house-raised dog will work for you to keep your love. *Which means you've replaced harshness with gentleness. You've got Pup working for smiles and words of endearment.*

The House-Raised Pup

The kennel-raised pup may have to be jolted to get his attention, but the house-raised pup will respond to being ignored. Read that sentence again; there's none more important in this book. To jolt a pup, the handler's frantic. To ignore the pup, the handler's reserved. Throughout pup's life, that's the way he'll be trained. The handler always at peace, the dog always seeking his praise. For our training is based on *love*. And love is that condition where another person's happiness is necessary for your own. A rejected pup suffers pain far more severe than any ever rendered by a whip.

That's why the chain gang is so effective (more on this later). The errant pup, now rejected, must watch the other dogs work and receive your attention and your praise. Like the coach who benches the player – the player finally enters the game with a force of ten.

Chances are there'll be other dogs already living in your home when Pup's brought in. Let it be known for the first two weeks they'll probably hate Pup's guts. And there'll be great scuffles and sounded threats where you'll swear Pup's going to be mutilated or killed! But dogs are not that way. They bluff. They display. They don't maim. Oh, there'll be that rare exception when a large dog will unwittingly hurt a

World's most-noted gun dog breeder, Bob Wehle, builds bond of love with each English pointer pup he whelps.

pup because he doesn't know his own strength. But mostly the older dogs just want to be let alone to protect all their conveniences and monopolize you and the treats. And let's face it, a pup can be a tormenting pest. Therefore, when Pup's being rolled under and he's squealing bloody murder (nothing is more shrill or unsettling than a pup's cry) don't, I repeat don't, go to his rescue.

To do so makes two things worse. First, it favors Pup in the old dog's eyes. Now he does have something to brood about. Second, it robs Pup of the chance of becoming self-reliant.

So stay out of it. Dogs have been working out family matters for centuries. They know how to do it. And what new kid on the block doesn't have to pay his dues?

But, I'll tell you this. When it's all said and done, in two weeks the dog that has given Pup the roughest time will probably become Pup's best friend. And that'll be for life. Now aren't you glad you didn't interfere?

The best thing you can give Pup when he's brought inside is a cave. Dogs love secret, dark, and sheltered places. Take some pillows and seal off an end space under the sofa. Now Pup can crawl under there and have a roof over him, walls, and a place where he can "hide" and peek out to monitor this strange new world he's just inherited. I have always advised putting Pup in a box or kennel crate with a pad for comfort. And that's still fine. But my emphasis was toilet training. I was discounting the fact that *a roof over a dog's head is very important*. Matter of fact, it is a very deep need.

Any enclosure is an aid in teaching toilet habits. Unless he's ill, Pup just won't mess his nest. So, the box helps the household bring Pup along. And that's what should be used at night. Either a box, a kennel crate, or a baby bed or crib picked up at a garage sale.

I bring so many pups into the house—and they're all different—that I've gradually learned tricks of the trade. Some pups will whine in their crate at night, but put them in a baby crib and wheel it up beside your bed where the pup can see you all night and he becomes satisfied and quiet. Remember, he has good night vision, plus he can smell the mood of you.

There's nothing so important to a dog as food. Consequently, here's where you can assuredly have a fur-flinging fight. For Pup will reject his bowl to go sniff out what the older dogs are getting. If there's any time Pup needs to be isolated, it's during dinner. But if you monitor your feedings, you can pull it off with all of them eating side by side. In some cases, you may have so many dogs wanting to examine the new pup's offering you'll be inclined to give up. Dinner time is just delicate. Keep control.

And I don't mean by yelling. You see the older dogs know exactly who you're yelling at. But not Pup. Every raised voice is his personal threat. And a voice-shy, man-shy, dog-shy pup will more likely prove himself a gun-shy and bird-shy dog. So keep order quietly.

Everything we're doing now is the basis for the final gun dog. It's all connected like links in a chain. The critic who thinks we're doting on a pup just doesn't have much fertilizer in his plot: he's not thought it out.

Take a kibble from Pup's pan and toss it. He'll run and fetch it up. We're teaching retrieving. Keep kibbles in your shirt and pants pockets. When Pup jumps up for love he smells your pants: he's learning to use his nose. Lying beside you on the sofa he scents the kibble in your shirt: and on and on. Plus, you honor him for each find: you're teaching him the value of discovery. You also can keep his pan on the counter until last. Pup'll learn to wait out the other dogs; in other words, he'll be learning to honor another dog's activity.

Sudden moves startle a pup. It can be a simple thing, but result in complex problems. Like reaching for Pup to take him outside. Do it slow and easy. Do it coaxingly. To thrust your hands out triggers threat, and Pup will either cringe or bolt. Now you've got Pup running from you, and this can't be. Better lie on the floor and have him come to examine you, then get hold of him and take him outdoors. He knows he's out here to do his business, but he can't remember how he got there.

Incidentally, nothing bolds a pup up like your lying on the floor and letting him have mastery over you. No longer do you appear to be a formidable tower. Now you're beneath Pup, seemingly at his mercy. He can climb on you and look down at you and discover you're manageable.

It will come to pass that Pup must take a ride in the family car. Take him alone the first few times. Older dogs are possessive of their respective places in a car. And for some family dogs, cars come second in importance to food. Matter of fact, what dog won't leave his food bowl to go for a ride? You can include Pup in a group outing after he's been accepted by the clan.

Now, there's hardly any of us who can resist the temptation of taking Pup to the back yard and introducing a bird wing on a fishing pole or throwing a wadded-up sock for a retrieve. Fine. Go ahead and do it. But never do it with another dog around. They'll distract Pup and break his concentration—just when you're introducing him to game! Or they'll barge in to take the play from Pup, causing him either to flee or to lunge on the prey. Both bad. And finally, the whole fiasco will result in you cursing and fuming, and now you've all destroyed the training session. Which means Pup's frightened and you're disappointed. The mood of you tells him this, and he may conclude, "I don't want to play that game anymore." So there goes feather and fetch.

There are many times the new pup must have time alone with you. And there are other times all the dogs can excite Pup to performance. That's dog training: that's you knowing how to read Pup, your dogs, and yourself.

Dog Door

In house training your greatest ally is a dog door and a house on the same level as the fenced-in back yard. But don't install only one dog door in the wall of your home. Make it two: one on the inner wall, and one immediately opposite on the outer wall. This means you'll need to frame and finish the tunnel between the two doors. The result is a four- to six-inch (depending on the thickness of your wall) air chamber between the two dog doors that acts as an insulation zone that will cut your energy costs. You can also install dog doors in your house doors, or screens, and manufacturers have even come up with a panel that fits into Arcadia doors.

Older dogs will teach Pup to use the dog door. You can also flip it back and forth with your toe. The door lets Pup get outside without your continually coming and going. But let's say Pup's made it to the porch and can't get down the stairs: his legs are too short, maybe he's a cocker spaniel – which can be a mighty fine gun dog. In this instance, place builder blocks on each stair step so Pup can get down a half-step at a time. He'll use the blocks going down but not coming up. Going down he's frightened, coming up he's not.

Now, there's nothing so unfortunate as a breeder who house trains weaning pups on newspapers (or forgets to cut the dew claws at three days). With paper-trained pups you're going to pick up your newspaper some morning and read the sog. But that's not the real problem. What in the world duplicates paper? Paper training has no transference.

If Pup's raised on concrete, he'll naturally go on a hard surface. Which means he'll think nothing of stooling on the kitchen linoleum. Let's pause a second and talk of picking up. If Pup is to be kennel-raised, he must be on a sloped concrete pad (for good drainage) that leads to a trough deep enough so it won't spill over and wide enough to take a shovel. Ideally, the whole thing is connected to the sewer line. If Pup is to go in the yard, then the best means of disposal is a flat pan on a pole to receive the feces and a springy rake (especially on grass) to flip it into the pan. If Pup's raised on gravel, the springy rake is replaced with a solid sheet-metal drag.

If Pup's been raised on grass before weaning, your carpet is a good substitute for dumping. So the concrete-raised pup favors tile, and the grass-raised Pup is triggered by carpet. Still, I'll take the grass-raised Pup any time. It's up to you to get him out when necessary. And he'll be giving you all kind of clues, especially running and sniffing and then starting to spin. But once he hits grass the urge will overtake him. And time may not mean much to you, but it sure does to me when the chill factor is below zero and I'm standing out there in the rain.

That's why I tell Pup, "Good Pup," or whatever his name is, when he dumps. I mean high praise. Really spread it on.

If Pup makes a mistake in the house—honest folks, it's not the end of the world. If he stools and it's solid, pick it up and flush it away. If it's soft, or you step in it, just scrape up what you can with two pieces of cardboard and salt the spot. Salt dries out the mess, just as it tans hides. Finally, vacuum and de-scent.

For an odor masker you can use vinegar or one of the new products formulated for that purpose—a so-called odor eliminator. Water accidents get blotted with paper towels, scrubbed with Alka-Seltzer water (I don't know why it does such a good job), and de-scented.

Not only do pups mess in the house, they also track the outdoors in. Keep a towel at the door. Pups love to dig, and here they come, claws packed. You may have to drop Pup in the sink and rinse his paws. He won't like this, so make a game of it. Also, pups can appear with smeared rear ends. Remove what you can with toilet paper and flush. Use scissors to trim feathers. Then wipe the area with Wet Ones, the moistened towels.

Finally, it's your obligation to keep the yard scooped up. Pups are inquisitive. They will examine stools. And this terrible practice can result in Pup taking stools to mouth, which can be a hard fault to cure. Don't ever let such a thing get started. Keep the yard clean.

We can achieve small and solid stools through proper feeding. This means less smeared rear ends and less material to scoop from the yard. But no pup is carefree. Continually check him for awns, spear grass, punctures, external and internal parasites, coat sheen, gum and eyelid color, and bloated tummy. I've heard more than one pro say, "The most important person in my operation is the kennel boy." The stool tells you the dog's condition. Be there to examine it.

So that's it for pups. Now to training.

8

Speed Training: The Destroyer of Gun Dog Pups

AMERICANS LOVE DEFINITE timing and definite answers. Remember the old days when you'd buy a new car, and the manual told you to drive it under fifty miles per hour for 1,000 miles before you could let her rip? Likewise, we take assurance today in thirty-day free trials, seven-year factory warranties, and no payments until next January. Our urban culture treasures time, and unique to that, the faster the better. Pizza in thirty minutes, one-hour Martinizing, overnight delivery!

Little wonder that as gun dog editor of *Field & Stream* magazine I've received hundreds of letters asking, "At what age can I take my pup hunting?" Or "put him on birds? Or "introduce him to water?"

All this is made especially unfortunate by dog authorities who have proclaimed, "You can take your pup hunting at nine months." Or "put him on birds at twelve weeks." Or "introduce him to water when you bring him home."

These same authorities usually promise, "Fast, radically new training."

Well that's the last thing on earth we need. And probably the last thing we could attain.

I admit the real answer to such questions poses a Catch-22. You can't train a pup until you know how to read him. And you can't read a pup until you've trained a few. That's why so many people say, "You always ruin your first dog." The same way, I suppose, you have to ruin several blocks of wood before you can make a working decoy.

Now let's take a deeper look at these dog gurus who propose to give definite answers and definite times to puppy training. It all goes back to a group of men, and especially Clarence Pfaffenberger, who did research work for the Guide Dogs for the Blind during the late 1940's and early 1950's. They were alarmed at the percentage of failures among donated pups put through guide dog training. Eventually they thought they noticed critical, developmental periods in a pup's life. Concentrate with intensive training during these periods, they figured, and it was likely the pup would have a much better chance of becoming a guide dog. Thus we were given a "neonatal period, the transition period, the socialization period, the juvenile period," and so on.

It was then stated that trainers should try and teach certain skills, or establish certain attitudes, during selected periods so the pup might become a guide dog.

Well, there were dog authorities who jumped on this possibility–not necessarily giving credit for their inspiration–and you began to hear such engraved-in-stone pronouncements as: "You must adopt your pup on the forty-ninth day. . . . The most critical period in a dog's life is from his twenty-first day to his eighty-fourth. . . . From his fifty-sixth day through his eighty-fourth day the pup has the ability to handle problem-solving tasks and is receptive to discipline."

Now let me say hard and fast, I have no problem with the Guide Dogs for the Blind. Thank God they exist to help the sightless and to have given us new and unique insights into dog behavior. And should you want to learn more about this valuable program, let me direct you to an excellent book: *Leader Dogs for the Blind*, by Margaret Gibbs.

My quarrel comes with those trainers and writers and whoever else took the Guide Dog findings and went off half-cocked to convince the world they could have a trained pup in ten weeks or six months or a year. And boy, was this a popular concept, for it fit the American psyche of no fuss, no muss, no waiting, no hassle, no commitment. Just grab a pup and go.

How many dogs have been scuttled because of this? And how many would-be trainers and eventual bird hunters were driven from the game? Well, look at the parent program and decide for yourself. In the Guide Dog system you have trained professionals working with selected pups in a controlled environment toward a specific goal. Now compare this with the average gun dog trainer. He's an amateur. He was given a pup or found a stray or got his dog from a classified ad. And this dog may be any breed or mix of breeds. This dog must fit into the man's environment, be it tenement, condo, tract housing, or what have you. And in all probability, the pup must live with other dogs, kids, and in-laws. And what's the goal for this pup? Sure, it is to take the man hunting. But isn't he also a playmate for the kids, a guard dog, a house pet, a whatnot with a bandanna about his neck that rides in the bed of the pickup?

Now, there is this to say. I know professional gun dog trainers who can have a retriever pup fetching at four weeks or can have a bird dog pup steady to wing and shot at three months. But they've done this one time, maybe. And they did it to prove a point. Having proven that point, they did not reconstruct the general rule. And that is, *training any living creature takes a lot of care and a very long time*. To train quick is like getting rich quick – it's all in the eyes of the armchair authority, not in the hands of the man who would try.

What's the Hurry?

What's the hurry, anyway? Who grabbed you out of the bassinet and said in three months you must be a welder, a brick mason, or an attorney! These can be the most delightful days and weeks and months of all. You and Pup out *Happy Timing*. Learning each other, learning the country, learning what love means one to the other. Sharing bed and bread. Finding out where in the car Pup wants to ride, and where he wants to sleep, and what toy he prefers. Telling people you've cornered at the shopping center just who Pup is – him standing there on lead – and what grand plans you have for his future. I remember Shakespeare and lesser lights telling us, "he who runs fast has a greater chance of stumbling."

I don't want you to stumble. I want you to succeed. You and Pup. And I know of no other way to do it than this: take a lifetime. Make Pup a grand devotion. Love him. Do everything with him. Be patient. Wait. Wait some more. Before you can teach Pup anything you want him to know, you must *make his world disappear*.

For how can you teach Pup to whoa if he's curious about the smell in the alfalfa? He should have become acquainted with that smell and traced it to its source in a nontraining situation. That is, *Happy Timing*. The two of you whiling away your days in fields and woods, jumping sideways from the leaping toad, ducking at the dip of the kingbird, mucking through the fresh cow pie, learning to avoid the lash of the snapped-back twig. Knowing what ice will break and what ice will hold. Recognizing that cucumber stench of rattlesnakes. When Pup has learned all this and more you will have accomplished at least two things: (1) he will have learned to love the country as much as you, and (2) it will have disappeared. That is, there'll be no more surprises. Which means there'll be no more distractions. Now you can start training.

And how are you going to put a calendar on this? Will learning the country be accomplished in two months?

But there's something else Pup must learn that's equally important. And that's you. Not you in a lounge chair before the TV, or coming naked from the shower, or sitting on a stool digging out an ingrown toe nail. Though all this is important. What Pup must really learn is your heart and soul and scent. What makes you tick – and the smells that tell it. What makes you mad. What makes your thoughts drift – to go away from him though you stand right there. For Pup doesn't know about marital problems or a job you're about to lose or a contract that isn't going to be signed. Pup must learn every strange thing that is you.

Then and only then – when Pup knows the territory and the man who's taken him for life – will Pup be ready to go for birds. And won't that depend on how complicated all those fields appear to Pup? And how simple you can present yourself? I think so. And how well Pup can learn. Just how bright he is. How mature. How eager. How bold. And how much time. This is the only place in training that time figures in – *how much time you've given to Pup to learn all these things.*

So you write and ask me when Pup should go hunting? I don't know. You tell me. *You're the only one qualified to say.*

But I know why you ask. You want to get started – as I suppose you were chomping at the bit to get through all the chapters I wrote on puppies. This is especially true with youth. The Bible tells us, "Your old men shall dream dreams, your young men shall see visions." That's it, you see visions of Pup and gun and gamebag filled. But wait. I think an Irishman I went to the moors with said it best. He pointed out to his brace of Irish setters that buttonhooked before him in their grand sweep for grouse and mused, "I never want to find the bottom of them." What he meant was he purposely undertrained. He didn't want to learn their potential. That was always a dream to be saved for tomorrow. He held a rope to life by not knowing that, just as he later held a leash to the brace of red dogs who went laughingly before him to the Land Rover.

But Americans have trouble with emotions and motives like that. Like a man I once knew who made a fortune late in life. With wealth, people would listen to him, and he loved to tell stories of his youth. As a child he learned the circus was coming to town. Why, the lead man pasted a jumping tiger on his dad's barn. And the boy worked all summer for the coins to see the circus. And the day arrived, and he rode the plow horse to town . . . but what's this? There's noise. A band is going down Main Street, and there are elephants and girls in spangles. He rushed up to a man standing on the corner and yelled, "Is that the circus?" And the man said, "Yep." And the boy said, "What does it cost to see it?" And the man asked, "How much you got?" And the boy told him, "Twenty-five cents." And the man said, "That's what it costs." And the boy gave the man his quarter and stood on the corner and watched the parade go by.

The wealthy old man paused upon relating all this, then said, smiling, "You know, Bill, I was thirty years old before I realized I never saw the circus."

Ignore the train-'em-quick gurus and see the circus with Pup and me. Otherwise you may spend all you got being part of the passing parade.

Let's move to ringside.

Communications and Control

All dog training is love. Stomping, yelling, kicking, beating, and cursing may be the way you stuff trash into a garbage can, but it's the last way we'll ever take Pup to birds. We're not training Pup for the demolition derby. We want him running before us with all his chrome shining, his headlights up, his antenna crackling—all happy in heart.

Now this is a gun dog training book: all gun dogs. We have no concern for breed. Except we'll teach upland dogs to point or flush and retrievers to retrieve. Yet that's not a fact, either. For I've hunted ducks with border collies, prairie chickens with cocker spaniels, grouse with Welsh springers, rabbits with English pointers, quail with Labrador retrievers (you must call them off or they'll vacuum the field), squirrels with a greater Pyrenees, geese with English setters, mountain lions with Australian shepherds, bear with feists, and on and on. All these dogs made their living hunting long before we ever came along. The most honest waterfowl retriever I have right now is a West Highland white terrier. And again, I repeat, because of cross-hybrid vigor the mixed breeds may be the best of all. The greatest quail dog I ever hunted over was an English pointer/German shorthair mix.

No matter the breed or the quarry you train it to hunt or fetch, there are some iron-clad rules in dog training. The most important contact between you and the dog is your scent. When you think, you stink. Second, there is no discipline with more power than eye contact. Hold a dog and stare into his eyes until he turns away: he's now yours. Third, man, horse, or dog, when you've taken their legs away from them, they're yours. Consequently, the most effective discipline is to take both hands, grab a dog by the skin and fur on both sides of the neck (just below and behind his ears), raise him up straight before you, stare him down, and tell him exactly what you think in a firm, quiet voice. All the shouting, choking, yelling, beating, shocking, and kicking ever done will not equal the power of the suspended dog and the stone eye.

But there can be an enforcer for distant discipline. That's a white, plastic fly swatter. Pop Pup with this when he does wrong as a baby in the house, accompany it with strong eye contact and definite voice, and Pup will cringe to that harmless piece of plastic the rest of his life. If he takes it into his head to turn you off at 100 yards, just yell him down with the command, "No," and take the fly swatter from its nestled position down the back of your pants and show it to him. He'll now be yours. Thus, the imperative – when raising the pup from eight weeks or so – in establishing your control early.

Finally, nothing can render Pup more helpless than a stainless steel veterinarian's table. That's why they use it. But those things cost from $800 to $1,200. You have a substitute in your house: the top of the washer and dryer. If Pup's really turned you off inside the house, plop him up there, tell him what you think of him, and show him the white fly swatter.

If Pup refuses to work a field, use the hood of your car. Any place where his feet slip. Any high place where you can look straight into his eyes, where he smells the doom of your breath and sweat, and hears the promise of your voice.

If he's still obstinate, then grab both sides of the scruff of his neck, lift him, and lay him down on the ground flat on his back. You can either kneel beside him or sit astraddle his chest. Now he's totally defenseless as you stare him down and shout straight up his nose.

And, that folks, is what I call dog training. Never once is Pup physically hurt, but he sure is intimidated. Mock malice. Remember momma dog. We're going to train as she trained.

The Old Way

Many years ago I was calling on one of America's most prominent gun dog kennels, gathering source materials for my articles. The owner had shown a dog that day, but it broke on wing and shot. The prospective buyer walked away saying, "He's not worth $500."

Yet the next day the guy called and said he'd decided to take the dog. The kennel owner told him, "Fine, he's yours . . . but the price is now $550." I guess the guy on the other end of the line sputtered and fumed, but he finally said he'd take the dog. A few hours later, however, he called back and said he'd taken the dog to have its hips X-rayed only to find there was bird shot in the dog's flanks. The kennel owner laughed and told him, "I had a training session with that dog after you left, and I shot him when he broke. That's what you paid that extra $50 for!"

Dog training?"

We were high in the mountains many years ago before the running of a major retriever trial. My buddy's dog had everything it took to win, but it was not listening to the whistle when distant on water. So my buddy got me up early and took the dog to a distant pond. He put an electronic shock collar on it and cast it to the center of the pond. Then he jammed the button on the transmitter and the dog went berserk: tumbling, screaming, and going under, frantically pawing at the water, white froth coming from its mouth. Its eyes were glazed with terror and still the electricity poured in on him while the man blew the whistle – which the dog could not hear.

Dog training?

A shepherd dropped by my house to talk dogs, and I mentioned to him that J.A. Hunter, the great African guide, once emptied several dog pounds to take the lot lion hunting. Those that survived made excellent lion dogs. My shepherd friend departed, but two months later I got a letter. He said he'd taken my advice and emptied a large city dog pound. He had to have sheep dogs. And boy did he find them; it was miraculous, and he wanted to thank me for the tip.

But he also wrote something else that puzzled me: though there were several who sure 'nuf worked out, still there were lots of "thirty-thirty" dogs. I called him and asked what a thirty-thirty dog was. I was told, "Those were the ones who wouldn't do it, and I had to shoot them with a .30/30."

Dog training?

So much for dog training, now back to our iron-clad rules.

The New Way

Pup must never have anything bad happen to him he can associate with you. So it's best he be self-trained or brought along—whenever possible—by other dogs (more to follow). *If anything bad happens to Pup we never return him to where it occurred.* Dogs associate pain with place. *Pup must be trained in short snatches of time.* No more than five- to fifteen- minute sessions. Hour-long or day-long sieges destroy Pup's curiosity, enthusiasm, and stamina. *To train a dog, you've got to be smarter than he is.* This is not some smart-alec remark. It means when one training method fails, you must be able to adapt and instill another. There are many dog trainers who have a system into which the dog must fit or out he goes. The smart trainer, however, adapts his training to the dog, not vice versa.

And there's a final law that may be more important than all the above: *always let Pup finish each training session with victory.* Retriever pros call it, "Sweetening him up." Say the session has been a shambles. Pup has earned your wrath—and he knows it!—but you never crate him this way. Let him win. Give him a puppy test. Put him away happy, not sulking. For the fact is he'll grieve all day and night if you don't. Like most rules, however, there can be an exception; if a dog persists in refusal, then he must be short-tied and isolated. We'll talk of this later.

So hooray! We're finally ready to train dogs. But I must remind you: *all previous methods were based on the handler controlling the dog. Not this one. Here the handler must control himself and the dog will respond.* It takes no smarts to beat a dog to death or to shoot or shock or kick him. But it takes the ultimate in thought for a man to control his emotions so he's sending the right scent signals, the right facial expressions, body stance, and tone of voice. That's why my system requires only a few inexpensive training aids. The primary aid is yourself. You got little to help you but you.

Pups are trained in yard and field. What happens one place does not necessarily happen in the other. In yard training we teach heel, sit, stay, here, all right, and whoa. Afield we teach whup, ho, and birds. That's for upland game dogs. For retrievers we teach heel, sit, stay, back, over, fetch it up, hold it, and give.

All gun dogs heel on your non-gun side, which gives you greater movement and directs the dog to come near your free hand when fetching (a hunter just won't put down his gun). A dog is heeled when his collar is adjacent to your pants seam. There are many ways to teach this, but my choice is Mike Gould's power bar.

The Power Bar

In the past, when we wanted to teach a dog to heel, sit, or stay or to cast, turn, and take hand signals, we used a slack rope, a check cord, or a leash. It was, if you will, the futile pushing of a wet noodle. But with Mike Gould's power bar we now have a lever. The *New Columbia Encyclopedia* tells us, "A lever consists of a bar supported at some stationary point along its length and used to overcome resistance at a second point by application of force at a third point." The stationary point is the fulcrum.

The power bar, then, is quite like the paddle used to propel a canoe. To merely sit in the canoe and splash with the left hand gets us nowhere, except wet. But to hold the paddle constant in our right hand (the fulcrum), dip it in the water (the resistance), and pull back with our left hand (the force), we can go fishing.

Using a check cord in the traditional way has, in a sense, been the splashing with our left hand. But now we take the power bar, anchor one end in our solar plexus, attach the other end to Pup (who is the

Power bar cord is looped through snap swivel snapped to dog's collar. The cord is drawn up very tight; allow no slack. Mike Gould is a professional trainer with years of experience and gentle hands. He uses a pinch collar with the power bar. A pinch collar is another power device: when the dog complies, the collar stays open; but when the dog balks or fights the handler, the collar contracts. The dog determines his own limit. But this collar doesn't fit my training program.

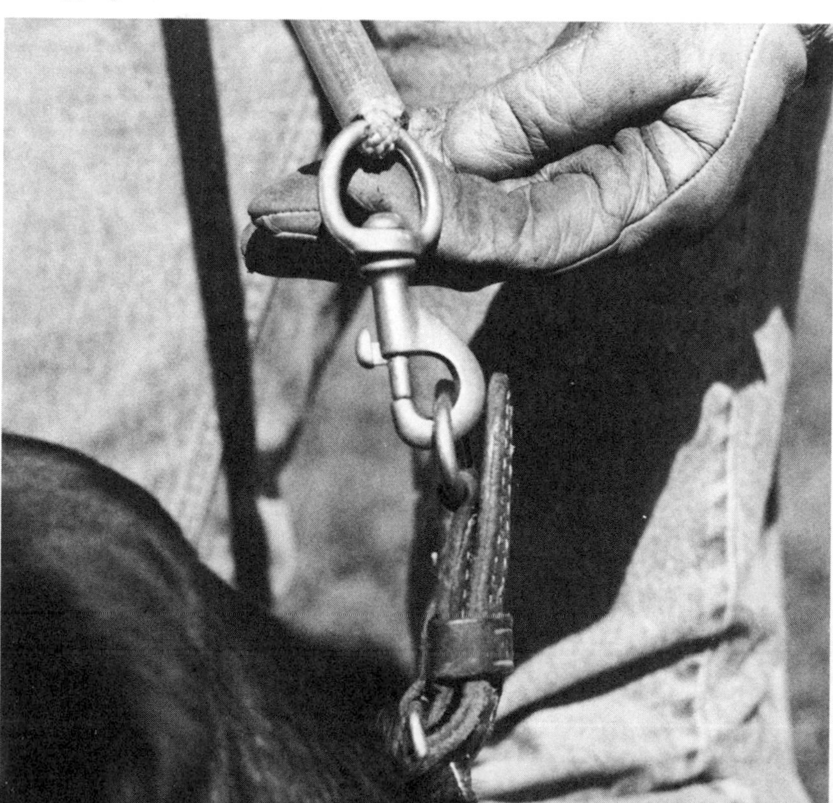

Mike shows the top of power bar, where looped-back cord is tied tight to trailing check cord.

resistance), adjust the bar with our left hand (apply force), and we start to get somewhere.

To make a power bar, cut yourself a piece of ½-inch electrical conduit and fit it to you as follows. Place one end of the conduit—grasped in your right hand if Pup's heeled to your left—in your solar plexus. Let the conduit drop straight down. Cut it off six inches below the fly of your pants. Mike is six feet tall, so his bar is fitted at twenty-eight inches long. That'll give you a benchmark.

Now take a ⅜- or 5/16-inch check cord and feed it through the aluminum pipe. Slip it through a snap swivel (usually brass, available at any gun dog or marine store), and bring the cord back up through the pipe. Now you have a round robin with the bight (a sailor's term) of the cord at the swivel. The loose end of the looped-back cord is tied in a granny knot to the main cord at the exact entry to the conduit pipe. Your only knot is above the pipe, and you merely have a bend in the cord down where the swivel must turn freely. There's nothing to bind; it's all free-wheeling. And it costs pennies. Incidentally, the main cord extends another twenty feet from the tied-off end of the power bar and is cast over your right shoulder so it drags the ground as you walk.

All check cords must be trailed slick: there can be no crimp or knot in the cord, nor can anything be tied to the end. The dog will eventually run while wearing this cord, and the slightest lump will hang up in rocks, V's of tree limbs, or barbed wire, and give Pup a serious jolt. A jolt so severe it could even kill him.

I don't care what dog collar you've used before; there's only one that fits the Tarrant method. That's a plain, flat, wide leather collar (built for stout) with a welded D-ring. Place the collar about Pup's neck just tight enough so you can slide two flat fingers between fur and leather. Attach your power bar snap swivel to the welded D-ring and you're ready. Incidentally, always let Pup smell everything you put on him. Scent makes sense. And always let Pup have time to settle when introducing each new rig.

Ready? Simultaneously step off and say, "Heel." Hold the conduit against your solar plexus with your right hand: there'll be drag. Be ready to bump either the conduit or the snap swivel forward with the V of your left-hand thumb and forefinger. The bump should startle Pup, and he'll leap forward. If he freezes, fine. Tell him, "Heel," and stand there. He's obeying.

This is very important. Any time a dog defies you, make his obstinacy your will. If he comes to you, say, "Come." Always put your

You can get all the power you want to yard train your dog with the plain leather collar and strong D-ring shown here. The pinch collar should be left in the hands of the pro and the seasoned amateur who are training dozens of dogs each year and may not always have time to follow the training program outlined in this book. Remember: it's intimacy we strive for, not intimidation. Use your head to train, not a heavy hand.

Dog is heeled to non-gun side while the power bar is held firmly against solar plexus with the right hand. The left hand is used to gently tap lower part of bar to guide dog through yard commands. Here, the Lab is told to "heel" as the handler steps off straight or turns to right.

command on what he's doing. If you command, "Heel," again, and step off only to have Pup freeze, show him the white fly swatter. If he jumps out sideways, tap him back to your side with the V of your left hand. At some point, you'll get it all started. You'll be walking and Pup will be heeling.

Remember, you're applying levered power. Never press and hold or haul off and slug the bar. Instead, slaps and taps and bumps will get the job done. And wouldn't all this have been easier if Pup had had the benefit of the litter-box check cord? See why all dog training is links in a chain? Pup would already have learned to give to the lead.

If Pup leaps too far forward, return him to heel by patting the bar back with the palm of your left hand. Should he crowd your knee, push out the swivel or bar with the V of your left hand. If he veers too far to side, bump him back with your cupped fingers. Also, continue using all your coaxing methods held over from the house and yard training. Pat your outer leg with your palm to entice Pup close, speak with a soft and gentle voice, tell Pup what a good boy he is when he does well. Remember, the force on the collar is our discipline, but directing the bar is our power steering. We're interested in steering, not discipline.

Now walk in a great circle. So great Pup won't be crowding your leg if you're going left or jumping way to side if you're going right. Keep at this drill, over and over. Stop, rest, say, "Heel," and step off. Repeat and repeat. For all dog training is *point of contact* (the collar), *repetition* (the drill), and Pup finally *associating* your spoken command with the desired action. The final result is Pup running free, reacting only to your voice on his eardrums.

Remember, always train in short snatches of time.

Well, you and Pup aren't going to hunt the world in a great circle. You've got to angle off abruptly sometime. So this is when the session can get tricky, for the circle gets tighter. Make sure Pup is heeling well, he's walking directly at side, no lagging or lunging, and he's keeping his collar even with your outer pants seam.

Now, when we turn *right* at heel (Pup is to our left) it stands to reason the dog's going to swing out–to keep going forward. And with everything that's novel to a dog, you're going to get some resistance. So just keep the top end of the bar anchored, and lead Pup around in a right-hand circle by directing him with your left hand.

To heel Pup in a *left-handed* circle is a totally different matter. As you turn left his body naturally crowds into your left leg. And, you no longer have the leverage of the bar, as it's held in an upright position. We must lower our right hand so the bar is *parallel* to the ground. Keep the right-hand end of the bar about six inches in front of your body and three inches to the right of your outer leg. The bar then crosses your lower lap and extends some distance to Pup's collar.

Your hold on Pup is now rigid. You have control. If Pup lags, you let the fulcrum of your lap drive him forward–the bar rests across the top of your thighs. If he leaps ahead, you bump back with your left hand. If he crowds you, then push him out with the length of the bar. If he drifts wide, then pull the bar across your body.

To repeat—for this is very important—when you want to turn right, you simply anchor the power bar in your chest and push on it with your left hand. But when you want to turn left, you must lower the power bar parallel to the ground and use your lap as a fulcrum to control and center Pup.

Now we're ready to teach sit. And never have we had an aid like the power bar to help us before. Remember how we used to pull up with the leash in our right hand while we stooped over and pushed Pup's rump down with our left hand? Now we just take the power bar and hold it to side like a canoe paddle—the bar coming straight over Pup's head, straight down his long nose. Raise your left hand, elevating the left end of the bar over Pup's head (*the left end is now higher than the*

To heel dog left, the power bar must be placed horizontally in front of handler's lap.

To teach sit with power bar, drop right end below Pup's nose, hold left end up, and push back. Pup can't do anything but sit.

right) and push back with your right hand to force pup to sit. To repeat: lift bar with left hand and push back with right hand. This forces Pup's rump to ground. Once in a while you will have a dog take a couple of steps back, but that's it. He will sit. Matter of fact, there's nothing Pup can do but sit. It's all simple, foolproof, effortless, and fast. In other words, it's perfect dog training.

But the benefit of the power bar does not end at sit. No. It also becomes the best device to insure, "Stay." Merely tell Pup, "Stay" (he's already sitting), raise your left hand like a traffic cop (you're holding the check cord in your right hand), continue to say, "Stay," and edge around in front of Pup, taking the power bar with you. As you back away, let the bar fall to the ground. The bar now makes a wedge, due to the angle of the conduit between Pup's collar and the ground. Should Pup try to move forward, the bar digs into the earth and holds him fast. But when you're quite distant, you merely have to flip the bar up as you order, "Come," then milk the check cord in fast (hand-over-hand) while Pup runs toward you. If you want Pup to heel to the left as he nears, then that's the side you present him.

But let's say Pup fights the wedged-in power bar. He wants to follow you as you back away. Okay, return to Pup, drop the bar so it wedges between earth and collar. But now you don't step away. Instead, step forward, place your left foot on the power bar, and press down. Do it short and snappy. Press and say, "No," all at the same time, over and over. And reinforce the effect by holding your palm up like a traffic cop, staring straight into Pup's eyes, and standing tall above him. With each press of the foot you'll see Pup's collar protrude to the rear of his neck. But we're not hurting Pup. That's why he wears a plain, flat, wide, leather collar.

Now back away, keeping your palm raised and maintaining the same intimidating stare. If Pup indicates he's going to move, then command, "No," and run forward, once again pressing the power bar with your left foot and saying, "Stay,"

And how do you know Pup's about to move? Easy. You read your dog. Before Pup moves his shoulder muscles will twitch: they must

You've walked to front of Pup and told him continually to "sit," but still he wants to move. Now you plant him firmly by pressing down with your left foot on the angle of the power bar. Pump the bar good; Pup'll anchor tight.

Standing distant with hand raised, handler tells Pup, "Stay."

activate before he can lift a paw. Watch the shoulders, they're your cue. Plus, Pup must lower his head to move forward. Watch for the slightest head movement. You also can tell by his eyes; they reveal his intentions. The set of his ears, the lifting of his chest, or the scooting out of the back feet are also signs. Body language: that's what we'll always be reading when predicting Pup. Especially in the bird field, where his cocked ears, perked tail, and eager race – everything – will tell you he's making game.

The Check Cord

All right, we've got Pup heeling, sitting, and staying. Now we remove the power bar and work only with a check cord, or we snap the cord to Pup's collar and mount the power bar far distant to be held in our hands. The whole thing's reversed. Let's cast Pup before us. If you want a retriever to fetch something, or cast to hunt, then stand beside him, extend your left leg to serve as a launching guide (the power bar is now in the right hand), hold your extended (flat) hand beside Pup's head, and command, "Back." To cast the upland-pointing dog you would command, "All right," and to cast the flushing dog you would order, "Hie on." The latter two commands are accompanied with a more relaxed cast, possibly the hand merely swept forward with a clicking of the fingers. We're telling the pointer and the flusher to go hunting: they can more or less choose their course. But the retriever we're sending with definite control.

As Pup leaves, you take off behind him: get the power bar up before your chest and hold it with both hands. When Pup hits the end of the twenty-foot check cord, either command, "Ho," which means look to me for directions, or give him a sustained blast on your Acme Thunderer training whistle. Pup will spin about at the force of the stop and will face you. You'll push the power bar across your chest, let's say, with the right hand anchoring it at the solar plexus and the left hand extending away from the body. This will give Pup a left-hand cast. Reverse it for a right-hand command. The amazing benefit of this training technique is you're teaching Pup two things at once: he's learning to quarter while at the same time he's being introduced to hand signals. You then step off in the direction you want Pup to cast and

Jerking bar from ground and keeping it high, handler tells Pup to "heel" as he milks in check cord and presents non-gun side so Pup can position himself.

Eventually, handler can work Pup distant on a check cord, using the cord as though it were a power bar held in front of his chest. Note extended right hand, which encourages Pup to cut across handler and hunt other side of field.

walk that way, Pup running accordingly.

Eventually you'll say, "Ho," or blow the whistle, and Pup will spin for the hand cast before he ever hits the end of the check cord. Now you've got him handling.

Always before we used a simple check cord with no power bar to cast Pup to hunt or fetch. The trainer really had to jerk the cord to get Pup turned and headed in the right direction. Also, a running dog transmits a lot of force back through the check cord and into the trainer's hands. But no more. The power bar before your chest both transmits and receives all the power in the check cord.

Amazingly, once you've learned to use the power bar to direct Pup in check-cording, you can leave the bar at home and apply almost equal power with just your two hands.

So the power bar is an amazing training device, and we owe it all to a very bright and innovative young retriever trainer and game-farm manager named Mike Gould of Rifle, Colorado. We'll meet Mike again, since he agrees with us that dogs should be trained by example and not

Note tight check cord as handler follows Pup in search of birds' scent cone.

punishment. With one piece of pipe, Mike took yard training from the stone age to the jet age and the total cost was pennies.

I took Mike's system and extended it to bird dog training. That's coming up. But first let's review this chapter before proceeding. We have reinforced our system of training gun dogs with intimacy instead of intimidation, listed the various vocal commands used on all gun dogs (more on flushers later), and explained the use of the power bar. The bar is used on every gun dog, be he flusher, pointer, or retriever. No gun dog can go to field until he's totally yard trained, until he's totally biddable to the power bar and check cord.

But now our training methods must part like a stream about an island. For pointers seek birds to show their position to the hunter and hold them until he arrives. Flushers lift game for the gun. And retrievers fetch deadfalls. This is not to say each dog couldn't (and doesn't) do what the other does. But for the sake of the purists we'll train them separately.

To that end, we'll go first to pointers.

9

Training the Bird Dog

A BIRD DOG must be taught to use the wind, seek out likely objectives, scent birds, hold them with his power, keep his point until the hunter arrives, stand steady to wing and shot, and then watch the covey down so he can relocate as well as pick up the deadfall.*

He will continue wearing the check cord far beyond yard training. This is our primary point of contact. There'll be times we must chase him down and the cord will help us. Pros even train their horses to run down a dog and stamp a hoof on the check cord to bring the dog to a sudden, somersault halt!

If you have an especially hard-driving dog, you might slow his pace by having him drag a twenty-foot section of discarded garden hose as he runs. But again, the hose must be slick so it can't wedge between any obstacles.

Through *Happy Timing* the bird dog has stumbled into gamebirds, *and we've paid no attention*. Eventually he's learned such finds constitute points of objective, so he'll begin hunting clumps in a clear field and he'll hunt the edges (for 90 percent of all game will be found

*Breeds trained here are the weimaraner, vizsla, Brittany spaniel, small Munsterlander pointer, German shorthaired pointer, German roughhaired pointer, German wirehaired pointer, Pudelpointer, spinoni, wirehaired pointing griffon, German longhaired pointer, large Munsterlander pointer, English pointer, English setter, and any dog that will point.

there). By the time he becomes an all-age dog he'll know when the birds are roosting or out feeding. This is all reinforced by the trainer. He casts the dog to likely objectives and follows him there holding the check cord. And to guarantee success he'll purposely build those objectives and plant liberated birds there for the dog to find. So now the bird dog is casting on command (left, right, out, in) for a foot hunter (and later one mounted on horseback or riding in a Jeep), and Pup's seeking out bird haunts. It's time to steady him on birds.

Commands

In yard training we teach Pup to heel, sit, stay, come here, all right, and whoa. "All right," is our command to cast from side, to get to hunting. The handler can actually grasp Pup's collar with his left hand and propel him forward, or he can merely tap Pup behind the head or high on the back (toward the neck) to release him from heel. When Pup's hunting distant and the handler wants his attention, he either yells, "Ho," or blows the training whistle. If the handler wants Pup to come in, he bellows, "Here." Blasted from a leather-lunged trainer, this word seems to travel miles.

Now we have four commands still to teach: whoa, whup, ho (used in a different context), and birds.

Whoa means stop. It has nothing to do with birds. Nor is it ever said when the handler is behind the dog (nothing is said, for any sound would be a distraction). Whoa is taught in the yard with two twenty-foot check cords and two leather collars around Pup's neck. One cord is snapped to the top collar and leads to the handler. The other cord is looped about a whoa post (making it ten feet overall from post to dog).

Stand Pup by the post (any steel post sledged solidly in the earth) and slowly heel him away. Keeping an eye on Pup, command, "Whoa," just as Pup comes to the end of his whoa-post rope. Should Pup try to continue – for you'll be walking away from him – the whoa post will hold him tight. Keep telling him, "Whoa."

Repeat this drill over and over. Later you can be twenty feet distant from Pup, command him to come to you, and tell him, "Whoa," just as he reaches the end of his ten-foot cord. Be considerate. Don't go distant until Pup's obeying well enough; otherwise, he'll get whipped around or tumbled end-over-end by the whoa-post rope.

Whoa is an extension of stay. Later you can use the power bar on the handler's check cord (attached to Pup's collar), dropping the bar to dig into the ground just as Pup reaches the end of the whoa-post rope and hears your command, "Whoa." Now he's wedged by the bar and held by the whoa-post rope – confronted by your upraised palm, your verbal command, and your no-nonsense stance.

The Bowline Knot

You must know this about check cords. They must have body. Nothing as unmanageable as a cable, I'll grant, but nothing as flimsy as a ski towrope, either. Good nylon rope is hard to find. So until you get a check cord with body, leave it overnight in a mud puddle and let it dry out to stiffen up. You'll learn what weight suits you best: 3/8, 1/2, or 5/8 inches.

The whoa post is one way to teach whoa. But there's another. A dog must lower his head before he can bolt. Check any acrobat. Where the head goes the body follows. So, we tie a bowline knot about four to six inches (depends on the length of Pup's nose) from the swivel snapped to Pup's collar. Any time we suspect Pup is about to move we command, "Whoa," and snap-roll the check cord so the bowline knot bumps Pup under the chin. This raises Pup's head, which lowers his haunches, and most important, breaks Pup's concentration. Now he must think through bolting or creeping all over again.

To get good at snap-rolling a check cord you need to tie the swivel-end to a fence post, or whatever, and keep practicing. All dog training depends on split-second timing. That bowline knot must bump Pup under the chin at the exact moment you command, "Whoa." You can practice this with a friend. Tie the check cord about his wrist, and tap the palm of his outstretched hand with the knot. He'll be able to tell you if your bump and oral command are in sync. But recognize this: many people never get the hang of snap-rolling a check cord. They should stay with the whoa post and the power bar to teach whoa.

All right, we're ready to introduce Pup to planted birds. He's running before you with a plain check cord snapped to his single leather collar, and you're directing him into the wind. You know where the bird is planted: it's in one of the tall grass clumps you mowed around. That's right, you've gotten access to some pasture and mowed it slick except for scattered clumps of tall grass where the bird is hidden. Or you gather branches and build a "beaver dam" objective for Pup to hunt. Or you work a low-grass pasture with a hedgerow along the side in which you've planted the bird(s).

In other words, Pup must be started in parklike cover with definite points of objective.

You continually check-cord Pup into the wind, casting him, telling him, "Ho," getting him to spin to you and changing his course to match your outstretched arm and the direction you step off. At all times the check cord is taut. Never let it drag, get caught between Pup's legs, or tangled about your own. If the cord does get between Pup's legs, you'll learn to snap-roll it free. Plus, as Pup gets field-wise, he'll learn to step free of the cord.

Now just a minute – think of this – *for the very first time you and Pup are now purposely hunting*. You've been working toward this moment for months. All the litter-box training, the house training, the yard training, the *Happy Timing* – everything! – has been directed to this outing. Enjoy yourself as much as Pup will. But for sake of man and Pup, do it right.

We call Pup a bird dog. Bird is half the name: the first half. The important half. You can no more train a bird dog to hunt birds without birds than you can learn to play baseball without a ball. Everything has pointed to this outing. Everything that happens to Pup in later life will be determined by this outing. Good luck!

As you check-cord Pup toward a distant objective you continually monitor the wind, snatching up grass and tossing it aloft, watching the smoke from your cigarette, or seeing how the dust puffs up from Pup's feet.

The Scent Cone

Suddenly Pup makes game: he enters a bird's scent cone. Pup has met his moment of truth. You immediately tighten the check cord and hold it so Pup can't take one more step forward. You say nothing: all Pup's attention must forever be directed to the bird. Now you walk forward, gathering the taut check cord as you go. Incidentally, the best way to do this is not hand over hand; instead, hold one hand constant and use the other hand to milk the cord through. This tends to leave a straight cord behind you.

As you walk forward you monitor Pup's shoulders. Should they indicate a step forward, jerk the check cord to break his concentration. If you let Pup bolt or creep, then that's what you're teaching him in the presence of birds. He'll end up catwalking on game, or leaping in and busting them. We want Pup forever on solid point.

Once beside Pup, and keeping the check cord taut, you slowly lower yourself – the gun-side leg bent, foot planted solid, with your gun-side elbow resting on your knee, your gun-side hand grasping Pup's collar. Your other leg is also bent, but the knee goes to earth, the non-gun-side arm circling Pup's lower waist, the hand either grabbing his off-front leg or wrapped solidly about the barrel of his body. Now

The moment Pup strikes scent the handler goes forward quickly, where he anchors Pup and himself for the upcoming feather dance.

Two Mississippi gun dog wizards introduce Pup to birds. Don Sides handles Pup while Hilliard Griffin walks a great arc around field to arrive at find.

wedge yourself. You're dealing with power. The bird's the fuse. Pup's the explosion. Be ready.

To keep things simple (you and Pup have a lot on your minds), I've not mentioned a key element until now—in all this check-cording Pup to birds you'll need a helper. This is the bird boy who's been walking behind you and Pup as you hunted the field. Now he comes forward in a great arc—walking away and around Pup's point—being ever so silent, until he arrives at the clump where you've planted the bird. Now he bends over, lifts the bird, and lets it fly in hand (see below).

Suddenly the bird boy lofts the planted bird into the wind as he commands, "Whup," which tells Pup to watch the bird down—*and you hold on for your dear life*. For Pup's going to go berserk. Power. Determination. Frenzy. Pup'll leap and flip and jump sideways and jerk, and I've seen more than one trainer actually dragged forward flat on his stomach. I've seen collars slipped over heads and check cords tangled around a handler's neck—and it's sheer joy. For you have a dog that shows he loves birds. You've got something to work with.

But mind you, should you let Pup break, then that's what you've taught him: to bolt at wing and shot. Should you let him achieve one foot forward, then that's also what you've taught him: to crowd or catwalk on birds. Hold him if you have to flip him over and lie on him.

Also there's another dimension. Should you be the second team to enter the scent cone (you're now training with a buddy and his dog), then Pup must honor. Everything said above applies. An honoring dog cannot lift a foot.

It may be Pup's honor is outside the scent cone. Doesn't matter. The pointing dog honors scent, the honoring dog honors sight. He sees a dog pointing. Should you want Pup in the scent cone, physically pick him up (he can't move a foot) and carry him there. Never, never, never let Pup move under his own power.

The Hobbled Pigeon

Now let's examine the planted bird that's launched. It's a pigeon hobbled with a piece of rubber hose, PVC, or even a long kite's tail of white rags. Let's use the rubber hose. Cut off a two-foot section of worthless garden hose and nock one end about ½ inch down. Now feed a three-foot piece of ⅛-inch cord through the nock. Equal the two lengths of cord—same as when lacing new boots—and tie the hose at cord's center. Then tie each end of the two hanging cords to each of the pigeon's ankles. The hose hangs like a necklace pendant.

When the bird boy goes to pick up the bird, he grabs the garden

Don and Pup tense as Hilliard reaches in tuft of grass to lift bird.

Hilliard gives Pup feather dance (note Pup's eyes) as Don braces Pup.

hose. This means the bird is free to fly out front. The more flap the better. For the bird boy is hurrahing, encouraging the pigeon to display and Pup to attend, making this feather dance the most fascinating thing Pup's ever seen. When the bird boy finally casts the pigeon to wind, the trailing hobble slows down the departing flight, giving Pup a lingering look to mark down game.

There can be no criticism with hobbling the pigeon. I've never known a bird to be harmed. Matter of fact, I've had pigeons make hundreds of such flights. Any they're soon back in their coop with their own private quarters, a meal of grain, and fresh water. The only hazard facing such a bird is dying of old age.

When the action's died down, coax Pup away from his point and continue hunting, the bird boy trailing along behind. It's obvious Pup will eventually start running to grass tufts, brush piles, etc. . . . Fine. He's learning to honor targets of opportunity. But too much work in the same field and Pup will start running milk routes on you. He's no longer hunting birds, he's hunting old finds. And this can't be. So you must continually seek new fields.

Bird flies and Pup starts long-departing gaze.

Any time you want Pup closer while he's backing, pick him up and place him where you want him. Never let Pup move a foot on honor. If you do, you're teaching him to creep.

A discarded bit of garden hose and a short length of cord make an excellent pigeon hobble.

Always let Pup watch flight of flushed bird. How else can he take you to singles or retrieve deadfall?

Most bird dog men are tempted to style Pup up on point. Don't. All Pup's attention must be out front. It stands to reason if you start piddling with his tail, lifting him up to brace his legs, or running your fingers against the fur of his back to tighten him up, then Pup's attention will be diverted from the bird to you. That's not what we want. Save your fussing with style until you've actually got an all-age dog. Then you can coax Pup to form.

Also remember this. When that bird flies, let Pup spin around and watch it down. The misinformed will yell, "That dog's loose on point." Bosh. That dog's just bright. The point's over, it's game he's after, and he's sure going to find it faster if he watches where it goes than if he hunts blind. But should you want Pup to hold extended point, then have the bird boy carry a backup bird in his pocket. When Pup's so frenzied in watching the hobbled bird down—or sadly, when we've drawn a Pup that's not too enthused about anything that's happened—the bird boy can throw another bird. Later, he can shoot it.

You may hear purists say, "I'll never train a pup on pen-raised birds." Why? Well, in the old days birds were not properly exercised in a flight pen and trainers didn't know how to check-cord into a scent cone. The tame bird would just sit and let the dog barge in on him. Which meant the dog was being taught to bump birds. Which further meant that trainers were letting the dogs move forward after entering the bird's scent cone. Well, now we know better. Birds can now be conditioned in flight pens to explode wild. And trainers are learning to read their dogs, to know when they make game, and to not let them crowd the find.

Consider, it's Pup's job to find birds. It's your job to kick them out. That's why you must work as far from scent as possible. For this accomplishes at least two things. First, it lets Pup work away from the muzzle's blast and keeps down incidents of gun shyness; second, at that distance Pup can see everything and watch all birds down.

Yet, one moment. I want to re-emphasize a point I've made before:

Dog trainer totes birds to field in plastic box, then transfers them to anchored mechanical flusher. (Note the wood plank.)

whoa is taught in yard training without a bird. Whoa is taught long before the dog is ever introduced to a bird in training. Whoa means turn to stone, stand dead, don't even think of moving—even if gnats swirl before your eyes and a flea stabs you under the tail.

Whoa is man's way of controlling point. Point is what God gave a dog to help earn his keep: to keep vittles on the table. *Point is natural. Whoa is man-made. A dog can point a bird, if he's scenting it, running fifty miles an hour. But he won't be whoaing at that speed. Understand?*

Eventually you'll train Pup afield without a bird boy. This can be done several ways. You can purchase a bird launcher (either cord-triggered or electronically activated by remote control) and launch the planted bird yourself. Or you can run Pup wearing the power bar or the bowline knot. With the mechanical bird launcher, you work Pup as before: going to him, gathering him in, holding him fast, then popping up the bird.

As Pup advances in his bird work, you can run him wearing a check cord and either stay with him for the flush or go out beyond the mechanical launcher. With the remote-controlled launcher, you can come upon the bird from any direction and trigger the trampoline that launches the bird. But with the cord-activated launcher, you must lay it all out before taking Pup to field.

You will check the wind and lay out the trigger-cord in line and under your feet at the spot you figure Pup will enter the scent cone. Should you lean over and pick up the trigger-cord you will cue Pup as to when the bird is coming up and entice him to break. Therefore, place one foot on the trigger-cord, and keeping the rope taut (and the launcher staked or weighted with wood planks), kick it with the other foot to launch the bird. There is also a rope on Pup, which you may or may not be holding depending on the progress of his training. Having to manage only one rope in hand certainly simplifies matters.

Another thing, dogs like to rush in and maul the mechanical launcher after the bird is lofted. They can, quite frankly, tear up the device. So get Pup under control and take him away immediately after he's watched the bird fly away.

But if Pup's wearing the power bar or outfitted with the bowline knot, the handler never stays with Pup for the launch. This is how it works.

The Power Bar

We check-cord slowly—Pup constantly in restrained power, the power bar attached to his collar, the check cord so taut the bar never

If you have a permanent set-up, you can anchor the launcher as well as Pup. You know where the dogs hit the scent cone, and you know the prevailing wind, so lay out your pull cord beside the dog anchor, heel Pup into scent cone, and snap him tight. That way you have both hands free while you kick the launching cord. You also can anchor Pup when he hits scent, then leave him, and walk around the launcher to shoot the flushed bird.

touches the ground. When Pup strikes scent, we give the check cord a tug, reminding Pup to hold his point, then we walk a great arc about him, keeping the cord and the bar from touching the ground. Never walk directly to Pup; that will only divert his attention. Instead, walk as far about him as possible, moving carefully so you won't become a distracting factor. Also, by keeping your distance you can fire without the blast affecting Pup should the birds flush. Many dogs suffer noise-induced hearing loss from close shots while others can become gun shy from a nearby shot.

When you're to the front, standing over the planted bird, drop the power bar to wedge Pup between earth and collar. Now he can't break. Pick up the bird, give Pup the feather dance, and let her fly. When you want Pup to release point, tell him, "All right," and flip up the power bar (keeping the cord taut) and letting Pup go by you to continue his hunt.

A word of caution: the power bar can't be worked with a running dog (too much chance it'll jam and really hurt him), nor can it be used in heavy cover—it'll foul. And if Pup is just flat too high-powered on birds, you shouldn't use a conduit-made power bar at all. Instead, replace the conduit with a three-foot section of rubber hose. Its weight will keep reminding Pup of the effect of the bar, yet should he break on point the rubber will give and let him pass safely by. Whether aluminum conduit or rubber hose, the power bar is the last training aid used on birds before we let Pup run free with just a trailing check cord.

Whoa

Still working without a bird boy or a launcher, we work Pup into the bird's scent cone, anchor him, then start our walk about him to the planted bird. But now we monitor Pup as we go, keeping the check cord ready to bump Pup's chin with the bowline knot as we softly say, "Whoa."

That's right, we can finally say, "Whoa," on birds, for we're no longer behind Pup. We're to the front the same way we were when working him on the whoa post.

All we've discussed applies: we constantly monitor Pup's shoulder muscles, and when we see them twitch we snap-roll the bowline knot to break his concentration, lift his head, and lower his haunches.

Once again we yell, "Whup," when we loft the bird. That means for Pup to pay attention, to watch the birds down.

There is another way to insure staunchness on whoa, and it's taught with what I'll call "reverse power." When someone pops you on the shoulder you fall away. But should he pop you again, you brace.

Here a chain-anchored Pup watches as bird catapults from mechanical launcher.

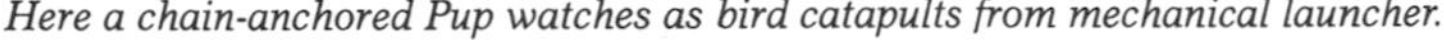

And the third time, you lean into the force.

The same applies to Pup on whoa. This is first taught in yard training, but then transferred to the bird field. You've put Pup on the whoa post and he stands whoaed halfway between you and the post—he's check-corded on both sides. Then you walk at angle to release the tautness of Pup being crosstied. Now, telling Pup, "Whoa," you pull the check cord, forcing Pup to take a step toward you (the first punch on your shoulder). Only when Pup takes that step, you scold him good, demanding he whoa. Then you tug the cord again. Now, what's Pup doing? He's rearing back. You keep tugging and Pup will set up like cement.

The same applies to styling Pup up on birds: giving him form and giving him confidence. When Pup's steady on birds you walk to him and groom him up. Most handlers lift Pup by the tail and set him down to spring up high on his feet, then they stroke upward on his tail, telling him, "Whoa," all the time. But the same thing can be accomplished by going to Pup and pressing down on his back. His eventual response will be to stand tall, to apply "reverse pressure" to your thrust. In bird dog parlance, this is called, "Pumping Pup up." It works; it bolds Pup on his game, gives him assurance, and—the bonus—makes him look good!

Finishing Pup Out

You'll recall that, "Ho," is used to get Pup's attention, or to get him attending. While check-cording we said it to tell Pup we were changing direction—or we blew one blast on the training whistle. But now, "Ho," must always be associated in Pup's mind with the promise something good is going to happen: especially when he's hunting distant without a cord. You're now telling Pup he's either missed something or you know something he has yet to learn. Pup must learn to rely on your judgment and the resultant command. Otherwise you just have a bird dog running amuck.

So, "Ho," is now taught with a ton of birds. They're seeded everywhere. Pup's running away from your planted bird, you tell him, "Ho," and direct him to feather. He'll soon start believing you. But he'll quit you (he'll self-hunt), or he'll go right under foot, if there's not a find at the end. So never say, "Ho," if you can't deliver.

If a bird flushes wild, we can stop Pup by yelling, "Whup." This tells him to get his head up, to hold his position, and to watch the bird down. Then we tell him, "All right," so he's released to relocate. But at wing and shot we tell Pup, "Birds." This not only tells him to watch the scattered covey down, but to mark deadfall as well. Now Pup can fetch what you've downed and take you to the busted covey. If Pup mismarks, you call him to you, keep him close, and make him hunt cover by saying, "Bird," or "Dead Bird," as you kick about with your foot. This is all done real serious: let Pup know how valuable the bird is to you.

Later you'll be working liberated birds without a bird launcher or a hobble. You'll dizzy them by holding their body in your hand and swinging their heads around. To stick them tight, tuck the head under a wing and plant them in a clump. Alas, these birds can revive before you get to them and either fly or walk away, yet they have left their scent and Pup's on point. So you walk back to Pup, tap him on the collar, and tell him, "All right."

When Pup's proven steady on point as well as wing and shot, you can remove the power bar and hunt him only with his check cord. Once he's made point, you walk to him, pick up the cord, and start your circle.

Still later, Pup'll run free of all fetters. Now is when association comes to the front in dog training. Only the sound of your voice vibrating on Pup's eardrums constitutes your control. Should Pup break on point, or on shot, then you'll have to start all over. So don't let this happen. Make sure Pup's ready before you ever release him to hunt free. Then take another month before you let him go. It takes only one second for Pup to goof, but it may take a lifetime to correct the fault. Never let him have the opportunity to fail. Make sure he's iron-clad, rock-bottom, sure 'nuf steady before you ever release him to hunt.

Men release their dogs to hunt too early, and that causes all the brutality in dog training. Suddenly the handler sees all he wanted to accomplish go down the drain: he's shocked, he's frustrated, he's dismayed, and he's mad. So here comes the whip, the remote-controlled electrical shock collar, or the bird shot in the rump. Everything disintegrates.

Each section of our country can pose a unique training or bird-hunting problem for the handler and his bird dog. In the Southeast we now have an amazing overpopulation of deer. There's hardly a handler in Dixie that doesn't dread turning his dog loose for fear he'll kick up a deer and blow the hunt, blow the field trial, or worse yet, blow the country.

Consequently, it is almost a universal practice to never turn Pup loose without first outfitting him with a remote-controlled electronic shock collar. The theory goes: if you can shock Pup just as he reaches for the deer, he'll think the deer did it, and thereafter he'll shun deer like the plague. But there is a substantial fault in this thinking: the cover is so thick in that country the handler can't see his bolting dog, much less know when he's closing on deer.

And even though most thoughtful handlers turn the power down on the collar so Pup just gets a tingle, there are better ways of taking Pup off deer than putting him in a shock collar. Hound men have been taking dogs off "trash" game for centuries. They do it one of two ways. First, they brace Pup with a figure-eight collar to an all-age dog that won't chase – in this case – deer. If the errant pooch wants to chase deer, the older dog will tell him in full growl and display of teeth to clean up his act. It works.

Second, the handler can make a drag of deer scent through the bird field and mark his trail with white flags to each side so he knows the precise line of the drag. Then the handler releases his quail into the bird field – all around the drag – and check-cords Pup into the area on a regular training session. Should Pup honor the deer-scent drag when he hits it, the handler stops him in his tracks with the check cord. Then, going forward to stand over Pup, he tells him in no uncertain terms of his displeasure. After this, Pup will hit the deer-scent drag and leap to one side like he's been snake bit.

Those fortunate enough to live in a rural area in Dixie can even corn-feed deer (where legal) in one spot, then release quail all around it. Now Pup is on a bona fide deer scent, instead of a chemical substitute, and the handler can take Pup off the real thing.

If the handler has trained Pup with the techniques and philosophy presented in this book, his voice will be sufficient to take Pup off deer forever. There's never been a whip woven that can come close to the power of a man's displeased voice when correcting a Pup at fault. That voice, plus the man's presence, his scent, and his facial expression.

Bob Wehle of Midway, Alabama, and Henderson, New York, probably comes closer than any other American bird dog trainer in epitomizing the basics explained in this book. I've seen him turn a bolting dog to stone – just with the tone of his voice. But what's more important is his bottom line: Bob builds a "love bench" in front of his kennels to give each dog a true and abiding "loving" each time he returns from the bird field. Says Bob, "They love to smell your breath." Once again, scent makes sense.

The Chain Gang

Sometimes we draw the wrong Pup; we can't light a fire under him, or we have a dog that quits us in training. Well, this is when you

Bob Wehle keeps "love" bench in front of kennel (note sunken dog houses). After every workout, each dog leaps to the bench for a loving. Bob says, "They like to smell your breath." Once again, scent makes sense.

have to sit down and analyze what went wrong and then try to take Pup back through whatever befell him and get it right. Yet we may not know what happened. We may be at wit's end.

Well, let's repeat: all dog training is connecting links in a chain. Also, all dog training is point of contact, repetition, and association. Plus, all contact with a gun dog is via his collar: we communicate through his neck until association builds where he responds to oral commands.

Which means all dog training is based on Pup giving to the lead. That's why we started with the litter-box check cord, then went to the power bar, the whoa post, the bowline knot, etc. . . . Well, I purposely left out an additional training aid that can help us now: the chain gang.

A dog's chain gang looks just like a trotline rigged to catch catfish or the old picket line used by the cavalry to hold their horses. It's two steel posts driven to earth with O-rings dropped down over them and attached to a length of welded-link chain. The chain runs from post to post, from O-ring to O-ring. Every sixty-six inches we bolt an eighteen-inch drop chain swiveled both top and bottom. The drop chain is terminated with a snap.

We use the chain gang in advanced yard work or we take it to the bird field. Remember, I told you it was easier to train thirty dogs than just one, and the chain gang proves that truth. Anchor the chain and snap your string before you as each pup is worked. The chain-gang dogs will go nuts. They can't stand for some pup to get your attention and be left out. They'll flip, leap, try to bite the dog next to them (thus the sixty-six-inch spacing), dig holes, spin about, bark, and generally go nuts.

This is where we put the errant pooch. We make him agonize as we train his kennelmates. But alas, what amateur trainer has all these prospective gun dogs? I once recommended you borrow the neighbor's dogs to really make the chain shake, rattle, and roll. But that's not likely.

So you do with what you've got, and that may just be a stake in the ground with Pup snapped to a chain and you out training his bracemate. Isolation also does wonders for a dog. You may have been viewed as the enemy before, but after days of being close-tied to a post, the lackluster dog (or the renegade dog) will start looking for you. Because it's you who brings him water, food, and maybe a pat on the

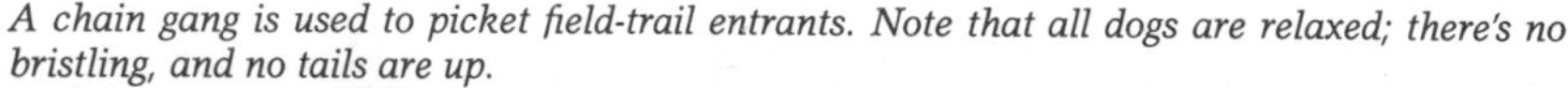

A chain gang is used to picket field-trail entrants. Note that all dogs are relaxed; there's no bristling, and no tails are up.

back. Most dogs will be enthusiastic about returning to work after a prolonged session on the chain gang, watching all the action, or being chained out back and totally ignored. Think it out. There's really a challenge in bringing each individual dog along.

So that's it, we've put Pup on birds. "But wait," you say, "I want my bird dog fetching . . . what about that?" Well, we're going to retriever training now, and what we say there will apply to the bird dog. Let's move along.

10

Training the Retriever

I WAS INVITED to Great Britain to attend the International Sheep Dog trials, and I was sitting with my English sheepherder friend, Ray McPherson. Ray won the world sheep dog championship the two times it was held, and he says to me, "At these trials you see a lot of mechanical dogs. But a good working dog must ofttimes disobey his handler and work the sheep as he sees it must be done. And the shepherd . . . who may be a half mile away . . . just can't see what needs be done. At these trials, it's like moving dogs on a chessboard."

Then Ray stood and said, "Well, I got to go get my dog ready to run." He jerked a thumb toward the contestant working the mechanical dog and said, "What good would that dog do you over a hill? You know . . . if he had to work on his own?"

Ray put his finger on a very grave American dog development: the mechanical dog. Though seen mostly in retriever trials, the mechanical dog is also evident in pointing and flushing circles.

And what is a mechanical dog? That's the dog the trainer has conditioned to do particular tasks because of rigid and sometimes preposterous demands by judges. Here's what I mean. Any retriever worth his rations will launch to water to fetch a duck. But in the field trial that's not enough. The duck may be placed in water so the dog is enticed to run the bank and then leap out for the retrieve. "Aha!"

exclaim the judges, "that dog ran the bank." And down go demerits in the judges' books.

But the dog that scores well launches to water directly before his handler (and the judges), then turns sideways and swims parallel to the shore to get the duck. What a farce. The judges say it shows control and that it also shows the dog is bold for striking the water. It shows, they say, the dog is not timid in going to sea.

But in a real duck-hunting situation (which field trials are required by charter to duplicate) taking all that time to retrieve the duck could result in: first, the duck, being a strong cripple, could swim away and dive beyond retrieving; second, incoming flights of ducks could spook from the retriever swimming the shoreline (at least some duck hunters think this is the case); and third, during the time it took the dog to get the nearby bird, any far birds—also shot down—might float away.

Now this is important. Field trials are required to simulate a day's hunt afield. Yet, in the example we've just seen, good common hunting sense is thrown aside so judges can make differences in dog performance that don't make any difference.

And there are several reasons for this, but first let me recall a conversation I had years ago with Talbot Radcliffe, premier English springer spaniel breeder in Anglesey, Wales. We were out training dogs and Talbot observed, "We must always remember field trialing is a game. It relates not to the field . . . it relates only to man made trials.

"It is not a hunt. It is a game.

"In this country we have fox hunting. And in fox hunting we have point-to-point. Now point-to-point is to test the horse running cross country . . . from point to point. All this done, of course, in the fastest possible time.

"Now, that is a test for a hunter . . . but from this we have developed steeplechasing over man made fences on a man made course with proper jockeys. Now this horse . . . this steeplechase horse . . . you never take hunting. Oh no! He is a specialized animal for specialized competition in a specialized game.

"Now . . . you come back to field trials for springer spaniels . . . you have a specialized sport, a specialized game, a specialized object, and to be successful in it . . . *you have not got to go hunting*."

My eternal thanks to Talbot for taking the plug out of his gun on this one: no one could have said it better. And so we accept Talbot's view of reality. But there's a catch.

If field trial dogs are not tested for hunting abilities in hunting situations, then that means they are not trained to be hunters, either. They're trained to pass non-hunting tests. Which further means that specialized animals win, and then they're chosen for breeding. Which means today's pups are out of field-trial winning, but non-hunting, stock. And then the naive guy or gal buys one of these pups to go hunting!

What does the hunter really need? He needs a dog that can hunt from dawn to dusk. Has the field trial tested for this kind of endurance? Or, the hunter needs a retriever that can work all day in cold water. Is this trait tested at trial? Also, the hunter wants a dog that will hunt from car, boat, or blind. Are these characteristics tested at trial?

In other words, are dogs really tested to duplicate a day's hunt afield? The rules say they must be. But the fact is they ain't.

Why is this? The answers are many. First, let's consider judging. In Europe a judge judges and his decision is final. He is held above reproach. Why, a judge over there is even permitted to judge his own son running in a national. It's happened in England. George Meldrum was the senior judge when Bill Meldrum, his son, ran the Queen's dogs.

But over here? Judges are suspected, begrudged, doubted. Therefore, they have to make graphic, and drastic, differences in dog work so all contestants can easily see the error of the dog's ways. For a judge to say, "I declare this dog's work to be best, for he pleases me . . . he shows style and birdiness and desire and stamina and. . . ." No way. It just won't be accepted. But I'll be damned if that ain't the way we buy a dog!

So birds are dropped right before English springer spaniels at trial, and though enticed to leap for the quivering, hot-blooded temptation – they can't.

Or, the number of covey finds is counted at a pointer trial. No contestant can gripe at the judge for that. One dog found six coveys, the best any other dog could do was four. "So we have a winner!" Hardly. The six-covey dog may have run in the afternoon with the earth warming and a moderate wind. He found the birds scattered at feed. But the four-covey dog ran first thing on a frigid morning, and the birds were still at roost. But this dog was bright, he hunted for roosts, scenting but the slightest hint of effluvia coming from the covey that was locked tight, wings pressed to side. These birds hadn't moved in fifteen hours, *they had done nothing to create scent*. It took an extremely field-wise dog with a miracle nose to locate them.

Point all this out to the judge and he may well answer, "Can't you count? The afternoon dog won."

Plus there's something else. There's the matter of variance. Retriever trials must be mechanical so each bird falls in the same spot for all dogs. How else can they be tested equally? Once again, the judges are not trusted. In England one dog may get a strong, running cripple (all dogs are walked forward side-by-side on line). Another dog's bird may fall before his nose. The first dog has a much better chance of scoring higher. Fine! That's the way it happens at field. That's hunting.

But over here that can't be permitted. No judge can be given latitude to judge. He must, rather, just compare.

And something else. There are way too many dogs running on the American circuit, yet only three days are traditionally set aside each week for trials. Consequently, every test is sudden death. Oh, the judges want to let all dogs finish the first series—that's a payback for the guy who drove 500 miles to attend the trial. But after that, it's put one foot down wrong and you're on your way home.

Which means the big dogs—the dogs that run constantly on the big circuit—must post faultless performance. And one way to accomplish such miracle work is to brutalize the dog into doing it. To kick and hit and shock and shoot the dog to, for example, keep him from running the bank to retrieve a nearby duck.

In my mail awhile back I slit an envelope and took a page in hand to have a lad exclaim, "Please help me . . . I've got to win." I laid the letter down, rose from the typewriter, and went to have a long draw of hot tea. GOT TO WIN!

That's what's killing the various species of gun dogs in America today, especially retrievers. That's what's robbing them of their innate instincts to hunt and fetch. That's what's turning hard-driving, free-wheeling, self-thinking gun dogs into mechanical robots in fur coats.

I drank another cup of tea.

Finally I returned to the typewriter and answered the boy. It matters not what I said. But now that I visit with each of you, you who are the gun dog trainers of America, let me say: Win! Win what? A ribbon? A trophy? A check?

What Really Matters

What about companionship with the one true friend God gave to man? The love and devotion of a good dog. What about years spent in training, bringing the pup to dogdom and the dog to season? To seasoned wisdom where he thinks out each field situation? Where he watches the ducks arc above you, and you can read their flight in his eyes? Where one jump sideways tells you there's a rattlesnake in the bush? Where the cock of the ear, the set of the tail, tell you the quail are coming up? Win?

I win every time a dog props his head on my knee and melts me with his soft eyes. I win when the gimped-up old warrior that I have to carry across ditches finally goes on point and, trembling, looks back over his shoulder to say, "I told you I'd find 'em." I win every time a coon dog can't be pulled off a den tree, or a terrier goes into a badger hole, or a beagle gives voice in a distant glen.

We now live in a world of man-made man. So it's only natural such a man should have a man-made dog. Something he can move on a chessboard. Something he can beat the spirit out of and render a remote pawn.

But I don't call that winning. I call that losing.

I also call that impudent. For, in all such thinking is the assumption man is smarter than the dog he's training. And the more we look at what man's doing to his dogs at trial, the more we realize this just ain't so.

You know there are field trial people who never go hunting? Who never permit their dogs to go hunting? Do you know there are field trial people who insist the handler never be called upon to fire a gun? Do you know there are field trial people who don't have a dog in their house? He's away at the trainer's.

And someone writes me, or calls me, and first thing he says is, "You gotta know the breeding of this dog . . . why he's out of Field Trial Champion Watergate Foulup." And I yawn. For I've been told nothing to indicate whether or not this dog will point or fetch. Oh, it may be the pup's sire was impervious to high-voltage, low-amperage electrical shock, or he could have a ton of birdshot and not go lame, or he could stand up under a BB-loaded whip and not buckle. But what's that got to do with whether or not he's a gun dog prospect?

You see, most field trials now demand the dog deny his instincts. And to deny your instincts you've got to be terrorized off them. The distant retriever is after the floating duck. He's not seen it fall, his trainer has told him it's out there. Out there somewhere – and the dog is looking and swimming. And the handler is whistling and giving hand signals and yelling for the dog not to go to shore. But where's the duck? It's planted beyond the hourglass pinch of water pressed between two points of land. The dog must swim a narrow channel. But any dog in his right mind would go to shore and run on land to hit the water again.

But that's not the point. Retriever field trial champions are not in their right mind. They're in the judges' minds and the handlers' minds. And should the retriever touch land he's out of the trial. He must go the distance by water.

So what follows during the next seek? The trainer sets the trial test up again–he may drive all the way to New Mexico to force the dog down narrow irrigation ditches–and this time when the dog goes to shore he's beat off it, shot off it, shocked off it. If he ever stays off it, he may become a great champion.

Champion of what? What God-given-dog-instinct has been tested here? Does the dog in the wild have to avoid land to eat? Hardly. These are tests devised by men to please men. They have nothing to do with the nature of dogs. And they have nothing to do with hunting.

And when you start to tamper with the nature of the dog–when you start twisting and reversing and denying natural instincts–you are essentially recreating the animal. Recreating him in your own image. Training up a dog not to be a natural hunter, but one that avoids man-made temptations in order to keep from being beaten to death. And the result is called a Field Trial Champion?

Well, across this nation there are men and women who aren't going to take it any longer. They're leaving the old established field trial circuits and coming up with more true-to-life, hunting-dog tests. It happened first with the pointer and setter breeds. People who no longer believe upland game has to be approached on horseback are activating foot-hunting clubs. People who feel pointers and setters are only half-tested by pointing (who also want to see the dogs bring deadfalls to hand) are establishing the new foot-hunt clubs, the new shoot-to-kill trials.

But let's step over here just a second. There's something you should know. In the early 1970's, after promising the editors of *Field & Stream* I would not bark at the moon, leap on their leg, or stool too close to the office, I got them to take me on as their dog writer. That magazine was (and is) a very big ship in a sea of world's sportsmen, but mine was a very small boat. Cast from the mother ship I paddled here and there. As the years went by I acquired a punt gun that I rigged to my bow: there were salvos that needed to be fired among dog men. Without Editor Duncan Barnes' professional policy of granting broad latitude to his writers so they may test the value of their judgments–and without *Field & Stream*'s power–none of what happened could ever have occurred.

I began to write of the fallacies of field trials, of the brutality to dogs, of man's turning dogdom away from a day's hunt in the field, of man demanding dogs trip over their own instincts or get thumped for being what God created. Nothing happened. One retriever pro did call me and say, "Somebody ought to whip your ass." Which I thought very strange, for I didn't even own a burro.

The Mechanical Dog

But then I began writing of the mechanical dog – some of the material you have just read – and as a direct result of an article that appeared in *Field & Stream* in April 1983, the nation's hunters were aroused. The movement began in Louisiana, swept up the Mississippi and then moved over to New England. Suddenly, there were two new hunting retriever clubs: the North American Hunting Retriever Association and The Hunting Retriever Club. Later, the American Kennel Club came up with its own adaptation of this new retriever testing concept: that is, retrievers would now be tested for a day's hunt in the field – not for their ability to keep from being retrievers, but for their ability to be that very thing.

Two of the new national clubs asked me to judge their first trials. Then I stepped aside. The movement had to take its own course; it had to be created by, maintained by, and directed by bona fide hunters.

The August-September, 1984, issue of "Hunting Retriever," the newsletter of the Hunting Retriever Club, Inc., carried a President's Message from Omar Driskill, of Simsboro, Louisiana, the actual spearhead of all the new hunting retriever movements in America. It said, "Bill Tarrant stood up against the nation for years and now he's being joined by thousands of hunters that are going to make this dream a reality. Bill Tarrant truly is the 'Godfather of the Hunting Retriever' movement. The Ruston Retriever Club in Louisiana asked Bill to judge the first National Hunt. He did.

". . . Bill wrote about us. All dogs running against a standard set of rules, where dogs ran all the hunting tests in their hunt. Dressed in camo we shot over our dogs and test hunted in a true-to-life hunting reality. We were learning and working together toward a Finished Hunting Retriever Champion.

"May we take time now and put to print our thanks to the 'Godfather of the Hunting Retriever,' Bill Tarrant."

So it was, and I paddled my small boat around and aimed my punt gun at other injustices in the world of gun dogs. But then it hit me, there are other national organizations in America where I've been told they gun down their godfathers. I glanced back over my shoulder only to see it's hard to create national organizations where you go to give, and not to get. Where the dog is more important than the man. Where the hunt takes precedence over politics.

And then I began to hear rumblings that once again the hunter would not be able to shoot over his dog at trial. What do they expect him to do? Throw rocks at the bird? And once again trainers were grooming their dogs with shock collars and whips and birdshot. But worst of all, the organizations began vying among themselves, trying to wipe out the other guy. And at least one of the clubs—at this writing—seems to be trying to reinstate the very system the new hunting clubs were created to forever destroy.

Well, I remember the point made by Bob Crosby, the first three-time, all-around cowboy champion, who said, "It ain't no sin to have lice . . . it's a sin to keep 'em."

We've all been party to driving gun-dogdom someplace we never intended. But no future sin can be permitted. The barbarism and inhumanity of training gun dogs to win on today's traditional circuit—like lice—have got to go. Now let's train hunting retrievers.

The Hunting Retriever

The purist works a retriever at heel, demanding he sit to wing and shot and hold steady until cast for the retrieve. Or, should a bird fall that the dog has not seen, then the handler will cast him to this "blind" retrieve by giving directions with whistle and hand signals. The fact you can work a retriever before you at quarter to lift game as a flusher, or use him as a toll dog on a pond bank to entice ducks to swim to your gun, or let him have a free head to hunt up quail, grouse, or huns (and sometimes even point them) will not be dealt with here.*

In great part we've already trained the retriever. We did it with the power bar. For that is the essential of a retriever: to be rock-steady and honest. He must obey every command. He must be under control at all times. The power bar accomplishes this: heel, sit, and stay (review that section before proceeding).

Tradition has established the practice of controlling a retriever more with a whistle than the human voice. Say, "Heel," and reinforce this with one, long, sustained blast on the Acme Thunderer whistle. Forever that will mean sit: either sit to side or far to field. One semi-short blast followed by a trill will tell the retriever to come in. Another long blast will tell him stop (and sit). And on and on.

So, the sequence is started as a part of yard training. Pup is heeled to side, a dummy is tossed, he's ordered, "Back," and cast with the non-gun-side hand. The minute he picks up the distant dummy, the handler gives the suck-in whistle: tweeeeeet, tweet, tweet, tweet, tweet.

*Breeds trained here are the Labrador retriever, Chesapeake Bay retriever, golden retriever, flat coated retriever, curly coated retriever, Irish water spaniel, American water spaniel, and any dog that will retrieve.

Pup returns to side, the handler bends over, and takes the dummy to hand.

"Well, that's great," you say, "nothing to that . . . I'll have my retriever pup trained in no time." Alas, it don't work that way. Follow me.

Equipment

We train with a dummy. We used to make our own, but every conceivable type is now available from gun dog stores. You want one that's stark white (so Pup can see it), small enough so he can get it in his puppy mouth, hard enough so he won't be inclined to bite down on it (causing hard mouth), and not too roughly textured so he can hang a canine tooth in it. Also, you want a cord attached to the dummy that is long enough so Pup has to hold his head high on the retrieve or step on the cord.

The dummies are canvas-covered kapok, cork, or whatever, pinched at one end with a brass grommet and sewn shut. You put a nylon cord through this grommet and tie it off at both ends. Dangling like that, you can give Pup a "feather dance" to pep him up, carry it easily, and give it a good toss.

But beware. Don't do what everyone does. Don't throw the dummy yourself. Oh, it's okay in early-puppy play. But no more. For when will Pup see a bird (the dummy is an imitation bird) flying from your hand? Plus, your motion of throwing takes energy and much movement, and that may spook a shy pup. Therefore, you need a bird boy to throw the dummy or a remote-controlled dummy launcher to flush it afield.

Consequently, don't buy one of those shoulder-seated dummy launchers propelled with a blank .22 cartridge. Again, the bird emanates from your hand – an unnatural consequence. And, the dummy may take on a foul smell from the gunpowder, and Pup may blink the dummy (play like he can't find it though he's standing right over it) because of the stink. Blinking is a severe fault.

So, we're still in puppy training and Pup's to side and you tell him, "Sit, stay," and toss the dummy – and nothing happens. Okay. Go get the thing and bring it back. Now get down on your knees and thump the dummy on the ground. Hype it up, cheer Pup to frenzy, twirl the dummy before him – make it as exciting as a scurrying mouse. Then holler, "Back," and toss the dummy six feet before you. Hurrah! Pup's off for the retrieve. But what's this? He's got it in his mouth, and he's running from you. Well, never, never, never chase Pup. Do just the opposite.

Turn your back to Pup and run in position the other way. When

Pup sees you won't play his game, he'll want to play yours. So here he comes. Let him pass, and as he does reach down and snatch the dummy from him. Incidentally, never grab the dummy and pull. It'll make Pup hard-mouthed. Instead, push the dummy in, gagging Pup as you twist your wrist, releasing the fabric from his teeth. If you're training an older dog that won't release, continue to push in and gag while you blow in his nose or reach over to his off flank with two cupped fingers and lift Pup from the ground: he'll spit the dummy out.

When Pup's settled again, reach over and dress his mouth: get the grass brushed away, the saliva cleared, and the gravel or sticks out of the way. Now send him again. As always, five minutes is plenty.

Before you're finished with this session you should know there's another way to entice Pup back to you: lie down on the ground. He can't resist coming back to examine you. But whatever you do, don't chase Pup with the dummy in his mouth. He's got to return to you on his own accord, for later, when he's fetching from water, to chase him means you'll be swimming.

The Mark

Now let's take our training session to the bird field. Leave Pup in his crate, walk to the area of the mark, and strew dummies all about. Pup's mark will always be away from the sun and into the wind. His field of vision will have a clear background. Now walk back to the car, release Pup from his crate, let him hike a leg or dump; let him sniff around. Then walk him from the car to your casting line.

Tell Pup to heel, sit, stay. Later you can tell him to mark. "Mark, Pup, mark," you'll say. He'll key to this command, sit taller, cock his ears, tense his pelvic drive muscles, sharpen his eyes. He'll know something's going to fly. When Pup's steady, you signal the bird boy to hurrah the bird (make certain he's got Pup's attention: remember the feather dance and the pointers), and then toss the dummy into the waiting pile.

Let's pause. Training sessions must always be exciting. The bird boy gives Pup all the chatter and hype a shortstop gives his pitcher. We want Pup to that state of delirium where one more, "Hurrah," and he breaks. Also, we have given the bird boy several bird-throwing drills before we ever went to field. Don't think an inexperienced bird boy can't throw the bird behind him, straight up, or completely over the seeded bird pile. He can. And we can't afford that. All we can afford is success. And one last thing: that bird boy must be all business. He can't make a noise, nor can he move, while Pup is hunting for the dummy.

No distractions. And finally, should Pup quit his hunt and leave the bird field to run toward the bird boy, that person must have all his dummies picked up so Pup can't find one and be guilty of switching birds. This will happen. Avoid it.

So the bird is tossed, Pup is cocked, and it's time for the cast. Well, Pup needs a launching pad, and you must build it. Pup's at your non-gun-side, your non-gun-side hand either above and directly in line between his eyes and down his nose or alongside his face. The hand may be held rigid or circled slightly: you know your Pup. You know what will make him concentrate or hype him up or even calm him down. Gradually you lower your body as you extend your non-gun-side foot to front, scooting it alongside Pup. Watch him! You can tell when he has the picture. When he leans forward, his head comes up, his eyes sharpen, and his ears cock—*send him!* Command, "Back," and lift your casting hand like you were throwing a bowling ball. Ram him. Get him launched.

Both you and Pup have marked the bird down, only you did not mark the spot of the fall. (Never!) Instead, you marked the fall in relation to the horizon: a barn, a gunsight pass between two mountains, a cottonwood tree—whatever. And you've dragged the side of your shoe sole in line with that mark. No matter where you move, you can come back to the casting line and know the direction of the fall.

Well, Pup's afield and he's surprised to find all those dummies. So he may pick one up and drop it, select another, and so forth. At this point we're not too concerned. All we want is for Pup to get any dummy and bring it to hand. But what if he gets hung up out there? At this stage of the game, there are three things we can do.

First, remove the seeded field and work with only one dummy.

Second, when Pup has a dummy in his mouth, command, "Heel," and coax Pup to you. Third, if he won't budge, walk out there and kick a dummy with your toe. All Pup's life he'll be more interested in hunting cripples than dead birds. The scooting dummy will arouse Pup to leap and pounce and take the dummy to mouth. Now you command, "Heel," pat your outer thigh to get Pup to side, and then walk him back to the casting line to take the fetch in hand.

Once Pup's delivered to hand, wheel him about, get him ready, and signal for a repeat mark. Five marks in total should do it, seldom more. Remember that it's like eating candy; we want to take Pup from the bird field wanting more, not fed up.

Finally, we'll advance to double and triple marks. One bird boy throwing two marks is called a "poor man's double." Pups can have trouble with them, even though the bird boy throws one straight east

Mike Gould launches a two-year-old Lab named Webb. This magnificent dog has so much drive he takes upright cast with little hand or arm movement.

and the other west. It's better to have three bird boys afield for triples. Or have three bird launchers, each one remote-controlled.

The problem is switching birds. And we can't have that. Pup will fail to find mark number one, look up to see a bird boy at mark number two, and head for him – sensing a bird will be close by. Should this happen, the number two bird boy must race Pup to the bird and get it fetched to hand before Pup gets there. Never can Pup be successful in switching birds. Why? Say you've got two crippled ducks on the pond, and the one Pup's after keeps diving. So he abandons it and starts for the other. But by the time he gets there both birds have disappeared. If Pup had worked the birds in order, you could have had both in hand. Now you have none. Pup can't switch birds.

From here on in you'll have to innovate. It all depends on how well Pup does. You may want to take your sessions to heavy cover, stop seeding the area of the fall, or you may even elect to go to water. Well, water is not Pup's natural element and you must note a couple of facts. Pick a windless day, and toss your dummies into sparse vegetation that'll hold the dummy in place should there be current. We can't have a drifting dummy. Ours must be a constant world when starting Pup on marks. Plus, it may be impossible for you to go to water and kick a dummy with your toe. Right? So Pup's never taken to water if he's switching dummies.

All in all, I'd recommend you stick to land far beyond that time you'd like to go to water. It's surprising how much Pup's got to learn bone dry. Take a ditch, for example. If Pup leaps to a ditch with a right-hand lead, that paw will stay extended and the left paw will strike earth first, which will tend to unbalance Pup, forcing him to bring his right paw over. The result? Pup is now cantered to the left. Consequently, to cast him on a straight line to the mark, you must cock him a little to the right of the bird's fall.

We used an open field to build confidence. But we must use heavy cover to teach Pup to both use and honor his nose. We cast him through briar and stubble to bold him up. And now what's happened? For the first time (except for *Happy Timing*) Pup pops out the far side of a hedgerow and you're out of sight. He'd better have the confidence to continue running a straight line to the mark.

Did you know dogs sour off hills when trying to make a fetch? They do. Run Pup on a 45-degree path up the slope of a hill and he'll fall away (fall down) from the mark. Consequently, we must cock him farther uphill on the cast to get him to come out on target (thus the reason for the launching pad).

Most dogs also are reluctant to cast into a strong wind. Remember this, especially on water. Most dogs will sour away from the wind, and some will flat quit you. So Pup must be worked at all quarters into the wind. Eventually he'll learn to use the wind to his advantage. All-age dogs will approach falls to the side of the wind in order to buttonhook birds with their nose.

And now we must go to blind retrieves: to teach Pup how to find birds he's not seen fall. But actually we're ahead of ourselves. For all dogs are natural retrievers. They can quit you, however, and if a dog won't hold the bird to deliver to hand, then he won't return a single retrieve. And can you imagine how messed up he'd be when sent for three birds down? So it's time we insured a guaranteed fetch.

The Training Table

We've already learned that taking a dog's legs away from him renders him helpless. Psychologists tell us all life is born with one fear: the fear of falling. So placing Pup high taps this instinctual fear; it renders him docile and makes him manageable.

The table you build must be stout. A 4 x 8-foot piece of plywood cut in two will give you two 2 x 8s. One can serve as the table top. The other section, cut in two once more, gives you two 2 x 4s for ramps. Nail dowels or ½-inch molding on the ramps at one-foot intervals to make a tread for Pup to use in going up or coming down the slick ramps.

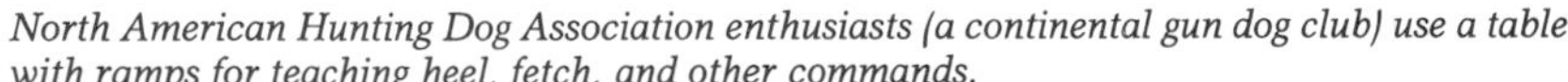

North American Hunting Dog Association enthusiasts (a continental gun dog club) use a table with ramps for teaching heel, fetch, and other commands.

The two ramps let the trainer lead the dog off and on the training table without having to pick him up. Table legs are built of 2 x 2s or 2 x 4s and cross-braced to stop jiggling. With a little ingenuity and some hinges, the table may even be made portable so you can easily carry it into your house or back out to the yard.

Making Pup fail-safe on retrieve – so he never drops the dummy, spits it out (oh, he may readjust his hold), or lays the bird down until he's placed it in your hand – has traditionally been called, "force-broke to retrieve." It insures a dog won't eat a bird, pick at its feathers, pick it up and drop it to leave it, switch birds, or even drop the bird at water's edge to stand and shake water.

A force-broke dog will never quit you because Pup's been forced to hand his self-will over to you. The effects are marvelous: the renegade dog is made biddable, but the soft or shy dog bolds up on the force-retrieve table. Why? Being made a constant performer, Pup now pleases the handler, which means the hassle is past. Pup now hears praise when he works, and this in turn makes a more confident, more self-assured retriever.

But I have an admission. This is a humane training book, and we've at last come to that impasse where the dog must be forced to hand his will over to you. In the past this was done horribly: the dog's paw was squeezed until he said, "Ouch," which means he's opened his mouth, and the handler plops the dummy in, commanding, "Fetch." For the point is the dog must open his mouth. Prying on his teeth only repels him, turns him away, and makes him take a stand. He must open his mouth without a fight.

Other trainers have pinched ears with fingernails to get the ouch. One barbarian threw a half nelson over the dog's right shoulder, dummy posed out front, commanding, "Fetch," as he heard the dog's upper leg bone break.

I wait for brighter minds than mine to get a dog's mouth open without him having to say, "Ouch." Until then, the most humane method I've come across is the nerve hitch. To use it we must modify our training table. At each end drive a steel post. Once they are firmly embedded run a taut wire between the upright posts. The wire should extend some three feet above the table. Put a turnbuckle on the cable and snug it banjo-string tight. Walk Pup up the ramp to the table top, snap his plain leather collar to the taut cable with a swivel-snap, and let him sit there to get oriented.

Now go find a worthless shovel handle and cut off several six-inch oak dowels, which we'll call bucks. We want hardwood so Pup can't be hard-mouthed. Plus, we want something Pup will never hunt; for that matter, never see again.

The standard force-retrieve table has stakes at each end to hold overhead cable outfitted with running pulley attached by chain to dog's collar.

Buy yourself some ⅛- or ¼-inch nylon cord and cut a piece three feet long. Go to Pup, tie a clove hitch just above the carpal joint—that's what we call his knee—on his right front leg for a right-hand gunner. Adjust the clove hitch so the cord hangs straight down and over Pup's foot. Now throw a half hitch about Pup's two center toes. Shove the knot up tight against Pup's foot.

Here's what we've done. The nerve hitch is the brainchild of Delmar Smith, of Edmond, Oklahoma, a dog trainer and ten-time national Brittany field trial winner. Delmar had always been awed by the force a pencil exerts when placed between your fingers and clamped down by a friend's hand. The pain is instant and unbearable, yet immediately upon releasing the grasp, or removing the pencil, the pain vanishes, and there's no imprint. So that's what happens when we pull the nerve hitch: it transmits nonprintable pain to the dog's two center toes. Yet, when you release the cord and loosen the hitch, the pain stops immediately.

So that's what we do. Holding the oak buck in our right hand just in front of Pup's mouth, we pull the nerve-hitch cord steadily with our left hand until, suddenly, Pup opens his mouth, we command, "Fetch," and we insert the buck. The nerve-hitch pressure is stopped, the buck's in Pup's mouth, we're pleased, and the pain's gone. (Incidentally, groom Pup's mouth, make sure you haven't caught a lip.)

Always put the buck immediately behind Pup's canine teeth: never back between the jaws. This would be too fatiguing. Command Pup, "Leave it," or "Give," and take the buck from his mouth by twisting it toward his eyeballs. Let him rest a minute and repeat the session.

You know you've got a force-broke retriever when you put a six-inch extension (chain or cord) between the snap-swivel and taut wire and command, "Fetch," and you see Pup jut his jaw out six inches, compulsively, demanding to take the buck to mouth.

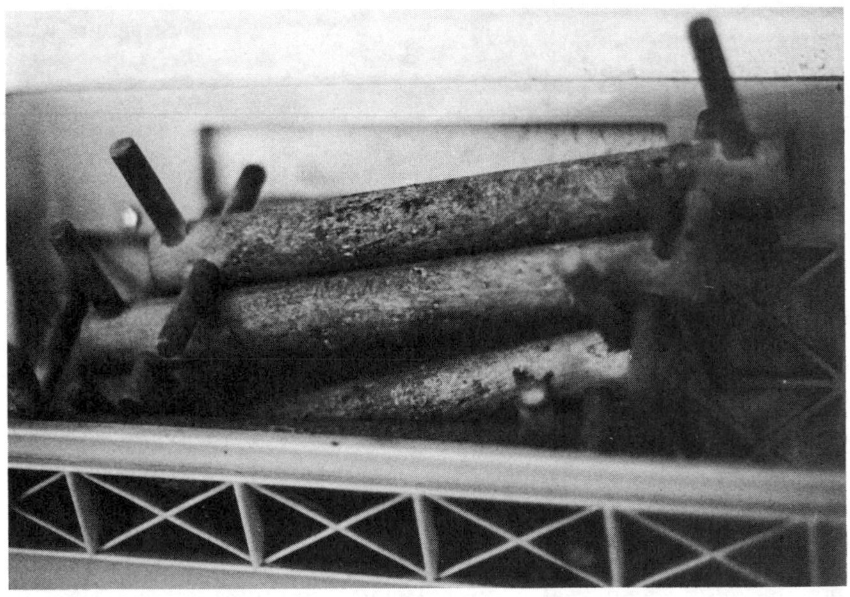

Dogs are first introduced to dowels at the force-retrieve table. Later, they go for bucks with Xs of wood pegs that lift the dowels for easy fetch.

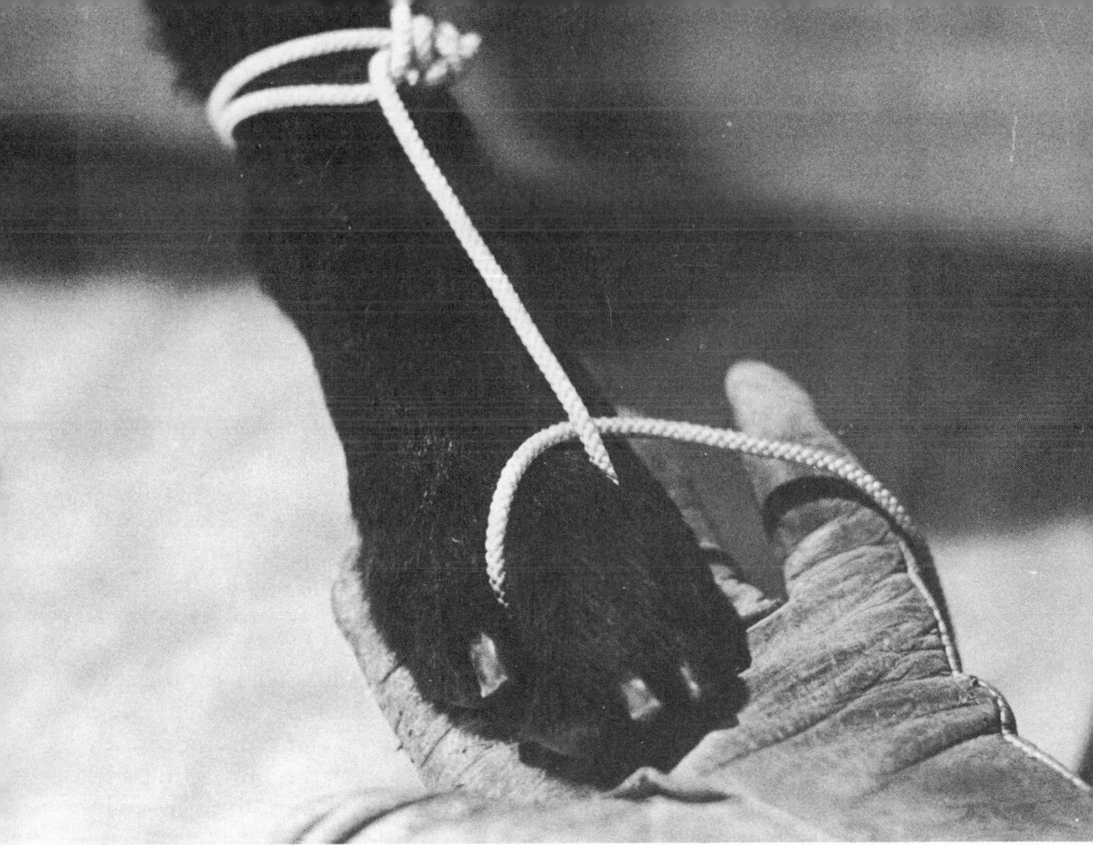

Nerve hitch is made by tying cord above carpal joint with clove hitch, then lacing it about two center toes.

The last time I published this training technique was nine years ago, and by mail I can tell there's one essential problem that plagues amateur trainers teaching Pup to fetch on the retrieving table. They quit too soon. They let Pup start running up and down the table, going to fetch an eight-foot distant buck (or dummy) that was planted down there, or they put Pup on the ground and started casting him for dummies or frozen birds. (Frozen? Yes, we're still concerned with hard mouth).

What I do with my dogs is this. I make a session of it. A hard session. Then I come back the next day. And, if necessary, the next. I figure it's nasty business, and both Pup and I want it over with. So that's how I approach it, and that's how I do it.

Years ago, I was a Marine recruit sitting at the end of my bunk with a galvanized bucket over my head, which the drill instructor would whack with his swagger stick every time he passed by. I was told to lie on the floor and do push-ups with the drill instructor standing on my back. I was being force-broke. And I wanted it done with. They were making a Marine. You're making a retriever. Same thing. Get to it. Get it done. And be done with it.

But oh, the results. Now when you tell Pup to "fetch," he'll grab a steel anvil if that's the only thing close. I once cast AFC Renegade Pepe at a retriever field trial to pick up a shot pheasant. But the bird was a strong cripple and ran out of the area of the fall. Well, retrievers are not permitted to hunt at an old-time-format trial. They must pinpoint the bird—or else they've failed the test.

But Pepe was a hunting retriever, and he wanted to trail the bird. No. The judge would not permit that. So I kept whistling Pepe back in to the area of the fall. Frustrated, Pepe finally ran to the bird boy and gunner, grabbed the wooden crate of live pheasants, and started dragging the whole rig to the casting line. Pepe had been force-broke to retrieve.

Now, when you finally take Pup from the table, you continue to have him wear the cord about his carpal joint. It trails and flaps as he runs. Should he refuse to fetch, just reach down and pull the cord. It needn't be wrapped about his toes. He'll leap for the bird. Still later, just tap that right-hand ankle as you order, "Fetch," and he'll get to it.

When cord is pulled, Pup says, "Ouch," opens his mouth, and dowel is inserted.

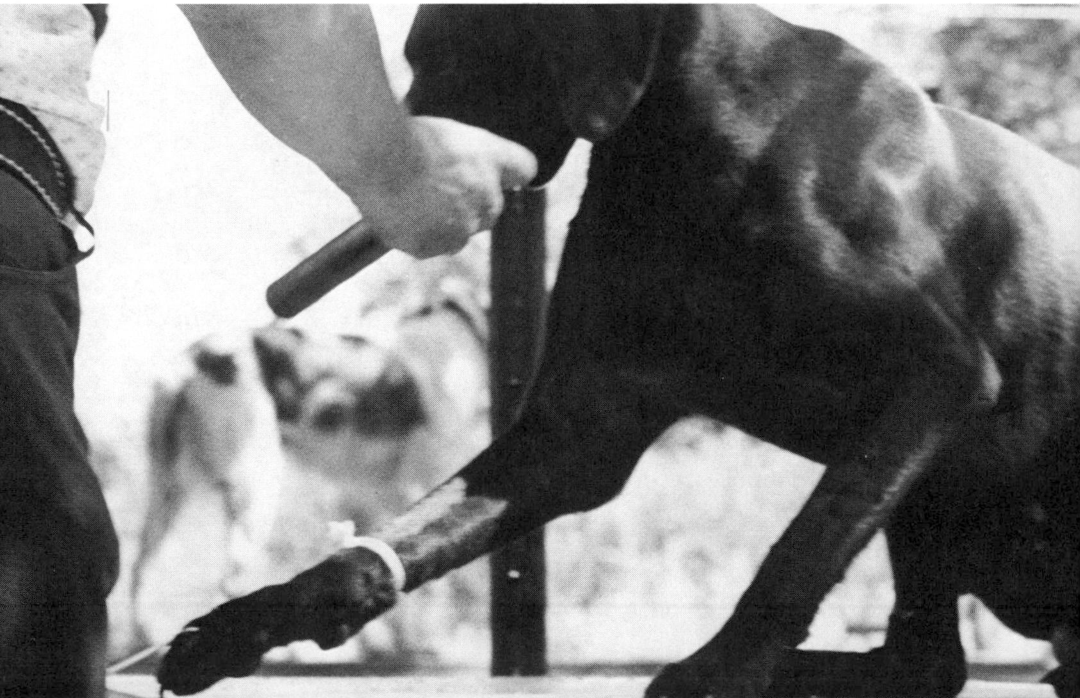

Should he forget, have him run with the cord attached a few more sessions.

The Blind Retrieve

The ultimate value of a retriever is to conserve game. What's shot is put in the gamebag. But not all birds drop at forty yards. Some ducks, when head shot, climb, glide, and sail a half mile. Geese can go farther. So Pup must be capable of blind retrieves.

We start with a baseball diamond. You and Pup at home plate, a dummy at the pitcher's mound. Cast Pup and have him make the retrieve. Next time, though, we put our dummy at first base. But once again we cast Pup to the pitcher's mound, only to give him the stop whistle, have him turn around for hand signals, then cast him right to first base. You can easily imagine all the remaining possibilities. Dummies at first, second, third. And later, completely out of the ball park. Where Pup must drive away 300 to 500 yards.

You can readily see why a precise cast is imperative. You're the bow, Pup's the arrow. He must go exactly where you aim him. Well, Mike Gould joins us again with a miraculous new breakthrough in retriever training called the Looking Glass Drill.

The Looking Glass Drill

We've got Pup sitting on the whistle because of Mike's power bar. Now we're going to make Pup cast precisely where we want him with the looking glass drill. Not only will this drill cast Pup through the eye of a needle, but wonder of wonders, it'll prompt Pup to come back the same way. And this is important. For too often, retrievers cheat on their way back. They start looking for an early landfall. Which means they may swim past a second bird down and want to switch retrieves.

Mike tells us, "A dog must be force-broke to retrieve before starting this drill. He must hold the dummy at all times. Here's the way it works. We drop a dummy, take three steps in a straight line, and drop a second dummy. Then we take three more steps and drop a third dummy, take three more steps and drop a fourth dummy. Make sure the line is precisely straight.

"Now we walk fifteen yards at a right angle to this row of dummies and lay out an identical column of four dummies. We now have two parallel rows of dummies fifteen yards apart.

"Now you heel your dog between the two dummies of the front row. We'll call this point A. Point B would be about in the middle of the corridor. Point C would be at the other end of the corridor.

When Pup's advanced through the looking glass drill, handler may stand distant and run Pup through corridor to waiting dummy pile.

"Leaving your dog to sit at point A—he's seven-and-one-half yards from each row of dummies, right in the middle of the corridor and facing away from it—you walk away from the corridor in a straight line twenty-five yards and plant two dummies. Then you go back to your dog and throw a third dummy toward the pile to hype the dog up.

"Obviously there's no suction on this drill right now (something to entice the dog off line). There are no distractions on either side . . . just grass and the pile of three dummies before him. You cast the dog, he makes his fetch and comes back.

"Now you move the dog back to point B. He's halfway into the corridor and there's a little suction . . . there're two dummies to each side, right? You cast the dog to the pile of two remaining dummies (he must ignore those right beside him) and he makes his fetch and returns.

"Now you move the dog back to point C. He's all the way through the corridor and there's more suction . . . there're four dummies to each side. You cast him for the last dummy you seeded twenty-five yards out there. Not only must the dog run through the corridor of distracting dummies, but more important, he must come back the same way. That's why I call this the looking glass drill. The dog sees the same suction, the same corridor, both coming and going.

"And the significance of it all is this. The dog learns to run an absolute straight line off your hand cast without paying attention to any distractions, and then he turns around with the dummy in his mouth and is obliged to come back the same way.

"This is especially important on water. With the looking glass drill you achieve the most critical angle-water entry, plus the dog comes back at the same critical angle. You stop the dog from running the bank when he's going for a fetch and you stop the dog cheating . . . you stop the dog from looking for the nearest land to beach when he makes his retrieve to hand."

"But how," I ask, "do you get eight dummies to float so precise like that in water?"

"Good question," says Mike. "I do that by taking two corral poles, painting them black, and then painting four white rings equidistant along the black poles. The white sections look like white dummies. That way you can lay the corral poles half in and half out of the water to start your casts. Later you can anchor the corral poles way out in the water and cast the dog through them."

I have to laugh, saying, "It's so simple it's amazing."

But Mike won't accept compliments, saying we ain't through yet. Now the dog must be taken 100 yards behind the corridor of dummies and run through them another 100 yards to the waiting pile of dummies. When the dog's doing that, then the two parallel lines of dummies are brought closer together until, one day, they are only six feet apart. Now the dog is running a 300-plus-yard blind with a latitude of six feet. "And that," says Mike, "is threading the needle."

But he's still not finished. Now he cocks the dog to the angle of the two parallel rows of dummies. The dog must enter the corridor just grazing the left-hand dummy and exit the corridor just grazing the right-hand dummy. Then he must come back the same way.

Finally you lay out three separate sets of corridors – one angling left, one straight away, one going right. And you keep moving the dog back away and keep seeding the dummies farther to the other side.

"Then we leave all this mowed-grass playground," explains Mike, "and go to the fields. We run the dog through ditches in the looking glass drill, up slopes, through puddles of water, whatever . . . we make that dog hold his line no matter what the obstruction is out there, no matter what the enticements might be to veer off.

"Later, when you take the corridor away, you have a dog casting straight down your extended hand on your cast."

"But what do you do," I ask, "if the dog starts avoiding the corridor?"

Mike says, "I yell at him to stop and sit. I verbally tell him in a loud voice, 'Nawwww, nawwww, *sit*.' Then I go out there, take him over to the middle of the corridor (all the time he's holding the dummy), and I tell him to sit and stay. Then I walk back to my handler's position and order him to come in.

"The reason I yell, 'Nawwww,' is I don't have these dogs on the whistle for casting as yet. I start the dogs young. They know nothing about whistle and hand cast. That comes later.

"I'd say the reason this drill is so good," Mike speculates, "is it helps the handler generate supreme accuracy on the cast without the handler having to do it all in aiming the dog. The corridor is also aiming the dog . . . the corridor is forcing the dog to hold his line. This makes the obstacle the target . . . the obstacle becomes a distant gun sight.

"But when the dog starts looking for the corridor, and all of them will, then I phase it out and never use it again. And we're only talking a few weeks here. But I'll tell you this, it's really an uplifting device for dogs that have a confidence problem. You know the dog that sits at heel and starts looking all around, or cringing down, and he's telling you he'd rather be somewhere else. After this drill they sit down and just go bing. They're aimed. They're eager. And they want to run."

The All-Age Dog

So that's it for retriever training. If you get Pup doing just those things we've discussed here, then you've got an all-age dog. Not for field trailing. But for hunting. And that's what it's all about. But in closing I'd like to note two things: First, a retriever must be stout on honor. Matter of fact, over in Great Britain that's most of the game. Retrievers are trialed or hunted in line, walking at heel beside the handler/hunter. When a bird flushes, the gunner(s) fire, the bird falls, and all dogs sit fast and solid. Then a judge at a field trial, or the head hunter on a day afield, calls out what dog can make the retrieve. That dog is cast and all other dogs must hold their positions. It may well be the bird has flushed and flown the complete line of dogs. They're set on ready, I can tell you. But they can't move, they can't break, they can't lift a paw.

So the bird lands immediately in front of a Lab at the far end of the line. Ho ho! That's the test. The dog on the opposite flank is sent for the retrieve. It's nearly unbelievable. That dog runs the whole line, runs before each dog's nose, then snatches up the bird before the far dog, and parades it back down the line.

Incidentally, flushers play the same game. I've attended the national running of the American English springer spaniel finals. Two dogs are down, beating cover for game. A bird is lifted, the flushing dog sits, the three gunners wait. They give the bird a long flight, then drop it under (sometimes) the most extraordinary circumstances. That's right, the bird falls immediately beside the bracemate. But both dogs honor. Then the judge tells one handler or the other to make the fetch.

And how are dogs made this rock-hard steady? It's all done in yard training; it's done with heel, sit, stay; it's done with the power bar and all the rest of our training aids. But there are some additional aids and techniques you should know about. Tie a nylon cord to your belt (say six feet long). Run the cord through the strong D-ring on Pup's plain leather collar. Gather the loose end of the cord in your fist. Now, walk along with Pup at heel. Should a bird lift, the guns fire, and Pup try to break, he'll hit the end of the double-backed cord. But when he honors, when he sits to wing and shot, then he's cast while the handler drops the loose end of the cord and lets it play through the D-ring and Pup casts.

Generally there are men about a retriever or flusher afield: and they're always there at a field trial. You'll always have two judges standing behind Pup and the handler. Well, take Pup afield and put him in a breaking situation. Have the guns fire and birds lift and pandemonium prompt Pup to erupt. Only get a couple of teenagers behind you. Have them scream and leap forward, waving their arms and making an undue fuss, chasing Pup down, leaping on him, false-wrestling him to earth, tumbling him, continually yelling at him. Now you come forward gentle, soft-spoken, and take Pup back from these two raving maniacs.

Don't think Pup won't spend the rest of his life looking back. Henceforth, when the guns bark and the birds fly Pup'll be hesitating to break, for he never knows when somebody is going berserk. And that split-second of hesitation will let you get a handle on him. Will give you time to say, "Sit," if you have to. Will give you time to threaten with a knee or a foot. Just time enough to give Pup a cue to stay seated.

Ideally, you would want to use a couple of guys Pup will never see again. They enter his life, go nuts, and disappear. If there are ten ways to get Pup to honor, and there may well be, I know none of them that can touch this method of the "two nuts" for absolute effectiveness.

The second point I'd like to make concerns the use of the remote-controlled electronic shock collar. I don't use it, and I don't run with those who do. Want to know why? Just strap one on your neck and have someone zap you. Dogs close their minds to panic and pain, and that's exactly what they experience upon being shocked. If you want a close-minded dog running amuck in pain and confusion and resentment, then use the thing.

Anyone can see the value of long-range command and enforcement, especially on running deer. But not through pain. Common sense tells us we should try to work it out where the trainer's scent is vaporized by a remote-activated collar. The scent being carried in an atomizer on the dog's collar and sprayed directly before his nose. For remember, scent makes sense.

The Scent Collar

If it weren't for a trainer, Pup would be hunting for himself. The only way he'll give to the trainer is through the man's presence, his voice, and his scent. We place the trainer before Pup's nose when we squirt a smell of ourselves before him. Pup knows he's doing wrong, he suddenly remembers the authority behind him, thus he hesitates (his action is broken), and this'll cause him to stop and think things over. "Where is he?" he'll wonder, and for darn sure he'll straighten up his act.

Now I give this concept of the scent collar to dogdom. It's the single most important contribution in this entire training book. I'm a dog man, not a mechanic. Someone else will have to perfect the scent collar. But when it's done I predict it will be the most important breakthrough in dog training ever conceived. There'll be a hundred applications all the way from yard training through advanced handling.

And that will not be the end of it. Consider the value of a scent collar that sprays bird scent. If a gun dog's out there skylarking and not concentrating on his hunt (especially a pointer) and you hit him with that bird scent – then *wham!* Pup recalls the reason he's afield. Also, if a dog is trained to stop the moment he enters a scent cone, then once that bird scent is sprayed from his collar the dog slams all four feet flat and sticks. That way, at least, the man can catch up to him. Then have the man always carry a bird in his pocket which he can roll out and reward Pup's point.

You'll eventually agree with me. The more you think on it the better it gets. The scent collar is the future of dog training. And I look forward to it with delight, for more than one reason. There is in dogdom a "borrowing" of men's breakthroughs with never a mind to recall who originated the idea. In other words, I'm talking about out-and-out theft. I've seen training books copied from training books. I've seen videos made from books. I've seen techniques "borrowed" and never a mention of the man who thought it out. That has always been my hallmark: to give credit where due.

So let's wait and see how it unfolds. Will the pages in this book that first brought the scent collar to the world of dogdom be recalled? Or will some high-stepping, fast-talking pitchman suddenly appear on the scene with "his" revolutionary breakthrough?

It really doesn't matter. My purpose is to take the whip from the trainer's hands. The scent collar heads us in that direction. That'll be reward enough. Still, I'll keep an eye out for the second-story man who offers the first scent collar for sale. Let's see how his ad reads. And let's pray the manufacturer ain't marked the thing up fifty times.

I've broached the scent collar and its applications with Mike Gould, one of the brilliant young retriever minds in America today. It will be young gun dog trainers like Mike who will throw off the dead hand of the past and make the most of the scent collar when it becomes available.

Now, most of my training devices are made from stuff abandoned in a junk yard or discarded about the house. They cost pennies. But that doesn't set well with most Americans. They covet gimmick devices; they love to push buttons. And they love to spend money and show it off: why else foreign cars and designer watches and label clothes? Well, expensive gadgets don't make gun dogs. It's patient, thoughtful, gentle trainers who make gun dogs. So I'll consent to the purchase of only a remote-controlled bird/dummy launcher (at this time), and that's the end of the exotics. Later I'll endorse the scent collar.

Twelve years ago I wrote a bird dog training book in which every training device was essentially made of junk. Well, most of that stuff is now available: ready-made. And talk about astronomical prices! Just leaf through your gun dog supply catalogs. What you can piece together from scraps is now built and sold for tons of money. So take your pick: I guess some guys hunt in rhinestone shirts.

In closing this section I'll readily admit you can go on and on with retriever training. Matter of fact, training retrievers can become an obsession. Yes, there have been divorces because of it. And I recall the time I was casting dogs on blinds into a blizzard where I couldn't even see the dog. But you need no more, the Pup needs no more, than what you've found right here in these pages to get him on birds and have them brought to hand. Happy doing it!

11

Training the Flushing Dog

NOW TO THE Pollyannas, the happiest dogs alive. Their tails beat 500 times a minute, and they're always laughing, always frolicking, always driving, always striving to please. These are the flushing dogs: the cockers and spaniels. The vest-pocket gun dogs that run a beat before the gun, lifting game, then sitting rock steady until sent to fetch. And more than that, sharing your duck blind to become little Evinrudes in water, pushing the duck (if they can't lift it) before them as they break sheet-ice to retrieve.

And, in a sense, we've already trained them. So much of what we taught the pointers and all we taught the retrievers applies to their training. But there is one notable exception – the flusher works within the gun's range to lift game, and does so by flushing. Consequently, they rely a great deal on foot scent, where the bird dogs with longer legs and higher heads continually search for body scent. And unlike a retriever you might use to quarter for game – and who might try to pursue a live bird and bring it to hand – the flusher will immediately sit at flush.*

*Breeds trained here are the cocker spaniel, English springer spaniel, Welsh springer spaniel, American cocker spaniel, clumber spaniel, Sussex spaniel, field spaniel, or any dog that will flush.

So this means two things: First, the flusher must really be yard-trained with the power bar. He must sit on command: no ifs, ands, or buts; and second, he must have a tape measure in his head—*a total understanding with his gunner*—so that most birds are lifted within the range of the gun.

This is how it's done.

Of course, there are different words for command: there are always different words when we change categories of breeds. When we want the flusher to sit, we say just that, but there's more. When we want him to honor a bird's flush we cry, "Hup," which goes back to the English demanding the dog to "Up." Strange? Sure it is. But they think we're strange, too. You see, the English had another command, which was "Charge." That meant for the dog to drop flat, chest to ground. It gave better control because it removed the dog two steps from breaking. He had to lie, then rise to sit, then move to break. And it kept the dog below the gun for low-skimming gamebirds. When the handler wanted the dog to sit, but to remain alert and watch the bird rise to drop dead or glide to new cover, the handler said, "Up," which eventually became "Hup."

Hup is usually taught with a training pistol held high over the head. This accomplishes several things. The bird flushes and the trainer fires the blank cartridge, the dog looks to see the man's arm and hand raised high, and he hears the command, "Hup." Consequently, the dog gets three simultaneous signals—a gun shot, an oral command, and an upraised arm—all of which tell him to sit. Many a flushing dog will stop afield by merely glancing back and seeing the upraised arm.

All this can be taught with the power bar. As you back away, the bar wedged between the dog's collar and earth, you command, "Hup," with your arm held high. You're telling the dog to sit and stay.

Later, working into a planted bird with Pup wearing a leather collar and check cord, you can immediately go hand-over-hand down the check cord to hold Pup for the bird boy's feather dance (same as we did with the pointers). When the bird's lofted, the handler commands, "Hup."

Or it can all be done with the remote-controlled launcher while the flusher runs without check cord. But the moment he makes scent, and you trigger the trampoline inside the launcher to loft the bird, you command, "Hup."

Should Pup break, we handle him nearly the same way we did the pointing dog on honor. We pick him up and carry him to the exact spot he vacated *before the bird*. (Remember, the honoring pointer was distant from the bird; the flusher is right on it.) Once there, we are very severe with him (Pup cannot break). Our wrath boils over, and we look mean and menacing as we command, "Hup." You can even produce your white, plastic fly swatter.

Traditionally the flushing dog's hunting sequence is this: The gunner's walking, Pup's making game before him. Suddenly Pup lifts a bird, the gunner fires, the bird falls, and Pup turns to stone. The gunner then walks to Pup and casts him for the fall. Pup fetches to hand. Then we purposely cast Pup away from the old fall to start a new beat. For returning to an old fall for all dogs (pointers, retrievers, flushers) is a fault: it shows lack of initiative on the part of the dog, and it wastes valuable hunting time that should be spent scouting new cover.

Should Pup break to flush, you can return him to the spot he vacated, and introduce as many as three additional birds from your pocket. Give Pup the idea there's no end to "sleepers" that may be out there, if he'd only wait to see. This is also good for making pointers hold point long after the covey has taken wing (it looks good to judges, gallery, and co-gunners); it also removes Pup one more step from breaking. It makes him linger over point.

The Controversy on Range

All we have left to teach the flusher is how to quarter—to make zigzags, kidneys, or bow ties, across the bird field. In other words, to hunt. Pup will always go to the left so many yards, then back across the front to the right the same distance, then reverse his course, vacuuming the field clean. Now, here's where needless controversy arises among flushing enthusiasts, and never before have I seen it discussed in a training book.

Most amateur trainers claim they want their dogs held to twenty-five-yard casts, thus giving them ample range to get on a flyer. But is this really what they want? Let's see.

During my lifetime as a guy who does things "doggy," I've discussed flushing dog range with many fine professional and amateur trainers, and I've considered, and respected, their conclusions. But the man who is most in tune with me doesn't by accident happen to be Mike Gould, of Rifle, Colorado. I usually find Mike clear-headed, practical, and to the point. You see, Mike has always been a poor boy. Consequently, he hunts for his table. Yet he's also a bright boy, and he pays critical attention to what happens about him. And like me, dogs are his love. So, my discussion of range becomes a consensus of Mike's and my findings. Spaniel trainers want to train very close as a matter of tradition: they want a flusher working within twenty-five yards. But not the pros. They want that dog ranging forty, fifty, even sixty yards before them, for that's the way the dogs are worked at trial.

The pro may ask you to gun for him with a thirty- or thirty-two-inch, full-bored 12-gauge shotgun so you can reach out fifty-five to sixty-five yards (more on this later). And there's a reason for it beyond field trialing.

The hunter who trains his dog to hunt no farther than twenty-five yards ahead, or to the side, is really cheating both himself and his dog. What you really want is a dog that can find birds, not one that's memorized a tape measure. As Mike says, "We want bird-finding talent."

This may mean the dog is driving 150 yards to front—and beyond. For by letting dogs run long and wide they start to form habits of circling birds and driving them back to the gun. Sure, you may lose a bird or two out the far end, or off from the side, but a high percentage are flushed to fly right back to you.

Mike says, "Usually when somebody goes grouse hunting with me they spend the first day telling me to call my dog in . . . then they spend the second day trying to get their dog to run out there with mine. Especially with blue grouse or chukars . . . you want to cover some country. If your dog is working only twenty-five yards to the front, you're going to have to walk ten times farther than if you were behind a dog that runs much longer."

As Mike notes, "I sit on top of those deep Colorado gorges and send my dog down to work it out. I don't have to go, he does. This gives me a great advantage shooting from on top."

He further says, "Dogs must learn to work birds, to manipulate them, to make the bird do what the dog wants him to do—all for the benefit of the gun. If the dog has the hunter's permission to work the bird out, even if it takes the dog out a little bit, the dog will produce more game on a day's shoot. So many people think this is a one-man team where the dog's out there doing his part and the shooting part is the guy's contribution. But it's important the hunter learns how to *move on his dog*.

"The most prevalent problem I see," says Mike, "among the dogs I train up for people is hunters who fail to recognize and discern the dog's body language." What Mike's saying is people don't know how to read their dogs. We've discussed this before. "Most hunters," continues Mike, "are not aware they have a real obligation to the team to harvest birds. The dog tells you, he always tells you, of his intent. And he tells you as well what's going to happen out there. It's your job to read him, to understand him, and to act accordingly.

"When the dog strikes grouse, you've got to get downhill. If he's hunting above you and he's making game, stay where you are: the birds are going to come right over your head. The hunter must be constantly reading his dog and paying attention and moving on what he expects to happen. If it's a pheasant, you've got to cut him off; if it's a grouse or a chukar, you've got to get downhill; if it's a covey of quail, you've got to get to the point of the flush fast, and take a stand where you can see and swing – you've got a job to do. You've got to move on it. For let's face it: if the dog's well schooled, he's going to hunt prime cover, and he's going to hunt for the gun. You be there."

The Dog Gives Commands

Mike concludes, "It all boils down to this. I think it's silly to worry about range. During the first one-and-a-half years the dog learns to move on your commands. During the second one-and-a-half years you should be learning to move on his commands." Yes, the dog is giving commands through body language. But to the uninitiated, Pup is sending a foreign language. Enough time afield, though, and you can easily learn to translate. Perked ears, beating tail, raised muscle over the shoulder, heightened and arched-down neck, tense pelvic-drive muscles, a rapid-pace – these are all Pup's commands.

Mike goes on to say, "Forget about consistent range . . . that's what I say. I say learn to hunt as a team. And somewhere along the way a range will develop. It might be twenty-five yards or it might be forty. And, of course, every dog is subject to working both ends of the spectrum. But I bet most will be working comfortably beyond twenty-five yards and some way beyond forty yards and the hunter will be shooting his birds."

This reminds me – many years ago I took a pack of proven field trial champion pointers into the desert and threw open their dog crates. They took one bewildered look at that barren landscape and then immediately took off running – one mile away. For they saw a windmill out there. That was the only objective they could size up to run for. That's what the great hunting dogs learn to seek out: points of objectives. Anything that might hold birds. This hardly equates with range; it equates with hunting. Understand?

So there it is. You choose. You're bringing this pup along. Work him fifty yards across. Or twenty-five yards. Or seventy yards. You decide. Or change the range as Pup grows field-wise and older. Do what you want. You've read what we say, now follow your own opinion.

British handler casts English springer pup within fenced enclosure. Dogs are taught hand signals as they are taken off rabbits and poultry.

I'd prefer you turn Pup at the end of his beat with one long blast of the whistle. When he hears your toot he knows he must come back, or work across, the gun. Consequently, Pup hits the end of the check cord, you jerk, he turns to see your opposite arm stretched out – the direction you want him to take – and he hears the whistle. So he takes a new course.

I've known serious flusher trainers to erect parallel chain-link fences eighty yards apart and walk Pup down the middle. He goes forty yards one way and hits the fence just as he hears the handler's whistle, then reverses course until he hits the opposite fence and hears another whistle command. Working the Pup on the ball diamond in yard training will help a lot in putting him on whistle and hand signals. For not only must Pup turn back at forty yards to side, he must also turn back when he's forty yards to front. Therefore, he must know not only the stop whistle, but also the come-in whistle (tooooooot, tweet, tweet, tweet).

Now a final word about range. I'll always recall attending the national running of the English springers in Camden, Arkansas, in 1973. The gunners were making fairly consistent pheasant kills at fifty-five to sixty-five (or even seventy) yards. I checked their equipment to find they were shooting Browning over/under Broadways. (Broadway refers to an elevated rib as wide as the barrel. It is a great aid in sighting.) The guns had thirty-two-inch barrels bored modified and full. The bottom barrel carried a charge of 3¼ drams powder, with 1¼ ounces of No. 7½ shot. This was backed up in the other barrel with No. 6's carrying the same powder and shot charge. The shells were Hi-Brass.

It must be understood these were not ordinary gunners. They had been selected by the field trial committee solely for their ability to give the dogs a long look at all birds and then consistently drop game at distances more than one coon hunter has said upon hearing his dog bay, "To hell and gone."

I was so impressed with one gunner at that trial I walked up to him and said, "I've never seen gunning like this in all my life." The man was Chuck Dryke from Sequim, Washington, a shooting instructor and trainer of gun dogs, especially English springer spaniels. He came back at me, saying, "If you think I'm good, you ought to see my fifteen-year-old son." I did just that. Only a few years later Matt Dryke became the first American to ever win a gold medal at the Olympics shooting skeet. So we're talking gunners.

And to conclude our discussion of range, I make this final clarifica-

Field trial handler casts English springer spaniel with upraised arm. This goes back to sheep-herder handling where the casting dog sits before the handler, facing him, and is told, "Get on," with upraised arm.

tion. When field trial gunners are dropping birds sixty yards out, that's not necessarily where the dog is hunting. To the contrary. The dog may be ten feet in front of the handler when he lifts a bird. The dog sits and the gunner purposely rides the bird sixty yards out before dropping it so Pup has a long look at his upcoming mark. The judges and handlers and gunners are "testing" the dog.

In a hunting situation you do as you want. It may be the dog is hunting sixty yards out and lifts a bird to flush right back over you. Or the dog may be ten feet in front of you and lift a bird only to see you knock it down before his nose. Okay!

So you lay out your check-cording courses and build your fences at those yards you and your gun can handle. All right?

Each of us must work with what we've got. Southerners can work a flushing dog in a pecan orchard—all trees laid out neat and straight and equidistant. Pup hits the row of trees and he's turned by the whistle. Or work him in a school yard with the fence to one side, or in a field bordered by a hedgerow. Use anything available to help you turn Pup.

Any time you want him to honor game, raise your arm, fire your training pistol, and command, "Hup." Pup should sit. Then go to him, laugh it off, and cast him in another direction (see the retrieving chapter for teaching Pup to honor another working dog).

Commands

We cast a pointer by saying, "All right," a retriever by commanding, "Back," and a flusher by ordering, "Hie on," which means in the Queen's English to hurry. So that's what we tell him. Now we're working sideways to the wind, the gunner trying to keep himself positioned between the planted bird and Pup. When Pup strikes game the handler commands, "Hup," but now he's in a position to step between Pup and the departed bird. Thus Pup is worked without check cord at close quarters before he's ever let free to really hunt.

You can see the difficulty in controlling Pup afield so far as honoring another dog. You can't get your belt-tied cord through his D-ring, nor can you necessarily have trailing teenage boys to leap forward and pummel Pup to ground. All that has to be done in a typical retrieving situation with Pup, never while hunting afield. And this is most practical. Many, if not all, flushers are worked on waterfowl, and they must duplicate everything a retriever does. Stands to reason, then, they must also have standard retriever training. It's just that they must be broke to honor before ever released to hunt.

Since the pistol is always fired when the handler commands "Hup," this now means Pup will stop to the oral command, a flushed bird, or the sound of the gun. At this stage, I'm always more concerned with having Pup stop on command; I'm far less concerned with style. For example, Pup may be to front, and a lingering bird jumps up behind the hunter; he fires, and the bird falls so the handler is sandwiched between it and Pup. Well, flusher purists say the handler must go to the dog and cast him back for the fall. As far as I'm concerned, it's their game; let them have their way. What's important is Pup stopped. He hupped. But I stand where I shot and tell Pup to go get the bird.

Working Pup from a duck blind is identical to working a retriever. We learned all that last chapter.

All dog work is based on yard training. If you can't control Pup in a fenced-in back yard, you're sure not going to get a handle on him in Farmer Brown's pasture. That's why I can't overemphasize the importance of fundamentals. Yet there is this problem, and I've committed it. Overtrain Pup in yard training without lots of *Happy Timing*, and you'll ruin him for life. I remember a Lab named Thunder that I drove into the ground with yard training. Also, I overlooked one more extremely important thing: birds. Consequently, I took Thunder to a derby and he was down, I mean he was hang-dog. So I pepped him up as I took him to the line, really got him leaping. Whereupon he hung a canine in one nostril of my nose, ripped it out, and there I am before the judge with a blood-soaked handkerchief and a dog totally confused.

Oh, I signalled for the birds to fly and the guns to bark, but Thunder—he was busy smelling human blood, busy worrying about the pain in my face. He never saw a bird. He never heard a gun. He never fetched a feather.

So you say, "Well, he finally got Thunder worked out."

Ha! I took that dog to eleven derbies and never fetched a bird. He had been destroyed by too much yard training. He became too dependent on both handler and drill to ever realize there was any transference to field and gun and bird.

Dog training is an art, not a science. There are no tape measures, timers, scales. You work it out in your senses, you feel it in your bones. It's a balance of work and play. It's your being mad along with your being happy. It's isolation and togetherness. It's every blasted thing you can think of that might work. But in the end it all boils down to one thing: it's birds. Tons of birds. With birds you will develop a bird dog, without them you'll develop a dog. Buy 'em, raise 'em, or snatch 'em from beneath bridges or out of bell towers. But you must have birds.

The Reverend Walt Cline lets English cocker savor pigeon. It takes tons of birds to make a gun dog.

Remember, breed of gun dog, fields of cover, birds gone after, it all comes down to whether that dog knows birds. We can spend our lives with Pup teaching him heel, sit, stay, over, back, come-in, stop, or whatever, and if we don't give him a ton of birds to work we've just built ourselves another mechanical dog. The one fault most committed by amateurs in gun dog training is that they skimp on birds and bird cover and hunting time. They skimp on the one thing they want Pup to be an expert at – birds!

Where else would they do this? Would they tell the race-car driver not to practice with a racer? A typist without a typewriter? A tightrope walker without a rope? No. But they will sure tell Pup to be a bird dog and never give him a bird to train on. I rest my case.

12

Gun Shyness

GUN SHYNESS IS very rare among dogs whelped from bona fide hunting stock. The reason: misfits have not been bred, so their beget don't see the light of day.

Looking at the whole spectrum of gun dogdom – mongrels through those bred in the purple – you will see a range in disposition that runs from terrified under the gun to dauntless. Now a gun-shy dog will cringe under the gun, or even run away. But this you must know: a true gun-shy dog is terrified of everything. He cowers before man, noise, weed cover, birds, taking a ride in the family car, a guest entering the house, or even the ringlets caused by lapping in a water bowl. God just wound these dogs' motors too tight; you shuffle a foot and they'll jump. I feel so sorry for them; their stomachs must be running hot with acid.

Such is the classic gun-shy dog, and there is no cure.

Now, there are extra-sensitive dogs that may cringe before the gun until they become accustomed to it. And there are other dogs, which because of accidents or misjudgment in the field on the part of the handler temporarily don't want to be around a gun. But these are not gun-shy dogs. Let me give you an example: Pup's on point, the gunner brushes past, a twig catches and slaps Pup's face just as the gun goes off. Now Pup is man shy, gun shy, bird shy, and cover shy. All accomplished in one second. But is this pup truly gun shy? No! A training error has occurred and must be corrected. Pup got hit in the face (we can handle this); he didn't get wired wrong in the womb (we can't fix that).

The problem is that there are people among us who say the dog that got slapped in the face is gun shy—and they can cure it. Ha. This is not gun shyness at all. The pup that's gun shy runs from his own shadow. He is neurotic. The pup that was slapped suffered an accident. We must merely erase the event, we don't have to physically rewire the dog. Understand? The gun-shy dog would have to be sent back to God for a rewind job: it's that simple!

Now, any idiot can take a young pup to field and fire directly over him. The blast would absolutely drive Pup to earth. And we could get something between the cross-wired dog and the accident victim.

But you and me, we start Pup on the gun by firing a .22 blank far distant from the kennel while Pup's eating (eating's a pleasure—we associate the gun with pleasure). We do not look at Pup. We pretend nothing happened. Each day we draw closer with the shot. Finally we can stand as far as a bird would naturally be from a pointing dog and fire. If Pup keeps eating, you're on your way. If not, start all over again—far distant—and be very careful and take a long time.

I recently trained with two young Texas pros who say they must take castoffs from other pros (for it's hard to get started in this training business). Consequently, they get the accident victims. Not gun-shy dogs (those should go to the hospitals), but victims of abuse and ignorance and impatience on the part of some handler.

The boys take the dogs into their home and make buddies of them. I'm glad I don't live there. They slam the front door, they slam the cupboard doors. They drop pans, they yell, they throw telephone directories flat to the floor. After one month, they say, the dogs firm up. I wonder; the dogs could also be stone deaf or punch drunk. But I pride the boys for trying and am pleased with their results. But the results don't come from slamming things: these two boys are very thoughtful and considerate. They have a soft hand and a soft way. Just being around this pair day after day bolds the dogs up: all that slamming just makes it harder for the boys to let their inner nature remold the dog.

I like what you and I do better. By not taking Pup to field for birds until he's well through yard training and had a ton of *Happy Timing*, we've got a dog ready for the gun. Then, when we do put Pup on wing and shot, we do so by walking a broad 180 degrees around his point, ending up far to front, letting Pup predict the shot, getting the muzzle's blast far from his head.

For as John Nash, sixth generation Irish setter breeder, told me one day on the moors of Ireland's Ballyfin where we were hunting partridge, "Did you ever notice, Bill, there are no bad pups . . . just bad dogs?"

Another way to avoid accident shyness is to kill your birds dead. The pheasant lofts, you fire, Pup's cast, and he gets a spur right on the nose. As Hunter Wells tells us in his book, *They Call Me Hunter* (Montague Stevens makes it even more dramatic in his magnificent book, *Meet Mr. Grizzly*), the bear knows what dog bit him, he knows where the hurt's coming from. Same with Pup. He knows you shot the bird that hurt him. He knows the gun had something to do with it. So you must use enough gun. And enough powder and shot.

Hal Jankofsky, a gun expert from Scottsdale, Arizona, has told me, "The best shot size on quail, pheasant, and dove is 7½ to 8 over dogs . . . because of the controlled shot [the short distance]." He adds, "A high-velocity load is actually slower. For example, in a 12 gauge it is actually fifteen feet per second slower than a low-brass shell."

So you're going to get on your target faster with low-brass shells (this does not apply to gunning with flushing dogs or going after waterfowl), and by shooting 7½'s you're going to be throwing more shot than if you were shooting 4's or 6's. Consequently, you'll have more sure kills and fewer kicking and pecking birds to make Pup hesitant to either point, flush, or fetch.

Another thing, beware of hunting pen-raised birds. If they haven't been properly flight-trained, they'll come up slow and skim the cover. You fire, but what's this? Pup has broke and he's chasing the bird—right into your shot string. That's why we're always to front of Pup when we shoot. Shooting Pup can surely destroy his enthusiasm for the bird and the field.

But pity the poor Lab. He must work directly under the gun. Yet they are seldom gun shy. Through selective breeding the spooky ones have been weeded out. Many a Lab, however, has gone stone deaf from gunfire. Best you keep Pup some distance from the blind when duck hunting. Some of the boys are now making a pad to which they swivel-snap Pup close to the blind. Only after the shooting do they get out of the blind, walk over to him, and release him for the retrieve. Makes sense.

Finally, accident shyness is caused by introducing Pup to the gun's blast too soon, crowding his point on flush, and shooting too close—or actually hitting him when hunting. We prepare pups for the gun by firing distant while they eat or while they *Happy Time* and are far away having fun. We never acknowledge the gun when they turn to find out what happened.

You can avoid creating accident shyness in Pup, for you now know the rules—but your fellow hunter might not.

Here's the way it goes. Your dog busts a covey of quail. The man asked along on this hunt—the expert dog trainer who doesn't own a dog—snorts in disgust, "Since you can't control that dog, I'm gonna give him a free ten-dollar training lesson the next time he does that." The dog does. The ten-dollar philanthropist slams the dog's head into the snow, striking him with his gun barrel. "There," the man gloats, "he'll not bump birds again."

Far-fetched? No! This incident happened in Kansas. What did the dog owner do? He was stunned. He did nothing. The dog? He folded for the day, and then for life. And the "trainer?" He got what was coming to him. He took but a few steps, kicked up a single from the busted covey, fired, and saw his $200 gun explode in his face. The barrel was packed with snow.

And then he knew: whenever a dog makes you mad he's defeated you. If it had been my dog in that field that day, the man would have learned more defeat than he ever thought could be assembled on the face of the entire earth!

13

Goin' Huntin'

WELL, THAT'S IT. Pup's ready. Let's go hunting. Pup running, laughingly, in the tall yellow grass. You with a handful of new shells in your coat pocket, a PayDay candy bar for lunch. You've worked hard for this, so enjoy!

And to make it all go better, here are a few suggestions.

Buy, fill with honey, and carry several ¼-ounce gelatin capsules you can get from your vet. Give one honey capsule to Pup every two hours to protect against low-blood-sugar seizure. On occasion, take one yourself.

However, should Pup suffer low-blood-sugar seizure, then treat for shock and hobble. Dogs are prone to bolt when recovering from seizure and may disappear, not to return. Hobbling Pup's legs prevents a runaway.

If the day is hot, let Pup run five minutes, then call him in and water him from a canteen. A dog laps water by flipping his tongue under. Pull aside Pup's lower lip (back toward his jaws), and pour water in the pouch left between lip and gum. Don't gag Pup. Take it easy. He will have to learn to drink this way.

After Pup's hunted another five minutes, water him again. Now he'll run cool and need only occasional watering. But should you neglect these two off-the-reel waterings, Pup's going to get hot. And if he

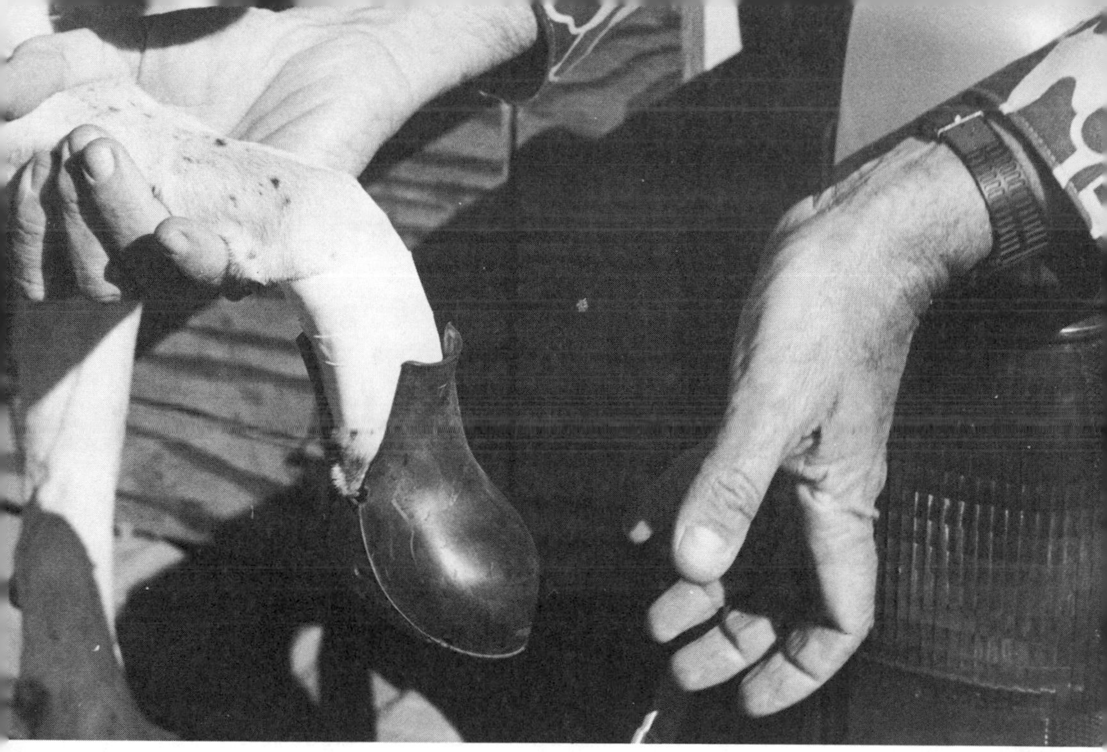

To put boots on Pup, first tape ankles . . .

. . . then tape boots to tape.

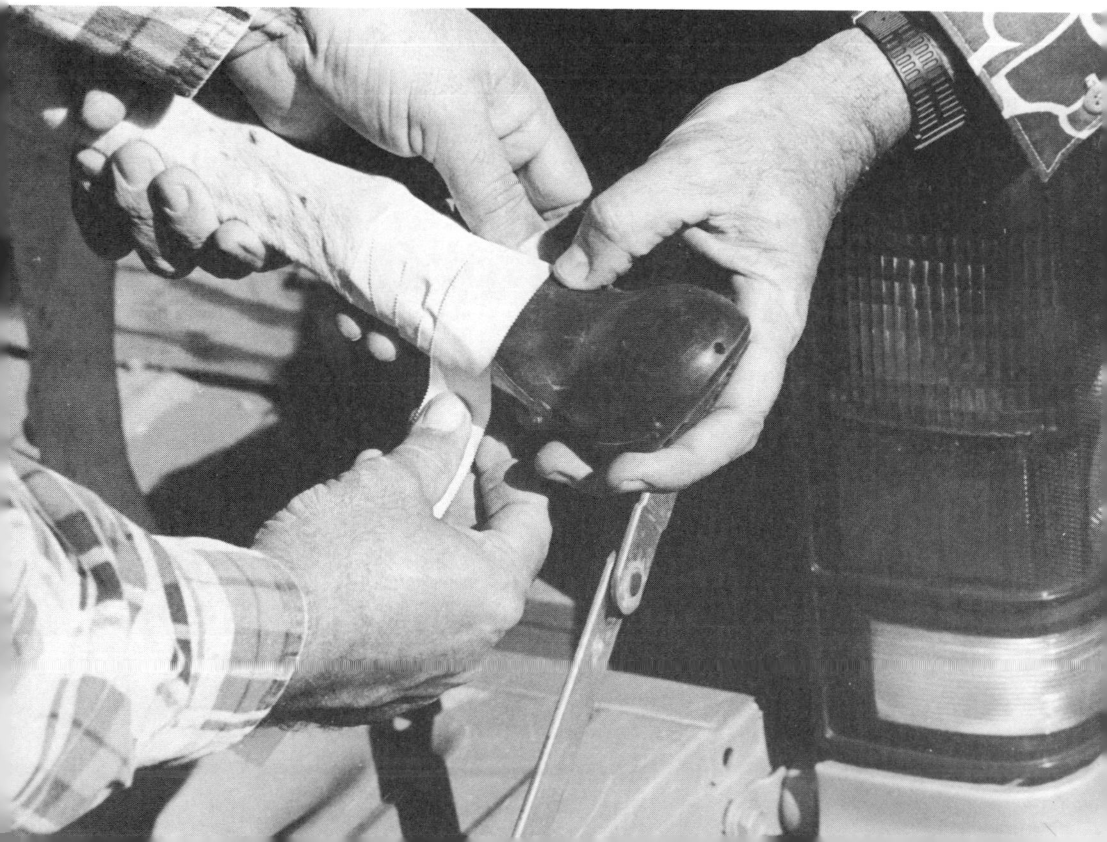

once gets hot, there ain't enough water in Minnesota to cool him down. It's the same principle as a car's radiator. Fill one before starting, and it'll run cool all day. Let it boil over, however, and you're going to sit there fuming most of the day.

If hunting in sandbur country, tape Pup's ankles before bird season. Use one- or two-inch tape and apply above, adjacent to, and below the height of rubber boots. Then when you go afield, tape the boots to the tape. Otherwise, you're daily applying and ripping tape off ankle fur, which causes irritation. This way you leave the tape on the ankle for days or a week (depending on moisture, dirt, etc.), and you're not pulling hair or in any other way harming the dog. Of course, the tape should not be applied so tight it cuts off circulation.

When traveling to and from the bird fields, be thoughtful where you kennel Pup. It's nearly impossible to freeze a dog to death, but you can smother one in a matter of minutes. Get air circulation through his crate. If it's torrid hot, then put a block of ice in Pup's crate. Licking ice has taken more than one pro's string of dogs across the circuit of the Southwest.

In old English, "quarry," meant entrails from game given to a dog as treat. If you want to treat Pup with bird heads, do so. Apart from the reward, they're nourishing. And they make Pup even more birdy.

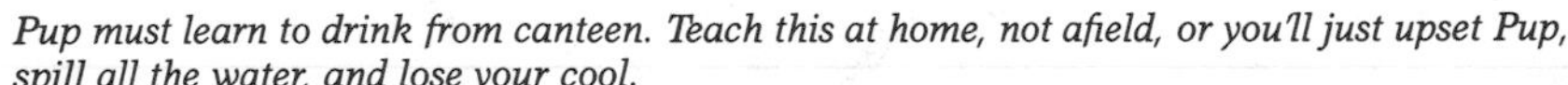

Pup must learn to drink from canteen. Teach this at home, not afield, or you'll just upset Pup, spill all the water, and lose your cool.

You say this may make Pup hard mouthed or actually cause him to become a bird eater? Not so! If Pup eats a bird, it's because he's hungry. Let him have it unless you've been thoughtful enough to carry some pep-burgers: one-inch round hamburger balls, each containing two teaspoons of sugar.

Pup's burning lots of energy: it's your job to replace it. Refrigerated pep-burgers, along with honey capsules, get Pup through those sinking spells man and dog alike suffer during a day's hunt.

Incidentally, give Pup his regular daily feed either morning or night. But should you feed in the morning, then don't hunt Pup for two hours after eating. Digestion requires energy, just as running does. To do both at the same time overloads Pup's heart.

During your hunt, call Pup in from time to time and check him over. Seeds in the eye can be a real problem. Flush them out with any solution your vet recommends. Tips of tails and ears will split from crack-whip force. I use A&D ointment to get Pup through the day. At home I switch to Tuf-Skin, the liquid athletes put on their shaved ankles to minimize tape burn.

Remove burs, stickers, and awns from Pup's foot pads with a pair of tweezers. Sometimes it takes scissors to cut foreign matter from his coat.

Look in Pup's ears. If anything's stuck to the flap, pick it off, but don't poke into the channel in hopes of dislodging some foreign particle. That's a job for the vet.

If Pup gets into a porcupine, you'll need pliers to pull out the quills. It's nasty business, but must be done. Be especially watchful for spear grass. This is the dog killer. It will enter and migrate, working completely through a dog. The result will surely be lethargy and could well be death.

Tomato juice poured over a dog doesn't rid him of skunk odor. Try the new formula Skunk-Off.

We've heard all the arguments against Pup wearing a collar afield, for there's the likelihood he'll hang himself. Having heard these arguments, forget them. Pup must have a collar with nameplate identifying him as your property and explaining how he may be returned if lost. There's no way he can get hung up if his collar is snug. And I mean snug – where you can just wedge two fingers between fur and leather.

Two tools you carry at all times are wire cutters and toenail clippers. Pup will one day leap, touch, and push off a page-wire fence. His back legs will slip through the void in the wire, go over the hocks, and he'll hang there. Hang there and die there, if you don't find him and cut him loose. Be all business about it. If you try to console Pup hanging

Llewellin fancier and desert bird hunter Bill Parton stops hunt to pull cactus thorns from Bandito with tweezers.

upside down, in his pain and panic he may bite you for your sympathy.

If Pup breaks a toenail, use your clippers to snip it all the way back to the fur. That's right, all the way back. Then get out of the way, cause blood's going to spurt six feet. Slap the area with a clotting solution you can get from your vet, and the bleeding will stop in minutes. Now you can go on with your hunt.

Should you work Pup with the nail hanging, each step he takes he'll feel pain. Just remove the nail. Pup can hunt all day with minimum discomfort. He'll be a little sore the next morning, but nothing like he would be if you left a partial nail dangling during a day's outing.

Remember, always keep your first-aid kit at base camp, be it lodge, car, or saddlebags. Every once in a while re-read the first-aid material that follows. There's just so much to remember, especially when we acknowledge whatever's going to happen bad is going to happen fast.

14

First Aid

THIRTY YEARS AGO I saw a cartoon showing a hard-rock miner lying on his back, clutching his leg. Off to the side a rattlesnake was slithering away. A friend stood over the miner, handing out a bottle. But the miner declared, "Won't do no good now . . . the liquor's got to be in you when you're bit."

Liquor and snake bite don't mix. That's not the moral of the cartoon. Instead, the cartoon tells us when disaster happens afield it happens fast. And a knowledge of first aid better be in you when it strikes.

Dr. Dick Royse, the premier Wichita, Kansas, vet who teamed up with us on puppy illness, returns now to say, "There's no substitute for professional medical care, but every dog owner should know the basics of first aid for the sporting dog afield. Everyone, sometime, will have an ill or injured dog fifty or a hundred miles from a vet. What eventually happens to that dog depends on what happens to him first. That's what it's all about, *first* aid."

Lacerations

"We had a seminar not too long ago," says Royse, "with Dr. Joseph Bojrab, professor of surgery, Department of Veterinary Medicine and

Surgery at the University of Missouri. He's a fantastic soft-tissue surgeon, and he talked to us on wound management. And what he said was this: 'Throw away your antiseptic, throw away your peroxides, throw away your distilled water . . . instead, use saline.'"

Doc explains, "Saline is an isotonic solution. In other words, that fluid is exactly the same constituency as body fluids. And you can get a bottle from your veterinarian . . . it's cheap . . . and it comes in 150- or 250-cc bottles. And that is what you want to clean a wound with. And I mean the first thing . . . and that only.

"Don't use anything else in your first aid. Now, if you've got a nasty wound–I mean it's really a deep cut or a wide laceration with a skin flap that opens up–go ahead and use your saline to clean it. If possible, bandage it–like on a limb. Take your bandage and get yourself some little three-by-three gauze packs. Moisten these with saline and put a moist saline pad on the wound, then wrap. You can get these three-by-three gauze packs at the drug store, or your veterinarian can let you have some of his.

"Now in all of this . . . the preservation of tissue and healing is just fantastic."

If the dog is bleeding, that flow must be stopped. Place a saline-soaked three-by-three gauze pack on the wound and apply pressure. Hold firm. Bleeding stop? Fine. If you want to stay afield, remove the compress, flush the wound with saline, and apply a new three-by-three gauze pack. Wrap with gauze, ideally lapping forty-five degrees to the lay of pack. Keep crisscrossing the pack, making a mummy wrap. Don't cover with tape. We want air to get to the wound. Secure gauze by catching hair with adhesive tape at the edge of the bandage.

But say Pup has a cut pad–you don't think it's serious–and you want to keep hunting. Okay. Cover bandage completely with tape. Secure bandage by catching hair of Pup's leg. Pull an old sweat sock over bandage and secure with tape to fur. But Doc steps in here to reveal: "There is a new compound for sealing wounds called VetBond; get it from your vet. It's excellent for small wounds on the ear or foot pads. But don't use it on large lacerations."

Remember, a rubber boot is good protection for Pup, but it's usually too small to cover a fat bandage.

But what if the bleeding won't stop? Or our compression bandage just won't stop the flow? As a last resort, apply a tourniquet. And only as a last resort. Tourniquets can be more dangerous than the wound. For tourniquet material, use a piece of rubber surgical hose, some two-inch gauze, Pup's leash, or any other flexible material that can be used to apply pressure.

Caution! Tourniquets should be applied just tight enough to control bleeding. No more. A tourniquet should be loosened every fifteen to twenty minutes, for about five minutes. Repeat the sequence until Pup makes it to a vet. For that's where you and Pup are going. This wound is too major for field treatment. The same applies to any large-area wound.

Large-area wounds are treated only with saline. Never use distilled water or antiseptic – not even if there's dirt in the wound. Antiseptics on a large wound may inhibit healing, because too many antiseptics destroy good bacteria as well as the bad. Pup needs the good bacteria to heal properly. Also stay away from powders. Most powders use talc as the vehicle to carry the medicine, but talcum inhibits healing.

And what about infection? Little concern. Takes about twenty-four hours for infection to become active, and by that time Pup will be in a vet's care.

In administering first aid to lacerations, there are several things you must remember. Never put cotton on a wound. The fibers stick. Also, remove a totally taped bandage as soon as possible. Let air in. Change bandages every day if Pup's kennel run is wet.

Also, never apply a bandage too tight. You'll stop blood circulation. Apply gauze firmly, but don't pull so the fabric stretches. When finished wrapping, you should be able to force your index finger under the bandage with minimal resistance.

On large-area wounds you may have to treat for shock (see below) and then move out fast.

And remember, a reflex dog bite is an instinctual reaction to pain. And a reflex bite makes a mean-dog bite seem as gentle as a bride's caress. To avoid being bitten, the dog must be immobilized and his muzzle closed.

Immobilizing and Muzzling

Precautions taken before attempting to administer first aid to a dog in pain include:

1. Approach Pup from the rear and toss a blanket over him. Possibly he'll partially wrap himself and you can finish bundling. The blanket warms Pup, which mitigates shock and assists in his immobilization so he'll not further self-injure through panic-stricken struggle.
2. Avoid reflex dog bite by applying a muzzle. Take in each hand

one end of a piece of gauze bandage, stand behind and above Pup, and toss a loop of gauze out over Pup's nose. Let it swing under his chin, throw a half hitch in the gauze, and tighten. Pull the half hitch as snug as you want. No way can you cut off Pup's breathing. Tie a knot. If wind blows the gauze (so you can't toss it out), then use a rawhide boot lace, a nylon check cord, or whatever else you have.

Vets have a tourniquet or muzzle apparatus with a slip-clip on it. The thing slides and locks at the desired position. Possibly your vet will sell you one. There was a time that Doc Royse and I recommended surgical hose for a muzzle, but strong dogs can stretch the hose and nip you. Therefore, use nothing that can give or tear.

3. If Pup's blanketed and muzzled, but still struggling, he must be totally immobilized. Staying to the rear, drop to your knees and place Pup on his side with legs extended – away from you. Now lean forward and pin Pup's buttocks to the ground with your shoulder. Extend a hand forward to crisscross and clamp Pup's front legs together. Use your free hand to clutch several folds of skin at the scruff of Pup's neck. You've got him. You're not hurting him. Pup can't hurt himself. And he can't hurt you.

Dr. Dick Royse begins clamping Pup to ground . . .

. . . then picks him up for trip to vet so Pup can't fall, squirm loose, or turn head to bite.

4. To lift and carry Pup, you must assure him a sense of balance. From the moment you start to pick him up, support him all the way. Don't let him feel he's going to fall; he'll panic and struggle. To pick Pup up, release your hold on his front legs and slide that hand back to the center of his chest. Tighten your arm securely about Pup's rib cage and over his rump. Pup's rear torso is now wedged in your armpit. Slide the near hand, now holding the scruff of Pup's neck, to side, adjacent to Pup's ear, so Pup can't turn his head and bite. Several folds of skin are taken in hand. You've got control. Now, lift by getting to your knees and standing. Pup shouldn't feel he's going to fall. He's not able to kick or squirm. Neither can he leap forward. And he can't bite.

5. To walk Pup away, slide the far hand up from his chest to grasp his far shoulder. Control is accomplished. Walk Pup to your vehicle and drive to the nearest vet.

Punctures

Puncture wounds are treated the same as lacerations – with one exception. The foreign object that punctured Pup – piece of wire, glass, thorn, nail – may still be in him. And it stands to reason that as long as the foreign object remains every time Pup moves the wound may be aggravated.

Try to remove the foreign object, but only if it comes easily – and I mean easily. Never use force. The only time force is acceptable is when Pup's punctured with porcupine quills – they must be taken out right then with pliers, and it is a painful and traumatic mess. It would be inconceivable to pack Pup up and tote him to town with those things sticking him. The porcupine is the ultimate peril for the gun dog man. With other punctures, you may have to immobilize and muzzle Pup; then keeping him quiet, head for town.

If the object stuck in Pup can be easily removed, then pull it out and stop any resultant bleeding. Should you want to stay afield and keep hunting, then apply a bandage. But note: puncture wounds can be deceptive. How deep did Pup get stuck? So deep his wound may eventually appear to heal on the outside but infect within? If so, even though the foreign object comes freely to finger-pull, Pup should be retired for the day and taken to the vet.

Doc tells us, "I recently had a hunting dog come in with a punctured pad. I flushed out the wound – cleaned it real good – dressed it, and put the dog on antibiotics. He stayed overnight with me, and the next morning looked great. So I sent him home with a supply of antibiotics and instructions for the owner. I told him, 'Watch it, and if any swelling occurs, call me.' Two days later the man came home from work and found the dog with the limb badly swollen all the way to the shoulder. The dog was toxic and down, and as a result he died in an emergency clinic that night.

"What it amounted to was this. We got hold of a gas-producing bacteria, or gangrene, if you will. And I think that's the first one I ever experienced like that. But it really shocked me that we lost the dog over a simple puncture wound."

So take no puncture wound casually. They can be potential killers. I'd say every puncture wound, by necessity, requires the treatment of a vet.

And a final note about feet. Each of us must winterize our dogs. That includes roading, which gets Pup in shape but also toughens up his pads. Plus, there are skin tougheners you can buy and apply. Doctor Royse's favorite is Coppertox, a product used to toughen up horse's hooves.

Furthermore, rubber boots are recommended in briar and cactus country. Plus, any place where there's lots of rock. A rock can literally sheer a dog's pad right off his foot. Over the years we've developed a good way to put boots on a dog. Tape all four ankles, slide on the rubber boots, then tape the boots to the tape. Each night the outer wrap of tape can be ripped off and the boots removed. The first wrap can stay for a weekend hunt, or even longer, and saves Pup the discomfort of pulled tape.

Fractures

Easy does it. Handle Pup gently. Keep him quiet. A struggling Pup can aggravate injury. Do not attempt to manipulate an injured limb—or feel about the torso, neck or head.

Under no circumstances should you try to apply a splint. You run a good chance of lacerating muscle tissue or severing an artery or vein with razor-sharp bone splinters.

In case of suspected spinal injury, slide Pup on a flat surface to be used as a stretcher and head for professional care. I once ripped off the door of an abandoned ice box to use for this purpose.

And don't assume Pup's without fracture just because he's walking or running. Not long ago I saw a house dog get hit by a car. The pelvis was broken in three places, yet this little tyke ran home, entered the house, and I'm told she crawled under a bed where she usually sleeps.

If you suspect fracture, treat for shock and head for professional care.

Shock

Shock is the dog corpsman's primary concern. Shock may occur with any serious injury. Symptoms are a docile Pup, depressed (depressed even to the point he can't lift his head—just flat knocked down), semiconsciousness or unconsciousness, possibly rapid panting, and a fixed stare to the eye.

Wrap Pup in a blanket and keep him warm and quiet. In most cases of shock, a dog experiences rapid drop in body heat. This must be brought back to normal—fast!

Approach Pup from behind and toss a blanket over him. As we said before, he'll possibly partially wrap himself and you can finish bundling. The blanket will warm him, plus assist in immobilization.

Generally, if Pup's hurt bad enough to go into shock, he'll probably need a vet's care.

Heat Stroke

Symptoms of heat stroke can be rapid, heavy panting or raspy breathing with acute oxygen deprivation. Another indication of heat stroke is if Pup collapses.

You must lower Pup's body temperature, and do it fast. Even control-dump him in a cold stream. Remember, Pup's underbelly is comparable to a human's wrists. That's where the largest supply of superficial blood vessels lie closest to the skin. This is where you concentrate your coolant. Should you have ice in a chest, wrap some in a cloth and apply to the base of Pup's skull (see below). Or, carry a bag of Kwik-Kold, the instant ice pack that's activated by striking the bag of white granules.

If Pup can drink, give small amounts of ice-cold water at frequent intervals. Too much water, however, and Pup may vomit.

You've got to work fast with heat stroke. Pup's normal body temperature is 101.5 F. Heat stroke can send this temperature soaring. When body temperature rises it causes tremendous congestion, which impedes circulation to the brain. This creates undue pressure, which, in turn, may damage brain cells. That's why we apply ice to the base of Pup's skull.

Incidentally, heat stroke can occur in the car as well as in the field. A closed car under a summer sun can reach temperatures of 130 degrees in most temperate climates, 180 degrees—at least it feels that hot—in the desert. When transporting Pup make sure he's got good ventilation, especially when your rig is stopped. You'll recall I mentioned earlier that a block of ice in Pup's crate can be a lifesaver.

Frostbite

The natural inclination in treating frostbite is to do the wrong thing. Your impulse is to rub the affected areas: ears, tail, feet. Don't! If you rub extremely cold or frozen tissue, you can easily fracture small capillaries in the peripheral blood circulation. When this happens it takes a long time for Pup's body to re-establish circulation in the affected area.

So here's what you do. Soak a compress in warm water and apply moist heat to the frostbite. Never apply and leave a dressing. This, too, can damage peripheral circulation.

You can get warm water out of your car's radiator or use coffee from your thermos. Remember, frostbite is a subtle thing. There's usually no pain or discomfort suffered by Pup while his extremities are being frozen. It's your responsibility to be aware of critically cold temperature and not expose Pup too long at any one time.

But there is this: when it comes to hot or cold, Pup can take a ton of blizzard compared to a pound of heat wave.

Poisons

Symptoms ordinarily take two forms: (1) incoordination, extensive nervousness to the point of seizure and convulsion; and (2) profuse vomiting and/or diarrhea. Unfortunately, with some poisons – and this is the bad part for the dog monitor – you see no symptoms at all.

A poisoned dog, however, must vomit. This can be induced by giving one tablespoon of peroxide orally. Lacking this, place one teaspoon of salt on the rear of Pup's tongue. Save the vomitus and give to the vet for analysis.

Also, if Pup goes into seizure or convulsion, you must protect him from self-injury. Wrap him in a blanket.

Toxic Exposure

If Pup contacts toxic or corrosive material – insecticides, crude pits in oil fields, acids, lyes – wash the skin with great amounts of water. Really flush him. And as with a poisoned dog, you must be prepared to wrap Pup in a blanket to avoid self-injury that may come from seizure or convulsions. You must also take the caustic agent to the vet for analysis.

Eye Injuries

It's difficult to evaluate eye injuries. They're usually more serious than they appear. You should do nothing more than flush the eye with common boric acid eye wash – if you do this much – and head for a vet.

In case of a seed or insect in Pup's eye, try to wipe it out – gently – with a tissue. Also, your vet can supply an eye lubricant many feel is imperative for the field. Lubricant makes the eye tear excessively, constantly washing out foreign matter.

Spider Bite

Hard to detect in the field, for a hunting dog will usually ignore a spider bite. Yet anywhere from three to seven days later Pup can likely show an area of dead tissue between the size of a dime and a quarter. The area will turn black, infect, and literally fall out. Don't attempt home treatment. Get Pup to a vet.

Snake Bite

Mandatory! Ignore the dog and kill the snake. Determine if it's venomous. If you can't find the snake, then look at the bite. Non-venomous bites generally have a U-configuration and are multi-toothed. Such bites appear as superficial scratches and cause little pain. Cleanse the area well with saline and seek further treatment.

However, a venomous snake usually leaves two fang marks. And, the victim may exhibit instantaneous, severe pain in the bite area. Depending on the potency of the venom – big snakes insert big doses, unless they've just killed; some snakes are more poisonous than others; and most snakes coming out of hibernation are more poisonous yet – the dog may become incoordinate, vomit, convulse, or go into coma. If you don't get the dog to a vet within four hours, the outlook for recovery is poor.

There's little you can do in the field for a venomous snake bite. Get the snake. Keep the dog quiet. Permit no exercise that will stimulate the venom's flow. Don't ever cut and suck: shades of winning the West.

Contain the venom by applying a flat, constricting band – your belt's fine – between the bite and heart. Impede the flow of venom, but don't block off arterial circulation; you are not applying a tourniquet. Plus, and this is important, if the bite is high enough on the leg, put a second constricting band beneath it. Keep the venom away from the paw. We are, in fact, isolating the venom in the area of the bite. The reason? Venom isolated in the paw by just one constricting band can cause damage resulting in amputation.

Now, a constricting band (or bands) is properly adjusted if a finger can be inserted with minimal force. The band should be left intact until definite treatment is provided, or a minimum of two hours.

What usually happens with a venomous snake bite is this. You're hunting 200 miles from a metropolitan area. You take the bitten dog to a rural vet for treatment, but the vet's a large-animal doctor. He can treat Pup, but he doesn't stock antivenin. But you do. That's right, you carry antivenin to give the vet to give to Pup.

Medical science is constantly improving antivenin. Present shelf life is twelve to eighteen months. That's under refrigeration. Yet your car can get mighty hot. So carry antivenin in a plastic bag within your ice chest or in the tire well. Anywhere to keep the temperature as low as possible. When not afield, refrigerate antivenin and buy a new kit often. Your vet will advise you.

And yes, once again you'll need to treat Pup for shock. Get him wrapped in a blanket.

One final thing, whether or not you apply ice to Pup's snake bite is up to you and your vet. It has been noticed, however, the iced appendages of humans suffering venomous snake bites result in more amputations than for patients who don't use ice.

Accidental Gun Shot

Important! How far away was Pup when hit? This determines extent of injury, how much shock to expect, and how deep the pellets penetrated. If you accidentally shoot Pup close enough to knock him down, you're going to be dealing with a tremendous amount of shock. So, back to the blanket. Wrap Pup, keep him warm, and get medical help as fast as possible.

But let's say you just sprinkle Pup so he yipes, there's only a few blood specks. You're probably not going to have any immediate problems. Cleanse area with saline and either keep on hunting or head for a vet. It's up to you.

But if Pup's hit hard, and he comes through shock, he's going to be so muscle-sore he can hardly walk. This can be expected with any dog shot forty yards or less.

So, if Pup's dusted with shot, you may treat afield. But if he's knocked down with the impact, treat for shock, and head for town.

Bee Sting

A bumblebee can knock Pup down. A flight of honeybees can drive him nearly mad. Make a baking-soda paste and pile on ½ inch thick to the affected area. Cover with a damp compress and hold for fifteen minutes. Follow this with an ice pack. The same treatment applies for wasp stings.

Burns

Move fast. For localized burns – say Pup touched the car's hot exhaust – apply ice, snow, or your handkerchief saturated with water from a winter stream. A large-area burn will cause shock. Now you've got to make a decision on priorities. Should you cool the wound or get the dog wrapped in a blanket? Large burns trigger Pup's body to consume great amounts of liquids. If Pup is not immobilized, he will aggravate dehydration. Make your decision and proceed accordingly.

Incidentally, never apply ointment to a burn. That's just something Doc has to remove so he can proceed with treatment.

Choking

If you suspect something's lodged in Pup's throat, and you can handle his jaws so you don't get bitten, then open his mouth and pull the tongue out as far as possible. Now, can Pup inhale air? If he can't, pick him up by his hind legs, hanging him head down, and give him a sharp slap either high across the back of his shoulders or across the front of his chest.

If a small object's lodged in the trachea, it may jar out, or you may stimulate coughing, which can blow it free. Remember, never stick your fingers down Pup's throat. He may reflex bite, and/or you might lodge the object even deeper.

To pull Pup's tongue from his mouth, compress the hinge of the jaw to force the mouth open, then continue to squeeze your thumb and forefinger on opposite sides of Pup's jaws, pressing the flesh of Pup's cheeks beneath his teeth. Now you can reach the tongue. Once the tongue's pulled out and laid to side (sandwiched between Pup's teeth), Pup can't bite.

Foreign Object in Ear

Hard to treat in the field. If there's anything in the ear deep enough to cause discomfort (Pup's shaking his head or scratching the side of his face along the grass or scratching at an ear with a paw), you probably won't be able to see it. You may remove anything from Pup's ear you can reach with your fingers. For example, you might see a stalk

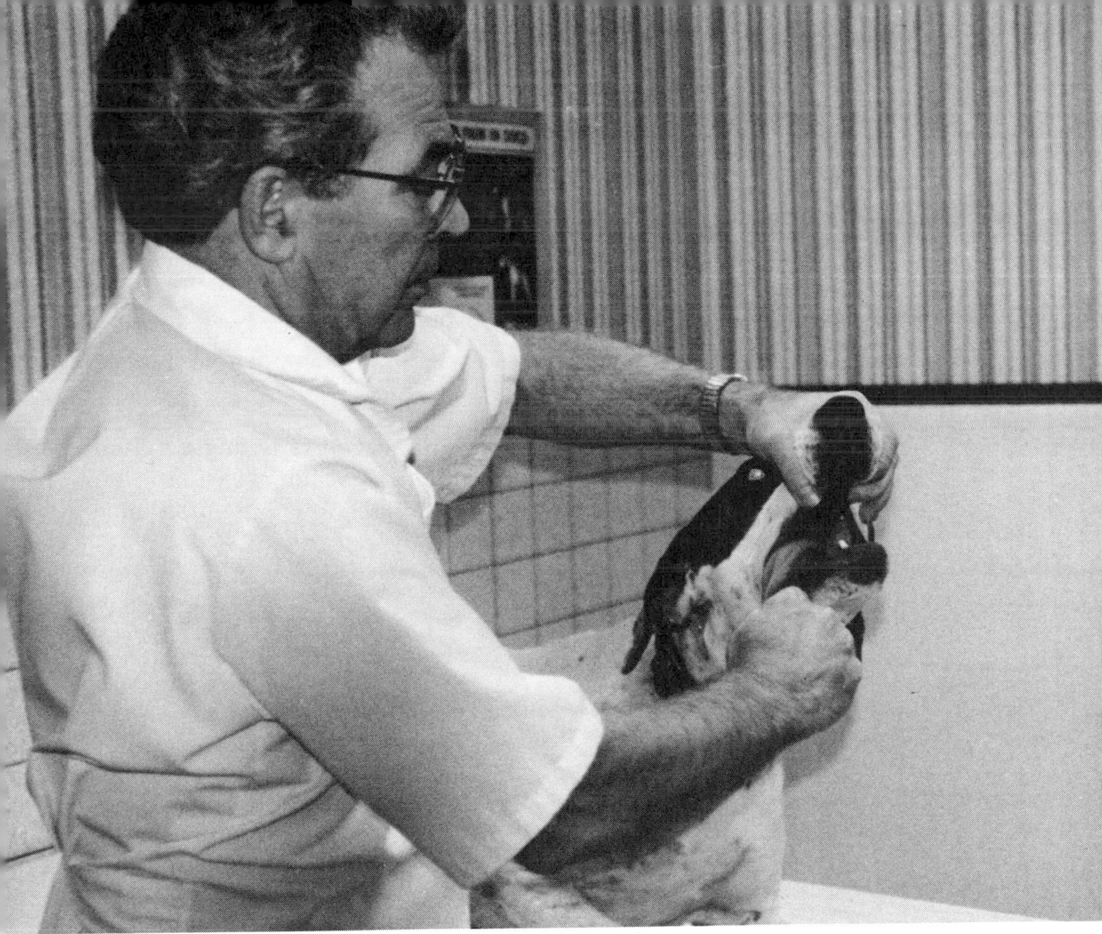

Doctor Royse shows how to pull Pup's tongue to side so you can look down his throat and not get bit.

of tickle grass in there. Pull it out. Nothing smaller than your finger should ever be inserted.

Electrocution

Drag Pup from energy source with loop made of leash, belt, or check cord—anything not wet and not a natural conductor. You may be confronted with three simultaneous emergencies: respiratory failure, shock, and burns. Induce breathing by artificial respiration. Lay Pup on his side, legs extended, and place one or both hands flat in the middle of Pup's rib cage three inches behind his shoulder. Press firmly, listen to air expire, and release abruptly. Repeat sequence twenty times a minute.

If Pup has stopped breathing, you've got five minutes to get him started. After that time irreversible brain damage may already have occurred.

Also, Pup has been shocked; he's in shock, so you must treat for shock.

And you may well have to treat for burns.

Drowning

Hard to drown a dog, except when a raccoon is taking a hound under. But strange things happen, such as car accidents where Pup goes underwater trapped in the car in his crate. Your only assistance will be artificial respiration (see above).

Royse places hands just where you want them if you ever have to give Pup artificial respiration in the field.

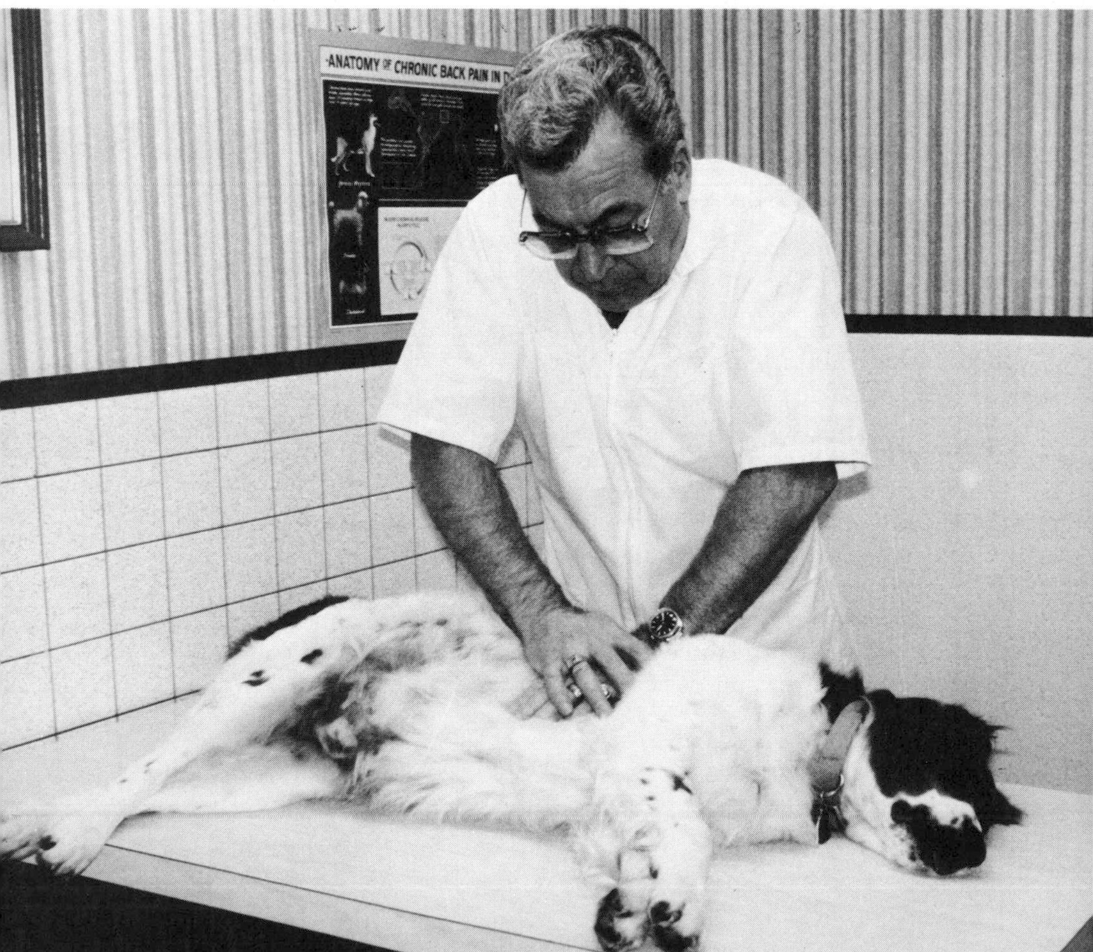

Dog Fight

Injuries resulting from a dog fight can include broken bones, pulled teeth, dislodged eyeballs, punctures, and lacerations. Be prepared to treat for shock. A dog fight can be a total calamity. Avoid fights at all costs.

Dousing fighting dogs with water sometimes gets them separated. But the sure-fire method is for two men, each grabbing a dog by his hind legs, to pull the dogs apart and swing each of them in great circles. For a dog, that's total disarmament.

But heed this advice. If your dog's been in a fight and all you see is a couple of little puncture wounds and blood spotting, don't dismiss it as a minor wound. Puncture wounds can come back to haunt you. When a dog opens his mouth and bites, he makes a puncture wound with his upper jaw, plus a puncture wound with his lower jaw. When he closes his mouth—this is a big, strong dog—he tears the tissue from top to bottom where he's biting. The result? The dog bite has loosened all that skin from wound to wound, and four to five days later you'll get a big abscess there.

So get your bitten dog to the vet as soon as possible to get the puncture wounds flushed out and to have the dog put on antibiotics.

First-Aid Kit

Our first-aid kit contains nineteen items called for above: fifteen in the kit and four either on your person or carried in the vehicle. In addition, include any other items your own vet recommends.

In the kit are gauze bandage rolls, two- to four-inch width; adhesive roll, two-inch width; three-by-three-inch gauze packs; tourniquet of your choice; blanket; Kwik-Kold instant ice pack; saline; boric acid eye wash; snake antivenin; baking soda; old sweat sock; salt or hydrogen peroxide; eye lubricant; rubber boots; and VetBond.

Outside the kit you need ice, hot coffee, tissue, and the belt from your pants.

The kit can be arranged in a tool box, the cut-away bottom of a bleach bottle with a plastic-film cover secured by a rubber band, a small fishing tackle box, a discarded brief case, or almost anything else you have around the house.

This kit is generally adequate for waterfowl dogs, considering they're traditionally worked in a marsh. But should you hunt upland game dogs, it will be necessary for you to carry two additional aids: a pair of bolt cutters to cut Pup out of a wire fence should he get hung up while leaping and a set of toenail clippers in case Pup splits or throws a nail.

In conclusion, Doc Royse reminds us, "A visit to your vet thirty days before hunting season will pay dividends. That hunting companion of yours deserves a complete physical examination, parasite check, heartworm check, vaccinations, etc. Then, once it's established he's okay to hunt, give him a break, don't break him.

"Work him every day, extending the duration of each work period until he's in shape. This will prevent a lot of sore muscles, possible seizure, sore feet, and styleless performance.

"And when the season's over, are you going to put your dog in the kennel and forget him till next year? Once again, he deserve diagnosis and tune up. He just spent several weeks (or months) in the field, working hard, enduring all kinds of weather and tough cover. It's just possible he may have picked up parasites, grass or awns in the ears, thorns in the feet. Let your vet check him out. And in that regard, your own vet knows what's best for your dog in your country. Go talk to him. Get his advice. Pup needs the knowledge applied through you."

15

Heartworm

HEARTWORM IS A parasite that lives on a gun dog's tired blood, for the adult heartworm is generally found on the right side of the host's heart, the part of the organ that receives blood from the venous system. Microfilaria, what I call "mini-worms," are heartworm offspring living in the bloodstream. Heartworm and mini-worms are father and son, but that's where the resemblance stops. What feeds one doesn't feed the other. What kills one doesn't kill the other. As a matter of fact, there's not a dad among 'em that can recognize his own son. Here's why.

The female heartworm gives live birth to mini-worms that cruise away through the circulatory system. Mini-worms are micro-sized; they're invisible to the naked eye. They can live in this dormant, infant state for three years, awaiting a new host–the mosquito. Since mini-worms have neither mouths nor intestines, during this period they feed off fat stored in them by the mother.

Should the host dog be taken to a mosquito-free environment, all the mini-worms will die at the end of three years, and that will be the end of the matter. But should one of thirty known species of mosquito take one blood meal from this dog and pick up one mini-worm through its proboscis–then here we go!

Three Hosts

Three hosts are required to transform a mini-worm into a heartworm: a dog, a mosquito, and another dog.

While in the mosquito, the mini-worm goes through three larval stages within fourteen to twenty-one days. In subsequent effect, these three stages can be characterized as: night crawler (harmless), garter snake (harmless), and boa constrictor (deadly). For a later blood meal of the mosquito will deposit the deadly mini-worm into the eventual host dog: a worm that will migrate through the skin, into the bloodstream, and make its way to the dog's heart, where it will grow and—as a boa constrictor—set about to choke, or clog, the heart to death.

Migration for the fourth larval mini-worm, from injection into the dog's skin to residence in his heart, takes six months. During this period the mini-worm grows into a female heartworm measuring twelve inches in length or a male counterpart about half that size. Life expectancy for these heartworms is five years.

Having set up house in the heart, the female heartworm reproduces and her children (the mini-worms) are released to cruise in the

Infected heart opened to show strangling heartworms.

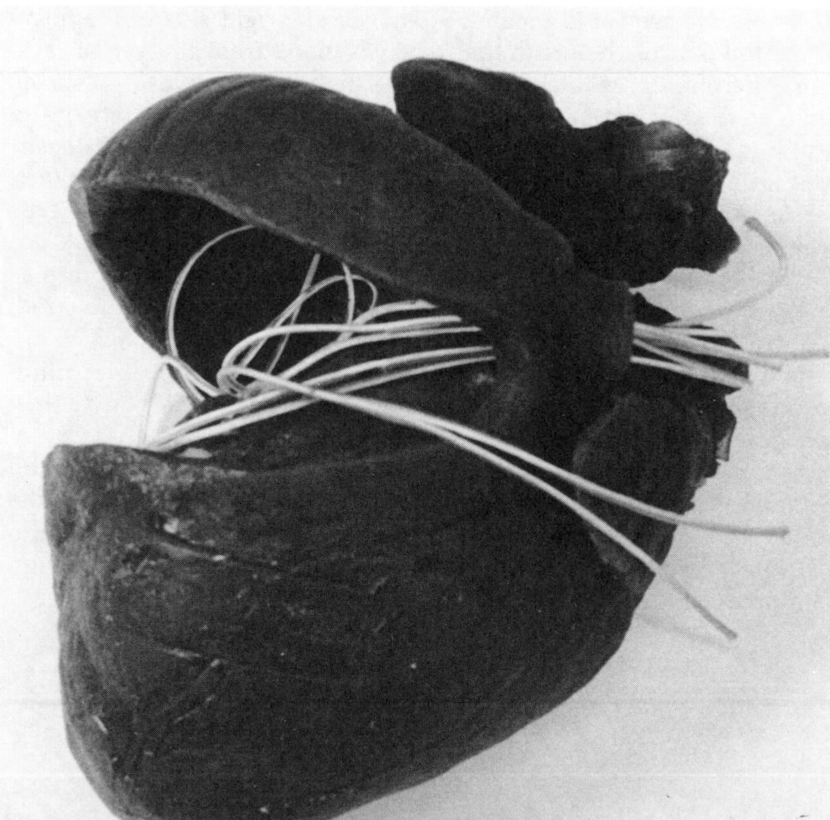

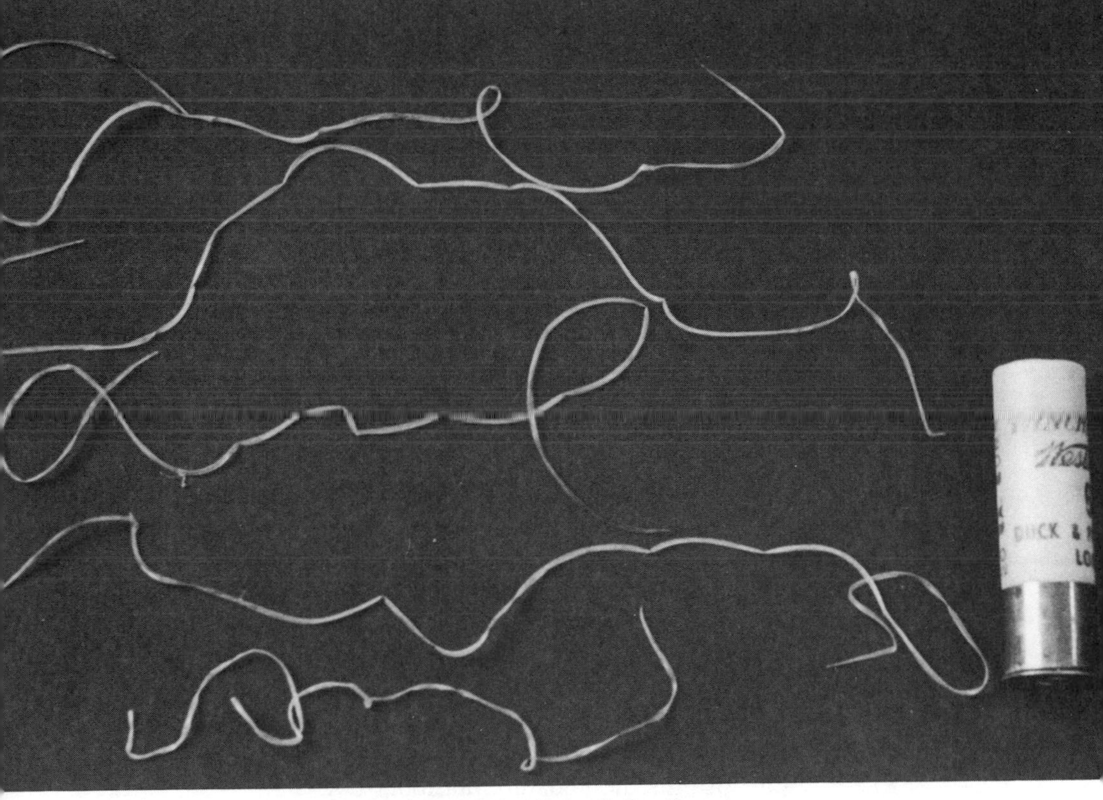

Heartworms placed on table beside shotshell to show size.

bloodstream. The cycle is now complete, and it will be repeated when the dog provides a blood meal for a subsequent mosquito. And on and on and on.

During the early 1970's, heartworm was considered "that problem" south of the Mason-Dixon line because the climate assured a good crop of mosquitoes year-round. But now, due to vast interstate travel, heartworm has been distributed throughout the United States.

All right, what a gun dog man wants to know is how to recognize this debilitating and deadly disease and how to prevent or cure it.

Symptoms

Symptoms of heartworm are listlessness, fatigue, and lack of zest and style. The dog moves at a reduced rate of efficiency, tires easily, and returns to heel during a morning's hunt. Or he may be running along, only to fall and pass out. The dog may or may not cough. Coughing used to be considered a sure sign. No more. The dog's coat may go flat, glossless, and appear dusty and dry. The dog may be restless and fidgety at night and will pace the floor.

Because the dog has so much difficulty breathing, his rib cage may become distorted. Instead of the ribs angling back away from the spine, they may protrude straight out, giving the dog a barrel-chested appearance. The dog may show liquid retention, become droop-gutted (or sag-bellied) to the extent of appearing pregnant. For you see, heartworm affects not only the heart, but other vital organs as well—kidneys, lungs, and liver.

Or, even worse, your dog may show no symptoms at all. One case history I recall involved a hard-going pointer that won a major stake on Saturday only to die in his kennel crate the following Tuesday. The owner couldn't believe it. The professional trainer ordered an autopsy. The veterinarian removed a heart filled with 344 worms (the record seems to be a figure in excess of 500). The owner flew 300 miles to verify the fact, and after seeing the dog, the heart, and the worms still refused to believe it!

Heartworm Tests

The vet has several ways of determining whether or not your dog has heartworm. But his methods *are not* foolproof. Why? Well, what stage is the worm in when the vet makes his examination? Is it a mini-worm? That calls for a blood check. And strange as it may seem, mini-worms can fail to show in a blood sample in the morning, but appear in the afternoon. Or, they may not appear in February, but infest the blood sample in August. Science is developing agents to increase mini-worm counts in a dog's bloodstream within minutes after administration so a vet can have a greater chance of spotting infestation.

Also, let's assume the dog has no mini-worms, but has just been bitten by a mosquito that put some of these boa-constrictor worms into the dog's skin. Well, that particular mini-worm may live in the skin for three months before working into the bloodstream and heading for the right ventricle. There's no test to tell if this worm's on his way.

Also, the dog may have heartworms, but no mini-worms, and vice versa. So let's check for heartworm.

The best test is a radiograph, an X-ray read out. Is the right side of the dog's heart disproportionately large or distorted? What about the pulmonary arteries? Yet, dogs have died from only one worm in their heart. The heart appeared normal in a radiograph.

So diagnosis is difficult, but fortunately cures and preventives are becoming more simple and more safe each day.

Until recently, the only sure way to keep your dog from contacting heartworm was to seal off his environment from mosquitoes. Today we're released from such chancy happenstance. There is presently available, through your vet, certain agents that keep a dog from contacting mini-worms. (This is not immunization.) One program calls for shots one month prior to, and two months after, mosquito season. Another preventive requires the dog take a capsule every day of his life. A relative new breakthrough is a tablet that needs to be given only once a month. Science will probably better that in years ahead.

As for treating the actual heartworm? Most cases are attacked with arsenic compounds. Arsenic is a poison. It poisons the heartworm and it poisons the dog. In order to successfully undergo arsenic heartworm treatment, a dog must have a master who will do everything the vet orders.

When arsenic kills the worms in the heart, they break up and head for the lungs, where the remains pile up. Also, a great amount of protein is let loose in the dog's circulatory system. This is shock compounding shock. Therefore, the treated dog must remain essentially motionless for a month or even longer.

The arsenic treatment is presently a two-day, four-shot process. The owner can take his dog home the end of the second or the beginning of the third day. But he may well take the dog home to die unless he keeps the dog totally immobile. Do not even go for a leisurely walk around the block.

And yes, heartworm may be removed by surgery. Several techniques have been developed—some through the trachea, some through the rib cage—but most vets today favor the arsenic treatment. There are at least two reasons. First, surgery cannot insure that all heartworms are removed. Second, the arsenic treatment produces fewer mortalities than surgery.

So, your dog has heartworm and effectively undergoes treatment. You're in the clear! Not necessarily. How advanced was the heartworm disease before treatment? Observe the word "disease." This is a parasite, you say, not a disease. Yes and no. When the worm clogs the heart, it reduces the level of oxygen supplied to vital, dependent organs. How did the lungs, kidneys, liver, and arteries fare while the dog had heartworm?

Heartworm debris can stick to an artery wall and act like a magnet that grabs hold of subsequent, passing debris and pyramids it all into a hamburger-mess—the way rust builds up in a pipe—that packs the artery shut. And the liver? Many dogs with advanced heartworm appear jaundiced. Their gums turn pumpkin yellow. The liver has failed, or is failing.

So heartworm, *you are the miseries.*

Miseries for reasons noted above and reasons yet to come. Did you know, for example, some dogs with heartworm are killed when dipped in certain solutions for fleas or ticks? That's right. More than one vet has had to explain to a baffled and incensed owner how a bath killed the family pet. Did you know some hookworm, roundworm, and tapeworm preventives can kill a dog that has heartworm? Did you know you shouldn't kill mini-worms in a dog until after you've rid him of heartworm? With today's drugs, to do it vice versa may kill the dog. So, two treatments are recommended for a dog with heartworm. First, you kill the heartworm; then, six weeks later you kill the mini-worms.

Now, there's a lot of lab work going on in the field of heartworm prevention and cure. For example, if you can eliminate the mini-worm (the larva), then no transmission of heartworm can be carried on by the mosquito. For let's face it, we're sure never going to be able to eliminate the mosquito.

So God help us, heartworm you may one day succumb to science. In the meantime, however, the only friend your dog's got is his vet and your daily (or monthly) guarantee that Pup gets his heartworm medicine. The life you save is the one that takes you hunting. Be vigilant and be responsible.

16

Allergies

IF DOCTOR ROYSE (our resident vet who's helped us so far with sick pups, first aid, and heartworm) had been cast of metal instead of born of flesh, he would have been a Swiss army knife: bright, neat, compact, sharp, versatile—all that stuff. He would not have been one of those tool-box jobs.

We catch him again at his Wichita, Kansas, clinic—I've just called to chat—and he sighs to say, "Skin disorders."

"What?" I ask.

"Skin disorders," he repeats, gravely. "Here in Kansas from April till . . . depending on what kind of fall we have . . . November, a good 30 percent of my practice is nothing but skin problems.

"You know, the guy comes in and says, 'My dog's got grass itch. Or mange. Or fleas.' And more likely than not the dog's got an allergy. Twenty years ago you were laughed at if you talked about allergies in dogs. No more. Allergies have become a serious subject for the vet, and a very vital area of concern for the gun dog owner.

"The reasons allergies are such a problem, if people will stop and think about it, is because of how large an organ a dog's skin is. Because that's where allergies show on a dog. He's different from people. People get red eyes, runny noses, that sort of thing. Not a dog. A dog gets the itch."

The Dog's Skin

"And just think how large a percentage of the dog's body can itch! Stop to think about it. Think of the dog's skin. How much surface area is there? From nose to tail. From ear to paw. It's all dog. It's all the dog.

"And think what the skin does – the skin is an enclosing barrier. It simply encloses the body. The skin is environmental protection against cold, rain, heat – whatever. The skin protects against bacterial invasion. It's a barrier. And temperature regulation. The skin helps regulate a dog's temperature. It's quite an organ in doing this.

"Take sensory perception: you're great on that, Bill. Touch, pain, pleasure. Or motion and shape. The movement of the dog. The skin allows the dog to flex and run and so forth. The skin is also an antimicrobial barrier against invasions from outside sources. And blood pressure control – very essential – because you have the central circulatory system, part of the larger vessels branching out to secondary vessels, on to periphery and cutaneous vessels all enclosed in the skin."

And to think I just stopped for a visit!

Doc continues, "The dog has secretions that exude through the glands in his skin. No, dogs don't sweat as such through their skins, but they do have gland secretions. Then there are secondary structures – hair and nails. These are extensions of the skin. And a lot of skin problems end up with hair loss and an invasion of the toenails.

"Storage," he exclaims. "The skin is a terrific reservoir of electrolytes, water, vitamins, and so forth.

"And pigmentation. The skin can protect against solar radiation. For example, just like a fair-skinned person, the white dog is more susceptible than the black dog.

"Vitamin D production – the skin is essential in absorbing sun rays. You've got to have natural sunlight to synthesize or make vitamin D in the body.

"So if you think about all the things the skin does, you begin to realize this is an important organ . . . and if it's affected to any extent, you've got a heck of a problem. Plus, it's a complicated organ. Why, it has three layers. And the top one, the epidermis, has five layers of its own. Then you've got the epidermal appendages, the glands, the sebaceous glands, the apocrine sweat glands, the claws, the hair – each of which has its separate function.

"So you think of all this. How big the skin is. How important it is. How complicated it is. And a guy comes through the door carrying Rover and says, 'My dog's got the grass itch.'

"What the dog probably has is an allergy. And an allergy itches.

And the dog's been scratching it. And if he's been scratching it long enough, you can have a heck of a mess."

Allergens

"Now allergies of grass, trees, weeds, man-made fibers – what have you – are carried by what we call allergens. This is the inhaled particle, or absorbed particle, that starts all the trouble.

"Allergic reactions are many and vary from the simplest to the most complex. Most of them are identified either as immediate reaction or delayed reaction. The immediate-reaction situation is seen in a dog that comes into contact with something that irritates him and sets up a sensitive reaction in his skin. Within minutes he's scratching or he's uncomfortable.

"Examples. Insecticide. The guy's spraying his yard. Paint thinner. He's painting his fence. Okay?

"Delayed reactions are the sneaky type. The animal is probably exposed to something over and over during a period of time. Finally, this repeated exposure sets up a hypersensitive state to a specific allergen, and this leads to tissue itching.

"Now most of these allergens are protein. Not all of them, but most of them. And if you think about allergies in people, you'll understand. Eggs and milk, for example, are high in protein. These can be the culprits. Same things in dogs. Common allergens that cause problems in dogs are all your pollens from grass, weeds, trees, molds, flea saliva, wool, feathers, house drugs, and food. Even drugs a vet may be using on the dog for a different purpose can sometimes cause problems.

"These and other allergens usually gain access through the body by four main routes: inhalation, which is probably the most common; ingestion, through the mouth (and includes food, or eating something that isn't food at all); percutaneous, which is through the skin, like rubbing against something or sleeping on something; and the injected allergen in the form of insect bites, or drugs, chemicals, etc. . . .

"Okay? So what happens? What's the process? Let's take an inhalant. Say a pollen grain enters the dog's nose. The dog inhales it. The pollen clings to the mucous membranes of the nose. Then it is sniffed on up into the deeper nasal passages. The nasal secretions and body secretions have soluble components that can penetrate that item of pollen. The pollen is broken down. The cell, or cells, are dissolved, so to speak."

Antibodies

"Now this thing . . . this foreign body modified by secretions . . . can penetrate through the membranes and be absorbed into the body. Once that's there, *it comes into contact with the skin-sensitizing antibodies forming an antigen-antibody complex.*

"That's important and should be repeated," says Doc. So he repeats it. Then he says, "That's when the trouble starts. When these two come together. The antigen and the antibody. That's when the gasoline hits the fire.

"Now get this. After this processed pollen has made its way into the body and the antibodies have come to fight it . . . *this releases various chemical mediators: histamine being one of them.* And this is the itcher. Histamine is what triggers the itching. You'll recall antihistamines were popular drugs for people. They were drugs used against histamine, which was being released by the cells in the body that cause itching.

"Okay. The guy's brought this dog to my clinic. The dog's got large reddened areas all over the body, his skin is hot to the touch, his . . ."

I interrupt. I say, "Pardon me, Doc, but why did God build our mechanism this way? That we have to scratch? Why do we get relief when we scratch, but just worsen the spot we're scratching?"

Doc's brow furrows. He explains, "It's the classic case of hitting yourself with a hammer to rid yourself of pain. The itching complex is a nervous sensation in the peripheral nerves in the outer layers of the skin. And it is an uncomfortable sensation. When you scratch, you usually scratch with much more vigor than the impulse generates. You bury the inner impulse—the itch impulse. You simply overwhelm it with your physical response. The dog does the same thing. You're both hitting yourself with a hammer. Okay?"

I smile and nod. He's just like a Swiss army knife.

Doc proceeds, ". . . the dog's skin is hot to the touch, he is miserable, he is really wild. And a typical story unfolds. I ask, 'How long has he had it?' The answer comes, 'Oh, two weeks.' Sometimes a month. Sometimes two months. 'Has he had any treatment?' 'Oh no . . . I put some of this drug-store stuff on him for mange. And it didn't seem to do him any good.'

"And this is where the dog owner, not realizing the seriousness of skin problems, makes a big mistake. No, the stuff he put on the dog probably didn't hurt him. *But the owner delayed.* He let this thing progress to secondary stages of inflammation. And I'll make a point on that.

"The simplest allergic reaction starts with some itching and some reddened skin. Then it goes a little further. And it becomes more inflamed. And the dog starts mutilating the area, or areas, with repeated scratching. The layers of the skin become inflamed even more deeply. And with all these layers of skin involved, their normal functions are inhibited.

"Then the dog continues to scratch until he has mutilated the skin to the point where secondary bacterial invaders can move in. And now it may be the dog is super-sensitive to the external bacteria that's entered. He's got allergy, plus, he's got bacteria.

"So he's scratching like mad and going deeper all the time. Plus, the dog's ability to respond with his normal skin function, which helps a vet treat the dog, has been smothered or wiped out. And time has compounded the allergy with secondary bacterial invaders, and the dog still has the original allergy problem no one's solved. Now, you've got to treat the whole animal.

"So this is why I emphasize this point. The dog owner must assist the vet two ways. One, get the dog in early if it shows signs of skin irritation. And two, acquaint himself with every aspect of that dog's daily life to help the vet pinpoint the cause of allergy. The dog can't talk. His master must talk for him."

Repeated Exposure

"Most allergic contact reactions require *repeated exposure*. The first exposure rarely causes any problem. That's the sensitizing dose. If you are allergic to penicillin and you go down and get your first injection, you'll not be bothered. But that second injection. . . . If you're allergic to it, that second one will get you.

"'The same holds true with dog allergies. Repeated exposure to allergens is what triggers it. What are the specific allergens? Only the dog owner can help you determine. He knows what the dog eats, where it stays during the day, what it sleeps on. This is where the dog owner can really help the vet assist the dog. Plastic can be a culprit. So can leather. Floor wax. Aerosol sprays. Synthetic fibers. Mop sprays. Fertilizers. Pollen from weeds, grass, trees. It goes on and on.

"I'll give you a case. I nearly missed one two weeks ago. A fellow brought me a nice Chesapeake retriever. Young dog, about six months old. Had a terrible inflammation in his muzzle and lips, on his front feet, and about his eyes. It looked like a classic case of pyoderma, which is a bacterial infection of the skin, mostly in young dogs.

I treated the Chesie. He responded beautifully. So I sent him home with medication thinking we were on the right track. The owner brought the dog back ten days later. He was much improved, but he was starting off again around his muzzle, though all the crust and debris had cleansed away.

"Now what I saw was a very clear, very definite demarcation around the dog's muzzle and chin. The light went on. 'Dummy,' I shouted at myself. I asked the guy, 'Are you feeding this Chesie in a plastic bowl?' The guy said 'Yes.'

"That was the problem. And I almost missed it because I had so many other overwhelming things going on with this dog. His condition had progressed so far I didn't think of it. The dog had plastic-dish dermatitis.

"So that's why, when you take an itching dog to the vet, you should be prepared to tell him everything, absolutely everything, about the dog's daily routine.

"Now to cure. Is there ever a cure for allergy? There's control. We can control the discomfort. But cure? I'll get a dog in, and he'll respond to drugs for, say, weeds, grass, or tree pollen. Then winter comes and the land goes dormant. There is minimal pollen. The guy thinks I cured his dog of allergy. But when spring arrives, back the guy comes with the dog on his hip, saying, 'Hey Doc, you didn't cure my dog.'

"But it's not that simple. What the vet must do is try to determine what might be aggravating the problem and eliminate it to the best of his, and the dog owner's, ability. For example, is the dog sleeping on a wool rug? Change that.

"Oh, there's clinical things we can do. We can send a dog for skin-patch testing or have him hyposensitized. I'll explain. Skin-patch testing is what we do first. Say we've got a dog with an itch we can't control. And this allergy proves totally uncontrollable the year around. We've got to do something for this dog, for we can't keep him on the pill."

Steroids

"Now let me explain that. The pill. Most allergy pills are steroids. There are a variety of combination drugs—antihistamine, steroid, and tranquilizer, for example. There are many, many different types of steroids. Synthetic cortisones are what they all are.

"But indiscriminate or prolonged steroid use can cause problems. If you give a dog steroids on a daily-dose basis, constantly over a long period of time, you'll produce irreversible change in the dog. You can suppress his normal adrenal function to the point you'll have a terminal case on your hands.

"So we've got to go easy on the pill, but this dog has year-round allergy, and he's itching and he's scratching and something must be done. So we go to the skin-patch test. From the owner we can assume what's troubling the dog, plus we know what's endemic (usually around) for any particular area. With an educated guess we make up separate allergen solutions. Say we decide to test the dog for flea saliva, wool, and elm tree pollen. We mix these materials, or suitable substitutes, in controlled solutions and inject them under the skin of the dog's shaved tummy with a very fine needle. It's just like giving a tuberculin test. In a few minutes, or a few hours, we'll be able to see if the dog reacts to any one of the injections. Eureka, we've isolated an allergen.

"I sent a dog for a skin-patch the other day. This dog showed sensitivity following the test to feathers, nylon carpeting, house dust, and kapok. Kapok? The dog was sleeping in the garage on an old life-jacket. I wish they were all as easy. And wouldn't that be something if the dog were a retriever and you were working him day and night with kapok-filled dummies?

"But things are seldom that simple. Let's say the dog's allergic to house dust. Now what are you going to do? Well, there's hyposensitization. What's that? Let's say through skin-patch testing we learn the dog is allergic to flea saliva, staph bacteria, and grass pollen native to the area. We mix a solution, so to speak, of these three entities – and we can combine them – and we go through a series of injections.

"In other words, we lower the dog's sensitivity. In still other words, we are inoculating the dog. We inject what's bothering the dog *into the dog*. The idea is to put these substances in there to block the allergens. The body begins to accept these foreign irritants. We're putting something in the dog he doesn't have.

"And some of these dogs with very severe and very prolonged skin problems – these dogs may well be what we call immune deficient. They just do not have an antibody defense system. They don't have the proper cells in the body to trigger up that defense mechanism. So they are really at the mercy of the allergen. All we can do is try to put something in there to help them. Thus, hyposensitization."

Doc pauses. He's thinking. I tell him to take a break. I tell him we ought to get a Coke. "I'll treat," I promise. He smiles, but will have none of it. He's got this thing to be said, and he's going to say it. "There are advances," he says, barely audible. "The University of Pennsylvania now reports they can substitute a blood sample from the afflicted dog to achieve the same conclusions as a skin-patch test. At least they've done it for ragweed. They don't even need to see the dog."

I sit back down. We're not going to have a Coke.

Cures

"Are there any cures?" he asks, again. "I don't know," he answers. "I've had people in my office with a dog I've treated for two or three years with really no hope of a cure. Just control. And then they move away to some other area, and maybe I hear back, 'Gee, I moved away and puppy dog is cured.' This is not uncommon at all.

"But I will make a point of this. People live with allergies in their children. The child's not cured. The allergy's controlled as best it can be, but the child's not cured. When the child becomes a teenager the allergy may go away. It's happened. What I'm saying is this is a control process through maturation. And in many of the dogs it is very much the same. A control process. I hate to talk about cures in allergies because it just doesn't happen as such very often.

"But this is what's really important. Listen to this. You can take a case of mange, a case of allergy, and a case of fungus, and you can stand these three dogs side by side, and they will defy you to diagnose them or tell their maladies apart. Because, depending on the stage of their respective conditions, they may look exactly alike. Yet the treatment for all three is 180 degrees from each other. Consequently, this is where the dog owner can get into trouble if he's not careful. Home remedies! For what? You don't even know what the dog's got. Okay?

"So skin problems require a vet's care."

Seasons

"Now let's talk about season of the year. When cold weather comes, your flea population is wiped out (anyway, it is in Kansas). That's a big factor because a high percentage of allergies are flea-bite induced. Or, if a dog is allergic to some other substance and he has a flea on him, it's like gasoline on a fire. It just compounds the thing.

"When winter kills the fleas, it also renders nature dormant. There is reduced pollen. The lawns dry up. It's cold and dry in most cases, and both fungi and molds don't grow in the winter. Plus, the ground may be covered with snow, and that is a good anti-allergen blanket.

"But come spring the infection cycle repeats itself. And I have a hunch – apart from all the spring pollen, dusts, molds, and fungi. What about the grass itself? You mow your grass and the cut ends exude grass juice, and you turn your dog loose for a run in the yard. He loves to run, and maybe he rolls in the grass, and you've seen him lie down and drag his belly in it and play . . . and he's bathing his feet and his belly in grass juice.

"In the growing season, we cut that grass once a week. And the dog gets out every night, let's say. And by cutting that grass at the same height all the time it gets like a guy's beard. It's stubble. Those grass stubs can be irritating to the skin. I don't know. But I have a hunch. It makes me think that here's an allergy problem: the cut grass itself.

"And many of the allergies last through the seasons. Those found in the house, for example. Or those in warm climates such as Florida and Arizona.

"Allergies are real, Bill," says Doc. His voice hints he may be winding down. "A dog's misery with allergy is self-evident. I told you before, we used to laugh at people who talked about allergies in dogs. No more. The open, raw, mutilated wound of a scratching dog has convinced us we've got lots to learn, lots to do.

"And it's all so much more serious and complex than the guy thinks who carries Rover into the clinic and says, 'My dog's got the grass itch.'"

"One day science may corroborate the guy's diagnosis. But unfortunately, science may also uphold our present knowledge that the poor dog has much more wrong with him than grass itch. And it's all bad."

Dr. Dick Royse has taught us much about sick pups, first aid, heartworm, and allergies. We thank him and turn back once again to the field. It's time you and Pup went hunting.

17

Let's Go Huntin'

LOOKING GOOD: THAT'S America today. Remember Dan Cushman's delightful book, *Stay Away, Joe*? Mama could not receive an important guest into her home without a flush toilet. The conversation went:

"Go to town and get a toilet. We can set it up in the shed off the back porch."

"But I told you they have to be connected up. How could we get water here from the creek?"

"You can fill its tank one time with a bucket. Who cares, just so long as we can flush it the once?"

Looking good!

In this little mountain town where I now live there's a teenage boy sporting a peroxide Mohawk and purple eye shadow who hangs around the grocery store with a ten-pound radio and a skateboard. He's looking good. Yet just eighteen miles west of us is a canyon that vies with the world for having more game per acre than anywhere else. Oh, if I could have been a teenager here. I'd left a toenail under every rock in that canyon.

We've all been a part of it—this going for show. Who hasn't had a daughter who couldn't go to the dance because she had nothing to wear. Or the wife who couldn't entertain with that old sofa and chair sitting there. Or the boy who couldn't attend college because he had no wheels.

Little wonder, then, I meet would-be gun dog men who say something like, "I can't have a dog because I can't afford the son of a national champ." It's part of our national psyche now: "I can't do something, because I don't have something." The thing is, we go for appearances before we go for doing. It's fashion, not function. You got to look good, it is believed in America, before you can do good.

Remember the drugstore cowboy? He'd hang around the pharmacy playing the pinball machine, dressed in cowboy boots, hat, 'kerchief, and hand-tooled belt with genuine turquoise in the buckle.

The cowboys I buddy with here in the Southwest wear feed-and-seed caps, frayed jeans, anything for a belt that'll hold up their pants, and a shirt with the elbows worn through and usually a couple of buttons missing down the front. They don't look good, but they can get cattle to market. So what's the bottom line? Do cowboys get cattle to market or play pinball machines?

Gun Dogs

So let's apply all this to gun dogs. If the big field trial circuit comes through your country and you should drive out and take a look, I'll bet good money an aluminum motor home will pull in there with a six-horse trailer hooked to the back bumper. This rig probably cost $80,000 and may have been driven 2,000 miles to get there.

Now watch the owner of this motor home bring out his mount. I'll bet good money, again, you'll see a fat horse. The bridle and saddle may be embellished with silver. Most everything will be new. Then listen to the man. He'll probably fuss about the drawing. He doesn't like where his dog's been placed. Nor does he like the bracemate his dog must run against. The man will also fault the cover, the terrain, and the weather. The sun will be in his eyes, the dew will have evaporated, the cottonwood seeds will be blowing, and the kids will be tooting car horns while the man's trying to get on his fat horse.

But look over there. See that rusty, blue, noodle-kneed, flap-fendered wreck? That old '72 Ford pickup. And that horse trailer in tow with the broken slats and sagging springs. Watch that guy get out his mount. The horse is gaunt, why you can count every rib. And here comes this guy's dog, leaping from the open crate. Why the dog's legs are dyed with red mud and his belly is scratched from stubble.

The man goes for his chaps. They stand by themselves. There's that much grime and time worn in them. He lifts himself into a saddle that ain't seen polish in twenty years. The skirts backing the stirrup leathers curl about his legs. The man has only a slicker tied behind the cantle of the saddle. The only gear he wears is a lanyard with whistle. He carries a flushing whip.

This man doesn't even look at the drawing. Matters not to him when he runs or where he runs or who he runs against. He trained to win. He came to win. He came to show the best in his dog, his horse, and himself. Not the best *on them*, but the best *in them*.

In horses you'll find a halter class and a performance class. We have the same in dogs. We call them bench shows and field trials. The halter horse vies in a beauty pageant. But the performance horse has got to do something (depending on his specialty) better than any other horse can do it in order to win. To me, that's the old America. Getting the job done. Not looking good as you fake it, as you fail to cut it.

We have this TV program in the 1980's, "Lifestyles of the Rich and Famous." Ha! The guys I hang around with would be featured in the counterpart, "The Poor and Obscure." We're not interested in looking good in the hunting lodge, we're determined on doing good in the field. And we all agree this emphasis on fashion, not function, keeps too many good people from ever entering the world of gun dogs.

Such people look at the sporting magazines and see where a dog-training widget costs $500, and they say, "Why, I couldn't afford that." Or they find it costs $45, let's say, to enter a field trial, and they say, "Who would have that kind of money?" Or they price farm land today and realize, "I'll never be able to afford a place of my own." And one last thing–as gun dog editor of *Field & Stream* magazine, with a worldwide circulation and more than ten million monthly readers, I get ten pounds of mail each year from people seeking obscure gun dogs. What's wrong with a raw-boned pointer, a feisty Brittany, a bench-legged Lab? But, oh no! They want a pink-eyed Appalachian tree climber that's being proved good on combination bobwhite and black bear. They want the new SeaCow retriever with starting rope about its neck that one pull and it leaves the blind in a white wake. Five gallons of gas will run it through a complete duck season. They want Thailand elephant-herding dogs. Why? Why can't they just want a proven, heavy-duty, field-capable gun dog?

What You Really Need

Well, none of this matters. That's the point. You don't need the fancy equipment, you don't need to run in field trials, you don't need to own your own spread, and you sure don't need a two-tailed Abyssinian goat herder and combination chicken plucker. All you need to have a good gun dog is to pick one of the standards and care for him and train him and love him. Have, too, a zeal for going after birds with this dog, and a helping way with your fellow man so you'll be there at the farmer's gate, wearing work gloves, and asking him what you can do to help out.

I wrote it once in a poem, "I'm worth their thoughts but twice a year: in the spring for my bass, in the fall for my deer." The point being, the rest of the time the farmer can go bankrupt; they won't care. The reason: what they want is a bird in hand. It's the killing that draws them, not the hunt. And I'd like to talk to you about that. Hunting is a total life. It lasts all year long. Making your own decoys, cutting grass for wrap-around blinds, building your own duck boat, planting lespedeza for quail, putting out Johnny houses for liberated birds, and working your dog all year long are all part of the life. But really, even when all this is done, it's not a dead bird that draws the bona fide hunter. Let me explain.

What's Really Hunting?

Like most young men, he was opportunity's nomad, pulling up stakes to seek something better down the road. He stood in my driveway with his head down, the soft, black hair falling like a broken crow's wing over his forehead. I saw he had an army cartridge belt and a canvas-covered, aluminum canteen in his hands. You don't find them in the surplus stores much anymore, and I'd admired this one when the two of us were out bird hunting. Such a canteen is perfect for watering a dog between puddles, but more than that, a canteen like this was part of my own youth when I wandered into the Marine Corps.

He handed out the canteen and belt, saying, "Here, take this."

I turned aside, looking over the crowns of junipers on down into the distant valley. "It's for Hattie," he said.

I dragged a shirtsleeve across my eyes and looked back to the young man. Hattie is not a dog I own. Hattie is not a dog anyone owns. But she existed once, and I took the hearsay glimpses of her and made a dream of them.

She was Home Again Hattie (the name can mean much to a man always moving), a white-and-liver-ticked pointer bitch whelped in 1957 and bought in part by Bob Guinn of Savannah, Tennessee, in 1962. Hattie won the National Free-For-All championship in 1960 and would win the National Championship in 1962. She only had eight placements in her life, but two of them were in the most premier stakes.

I never saw Hattie run. But there were days I'd sit in Mister Guinn's bedroom on the second floor of the Cherry mansion, and he'd talk of her. I'd listen and look out the hand-blown window panes, out on the turbid Tennessee River as it swirled north.

General Grant had stayed at the Cherry mansion before the battle of Shiloh, and later the wounded came there. You can still see where one Yankee carved his initials in a living room window with the diamond of his ring. He probably had a premonition and wanted to leave his mark. Like the young man in my driveway with the canteen, that soldier was pulling up stakes for an unknown journey.

Mister Guinn would lie there in the big bed with his Bible, opened and folded down against his chest, his thin hands flat on the book, and he would talk of Hattie. She was gentle when taking her share of a sandwich, but would go like a kite in the wind when cast for birds. She had dainty feet, a delicate nose, and deep whiskey-colored eyes. She was light like a hawk and nimble as a doe. When braced against a competitor at a field trial she would but glance sideways, one eye looking over her nose, as a proper lady does before she's introduced at a formal tea.

Then Mister Guinn would tire and his voice would lose some of its timbre, and I'd sit a moment longer seeing Hattie as a picture in my head, moving silently through the tall yellow grass in the effortless way a tern flies from the Arctic to the Antarctic: 22,000 miles there and back.

When I could move without disturbing the man, I'd go down the creaking wood staircase and out the front door to stand on the porch with the peacocks walking mechanically in the front yard. And I'd say the name, "Home Again Hattie." To me it meant that no matter how far Hattie cast, she would make it Home. There was always Home for her, and thus for us. It meant that no matter how far we went in search, or how totally we got lost, or how interminably we had been gone, we could always go Home.

But it also meant that if we did go back only to find home actually gone, we could build a new home. The chirpy name, "Hattie," which when said seems to form the lips to smile, assured this. Plus, Hattie denoted—for me, at least—a rolled-up-sleeve, barn-raising, never-say-die sort of gal, who'd blow a wisp of hair from her face, grab an ax, and build a home with grit, then oversee the finished structure with charm.

Recalling these things, I took the belt and canteen from the young man and said, "Hattie thanks you." He shook my hand, climbed into his battered old Nissan truck, and backed down the drive. I could not see his face for the bug-grime of the windshield. But I waved. And when he had gotten the truck headed west on the road, he tapped his horn three times.

Then it was silent and the breeze shuffled in the piñon and I felt the sun pressing on my shoulders. They were all there, now, in the drive: Mister Guinn (long since passed away); Terry Smith, the young retriever trainer who introduced me to Mister Guinn, and who was senselessly killed in a car wreck; and now the young man with the gift of the canteen. And a hundred others. Men–and dogs, too. Come to touch my life a moment, then gone forever. Never to find home again.

Walking up the drive and into the garage I remember–for no reason–a bathroom tile I bought years ago in Jackson Square, New Orleans. The wizened little guy–he looked like a scrubbed chimney sweep–who wagered he could make a living selling tiles with quips inked on them had caught my eye and my ear. I liked his pluck, making art of scraps. So I picked up one of the tiles on which he'd scribed, "Happiness is not a destination, it is a way of travel." I turned back quick, toward the direction the Nissan had gone. If only I had told the boy that.

I stood in the dark of the garage and looked out at the sun. Dog men, like the boy in the Nissan, aren't that easy to find. They're no more plentiful than good dogs. Oh, you'll meet men with dogs. That's not the same thing. I'm saying Dogmen, now. That's different. To begin with, Dogmen become remarkably like dogs. They have those same virtues: honesty, loyalty, devotion, steadfastness, selflessness, care, love. They can endure the same suffering, the same misunderstanding and rejection. They can abide man and time and circumstance.

I recall the old man I met one morning walking the dikes of Cheyenne Bottoms (a great wildfowl warehouse) near Great Bend, Kansas. I shouted ahead to him, "Did you get your limit?" I was very young. He answered in a voice barely audible, "My need is more to see them than to shoot." He stopped to rest cross-elbows on his gun barrel. I laughed and asked, "And what of the dog? Does he feel like you do?"

The old man smiled when he told me, "He and I usually agree on most things."

We stood then, he and I and the old Lab with the white muzzle, and we talked. The man told me he could hunt all day and never pop a cap. The poet of the man, he figured, harks to the creak of leather, the stench of sweat-stained canvas, the reassurance of feeling leg muscles flex and reach and pull. He made me believe that even the sog of wet

Hunter's hunter, the late Terry Smith, walks in sogged pants and socks toward camera. When the mallard in the Lab's mouth flew over, Terry plopped down in the muck, up to his cartridge belt. I yelled, "You're going to get all wet." He replied, "What?" He was incredulous that I would speak so, then added, "I'm huntin'."

socks could have appeal.

I remember him leaning down and pulling on the old dog's ears. "There's always love in their eyes," he said, then added, "When he was young he struck out ahead. I'd see him beckon from a far hill, or find him waiting, laughing, slopped to the gills in a mud puddle or, God forbid, rolling on a dead carp."

I nodded to affirm the truth of all this. Then the old man said, "You send the dog to a pile of tumbleweeds for pheasant or into the tules for a duck . . . that will excite him. I do that now and then to please him. That's what hunting is for an old man and an old dog, you know? Chuckling over the other's success. And in truth, the good hunts are always seen through the other's eyes and felt in the other's admiration."

So saying, the old man patted his outer leg, calling the Lab close, and the two of them went down the dike – heading home.

That's it, you know. That's what I've lost. I'll never again see the hunt in Mister Guinn's eyes, or in the eyes of the boy who gave me the canteen, or in all the other eyes of a hundred men and a hundred dogs with whom I've raked the fields and waded the bogs.

I shove in the back door of the house to enter, but the dogs pile up against it, refusing to let the door open. It's a melee of barking and spinning dogs. "Get back," I say, "Let me in." But they are not going to give way. They've laid against that door since I went out and now must be paid for duty. This one has to have an ear scratched, that one will roll over for a belly rub, a third will insist on standing and looking me in the eye while its flanks quiver, a fourth will run ahead in circles, imploring me to enter the kitchen and open the goodie jars.

I stop to sit in a chair and they pile on, butting each other with heads and shoulders to maintain position, issuing growls, dropping down, spinning, and coming back up for better advantage. "You're all right," I tell them, "You know that?" On my leg I can feel the beat of a tail, another dog licks me from finger to wrist.

"Okay," I concede, as I try to stand and motion them on, telling them by hand we'll go to the kitchen. They like beef jerky and rawhide chews. They get way too many of them. I pause long enough to lay the cartridge belt and canteen over the arm of the chair. The dogs run ahead only to stop and come skidding back, begging me to hurry. I ask them, "Anyone here named Hattie?" They laugh at me with parted mouths and perked ears. "No, none of you is Hattie. I can see that." I break the jerky in twos and hand them out. The dogs chew and gulp and sniff the floor for more.

We go out the front door to sit on the porch so I can look down the empty road where the Nissan's gone. The dogs run to the fence in hopes of seeing what I'm looking at. They don't know I'm looking at everything there ever was, or ever will be. Nor do they realize how important it is that they and me aren't going down that lonesome road. They don't realize how important it is . . . we're already home.

Calendars of Our Joy

I sit on the porch as the sun works west and think of the dogs that have led me, and abided me, through a long life afield. Through the slant of the sun, in the shadow of the trees, coming up the gravel drive – I see them now. Old gun dogs that have stood the test of time and event and circumstance. They come now, slowly, and lay at foot or close to side, jowls flat, eyes faded with the fog of cataract, their muzzles and paws white or speckled salt and pepper. But they come. They want to be close – as they always did.

They are great treasures, these old dogs. For they are more than themselves lying there. They are us. Parts of us. A hill climbed together and the crimson leaves of sumac danced in the morning sunlight. The well looked in and the rock dropped and the chill of the dark hole seemed forever before the splash was heard.

They are sweaty palms, for you were hosting your boss and he'd never gunned over a trained dog before; yet Pup was so birdy you couldn't be sure he'd hold for wing and shot.

They are the iced mace of wind thrown by bad-dad winter, off to the north, blowing the redleg mallards off their last haunts. Blowing them south, flying like buckshot. And you're gripping Pup and whispering, "No head up," as you fit the duck call to your lips. But it is cold and you know it will freeze to the skin. But you call. And the lead hen throws her body high, looking down and back, seeing the iced-in blocks pointing bill-up to the slate sky.

And now they come, shingles ripped loose from some old barn, and the wind is driving them crazily toward your decoys and you stand and the old gun barks and the dog launches. He's breaking ice and standing high in the water, though his feet don't touch bottom. And you wish you'd never shot. For nothing can live out there. Not even Pup in the prime of his life. Yet he clomps the big bright drake and spins about, throwing water with his whipping tail. He comes for you – swimming, by instinct, for the drake covers his face.

And you're out of the blind now and running the bank, yelling out. And the retriever comes to shore, not stopping to shake, and heads straight for you. But the black dog turns instantly silver. The water has frozen that fast. And you take the duck and the dog shivers, his teeth chattering, and the pelvic-drive muscles convulse. Then he spins in the tall yellow grass – he runs and rubs the side of his jowls in the mud and stubble.

No duck is worth this – remember saying that? – and the two of you go back to the house. Back to the towel you rub Pup with and the fire you sit before, and the wind makes a harmonica of your house-siding and whomps down the fireplace to billow the ashes.

But the duck does lay on the sideboard by the sink. You entered nature and went duck hunting and tricked the wild fowl to your trap and the dog closed the door.

Still, you're sorry you went; but years later, when the smell of that day's wet fur is forgotten and even the curled tailfeathers from the mallard have long been blown from the fireplace mantle, you'll remember – you'll remember that retrieve and old Pup will come to side and you'll fondle his ears and the memory of that cold day and that single duck will become the most important thing that ever happened in your life.

For Pup is dying.

And you can't see him that you don't have to smile and call him to you. It may be the last time you ever touch his ear. But that's just part of it. You're dying, too. Pup will just go first. As he always went first in the field or at the blind. You followed him, not the other way around. It was he who entered the unknown and learned its bareness or its bounty.

And you love the old dog, for he lived your life. He was the calendar of your joy. Why, you could leap the stream when you got your first pup. Remember? And you could hunt all day. Cold? Bosh! And the apple in your pocket was all it took to fuel you from Perkins' fence to Hadley's barn – a limit of bobwhite later.

But now the arthritis hobbles you. And the cold. It seems to come and sit in your bones like an unwanted stranger.

So you don't just call Pup to side, you call your life. You run your fingers through your past when you fondle his ears.

And you stand and go to the gun case. Why, the bluing's gone from that old Superpose. Then you remember when you bought it – long before Pup ever came into your life. And look at that duck call. There's no varnish left on the barrel. And the barrel is cracked! And the string that holds it – it was a country store back in the hills and you stopped for a loaf of bread to feed Pup. And the duck call was in your pocket, just out of its cardboard box. And you asked the proprietor for a piece of string, and he went to the meat counter and drew off a yard of it. You were always going to get a bona fide, braided lanyard.

But that's like life. You were always going to . . .

And there's Pup. He was not a going to. He was a was. Not a put-off till tomorrow. Pup was planned and bought and trained and taken to field. That happened. And the million dollars was never made, and you never became branch manager, and your kids didn't make it through college. But Pup did all you imagined for him.

Pup was your one success.

And he is dying.

How many pups ago was it your sweater fitted loose on your belly and your belly was hard like the barrel of a cannon? But look at the sweater now. Stretched tight and tattered and faded. Why do you still wear it? There are Christmas sweaters still in their boxes, on the shelf in the closet.

And the boots. Remember? They had to be just so. But look at them now. Toes out, scuffed, heels run over. And yet you shuffle about in them.

Is it because you're holding on to the past? Is it because looking back down the road means more than looking on up ahead? Is it because the birds you went with Pup to get were got? And now? What do they say? A bird in the hand is worth more than two. . . . Maybe that's it. Pup made you a bird-in-the-hand man.

The Royal Flush

It had snowed the night before, and you and Pup had crawled under the barbed wire fence to enter the apple orchard. The tree limbs were naked and bleak and your breath rose before you – the white of steam. Then Pup, while making a back-cast, went in point mid-air and twirled and came down contorted so his left leg stuck out with that foot barely touching the snow. You passed him, acknowledging his point, and up they came. It was a bright, new 20-gauge Franchi automatic you carried, made partly of aluminum so it was supposed to be lightning fast, and you always dreamed of the day you'd take five on the rise – the magazine was legally loaded. And up they came, and the gun stabbed at your shoulder and the smoke mingled with the steam of your breath and neither you nor Pup could believe the falling. But they were down: five bobwhite. *A royal flush.* And Pup had to be convinced to go get number four and number five. For you had never shot that many birds at one time before.

Yes. Others in those days may have been two-birds-in-the bush hopefuls. But you and Pup did it. You went. No sunshine patriots then. No sir. The five birds lay in hand, and the snow started falling again.

He's got bad teeth now, you know? Pup has. And let's admit it. His breath stinks. And look at him, great blotches of hair stand here and there like some derelict mountain sheep that's taken to roadside begging at a national park. And he does little but sleep – he does lots of that.

There are pups to be bought, you know? Why, ads are everywhere. And some say gun dogs have gotten better than ever. Or at least the training methods have gotten so sharp you can even bring a mediocre pup along.

But no. It's always been you and Pup. And you'll wait till he's no more. But have you ever wondered? What will you be when he's gone? If he were the best part of your days, then what will there be when he's dead and buried? What will there be of you? Some grumpy old mumbler who sits by the fire and harrumphs at those come to be kind?

He's by the Gate

No, not at all. For you were a gun dog man and you went to field. Your Pup was the best gun dog you ever saw. And you watched the flash of the great black Lab as he leaped through bramble and you saw him once atop the hill – how far away was he on that cast? A half mile? And all you must do is close your eyes or, better yet, just go to the window and watch the falling leaves. Pup's out there. He's by the gate, see him? And he's leaping that way he always did, urging you to get on with it. And he darts now, to the field, and sniffs the passing mice, the dickey birds.

And then you're with him, the weight of the gun reassuring in your grasp, and your stride is strong and the wind bites your cheek but you laugh and blow the white steam of cold. Always you can do this, just standing at the window – for you did this.

What of that smell of straw at the old duck blind and pouring the coffee from the thermos. Then learning how to pour the coffee from the steel cup so you could put the cup to your lips. And you never knew why the pouring made the cup manageable.

And the pride in your decoys, watching them run to the end of their cords and spinning about, ducking their heads and bobbing to drip water from their bills.

And off to the left, in that stand of multiflora rose. Hear him! The cock pheasant *car-runks*. Bright as brass he is. And you could heel Pup out of the duck blind and go get him, but you like the bird's sass. You like his arrogance. And anything that gaudy can live out there in the back of your place.

And what of that morning you and Pup were sitting there? Duck

It all boils down to this. When Don Sides finally gets Pup trained, it's the memory of dog, bird, and gun he'll always cherish. So much can be taken from you, but not this!

hunting–for you–didn't mean shooting ducks. It meant being there. Hearing the rustle of your heavy canvas pants and the tinkle of the dog whistles and duck calls as they danced on your chest. Blowing in cupped hands, beating them against the sides of your chest. And standing and stomping on the wood pallets you brought in, for the water rose with the late rains. And yet for that moment you and Pup were silent, and the redtailed hawk landed, right above both of you, on a bare limb.

And you were ornery. Jumped up you did and yelled, "Hey hawk!" And the hawk was so startled he hurled himself to the air with a great squawk and left a white stream all over your blind as he beat his departure. But it was still funny and you sat in the draping of hawk feces–and laughed.

Not another single living thing had that moment but you and Pup and the hawk. And the three of you made that moment momentous forever. Now the hawk is gone and Pup is going, but that moment makes you all vibrant and alive. And in a way it makes you important. How few people have an exclusive moment?

And if Pup had not taken you to field you'd not have had it. So he lies there now, that generator of meaning and memory. That's what a gun dog comes to be for us. An enricher of life. Something to take ordinary moments and make them miraculous.

Of Miracles and Memories

That's why the love for Pup is so great. What matter if he passes gas and has bad breath and groans in his sleep? He's earned his transgressions. And he tells us of our own end. For sharing the best with him, we must now share the worst with him, and we lie there, too.

But dog men push that away. Their Pup was a springer spaniel, you know. Oh, how happy he was afield. Why the stub of his tail couldn't be tallied as it wagged. And it wagged that way when idle or working. He was just that happy. And he made the man happy. For happiness is infectious, and there's no known cure. Not even disaster. For you'll walk around the knowledge of disaster to peek in memory at that happy tail.

And that man's Pup was a beagle. A mellow-voiced ground snorter if ever there was one. The bow legs, all that massed muscle. And he used to launch the rabbit and then dart out in pursuit, giving the man instructions–loud instructions!–to be sure and shoot the next time they came around.

But that's not the Pup I was thinking of. No. That Pup was your cocker with thick hair the color of wheat tassels, and he'd run to launch the bird, down in the mud, going under the highwater log. And up he'd come with mud balls hanging from silver whiskers, and in a turn – which was more like a complete flip – he'd tell you with his body signal there was nothing down there and you'd best be off.

But who am I to talk like this? You know your Pup better than I ever could. For there was just the two of you – oh, maybe a hawk! And what happened can never happen again. No man and dog could ever be that rich again, that lucky again, that blessed again.

Yet each year several million new pups are taken into American homes, into American hearts. All on the knowledge there are some miracles and memories left out there yet.

Well, I started all this with the question, "What is really hunting?" You prize the hunt the way you want. The biologist fans the wing to age the bird by its coloration, by its strength of feather. The gunner logs his hits and misses. The epicurean hunts to eat and is as much involved in cooking the bird as shooting it. The artist puzzles at the bird in hand, trying to fathom how he could ever paint the speculum of the wing. The once-a-year hunter knows the legal limit and fails the day (fails the year) if the full amount is not tossed in the gamebag. The social hunter sips his toddy, plays poker, and tells off-color jokes. We all go to the bird field for different reasons.

But hunting for me is spending my life afield with a dog.

This book was written for you who feel the same way.

18

Opening Day

TAKE NOTHING NEW to the bird field. You know how new boots blister, new pants chafe, new shirts bind, new guns founder, and new dogs blunder. Oh, take new hope. That's what draws us all there. But have everything else as old and used and trustworthy as yourself.

Fragmentation hand grenades! That's how bobwhite quail explode. Shrapnel here, shrapnel there, then gone. And you stand there with your gun at bayonet charge and feel dumb and damned. The dog can't believe you missed all those birds. He looks left, jerks right, then up to you, his face saying in wonder, "Is this what you trained me for?"

But you were not ready. You could not be ready. For though this is opening day, your quail hunt should have started months ago. Only then could you have been ready. Not only in conditioning your dog, but in getting yourself in shape. For today you've walked too far, sweated too much, went on past having lunch, forgot to drink water—with all your excitement—and the quail were too fast for your reflexes. Months ago you should have started on short, followed by long, walks; and you should have exercised, rode the bike, and cut down on calories, too.

And Pup should have been roaded: outfitted in a sled-dog harness and held back as he drove into the leather of the thing each day until his tail drooped. That's your sign. The sagging tail.

Red setter (cross between an Irish and English setter) is but a blur as he drives in sled dog collar, roading before a pickup.

And even if you were in top physical shape—just out of training camp with the Pittsburgh Steelers—you're still not ready for bobwhite. You get ready for this type of psychological warfare at a shooting preserve. That's where you not only learn to handle the startle but learn to insulate yourself against the "BDBDBDBDBDB," the scat, and the 360-degree scramble as well.

Trap and skeet won't prepare you for bobwhite encounters. You'll learn to shoot there, to pick up your target, lead it, fire, and follow through. But only if someone gooses you with a broom stick, or throws a snake at your feet, will you get as excited and discombobulated as you will when bobwhites scatter.

The released quail at a shooting preserve will hold longer for your dog—and for you—and will let you look deep into the thicket so you might spot them. They will set longer while you beat about the bush, while you prepare your psyche, take a deep breath, and remember to release the safety on your gun. And being pen-raised, when these birds do get up they won't fly all that fast. And you can get on 'em and gain confidence and learn to short-circuit the panic they create in a gunner by their crazed and garbled wingbeat.

The Shooting Preserve

Besides, there's sheer joy at such a hunt club. Like the Estanaula Hunt Club & Kennel, near Brownsville, Tennessee, owned by Harbert Mulherin and his son bearing the same name. Wilson Dunn, of Grand Junction, Tennessee, and I are riding a mule-drawn wagon, leaning back, looking up at the passing clouds. Out front the elder Harbert is scouting on a Tennessee walker in trail of a pair of dogs running from "kin-till-kain't," as Nash Buckingham, from these very parts, used to say.

Our eye is on the Brittany: Ely is his name. And he's been down three hours and seems fit for three days. Look at him go, that little rocking-horse gait all Brittanys have. And that built-in laugh, the pink lips perked in perpetual smile. And the ears flapping and the stub of his tail beating a drum to his step. Oh, he'll handle birds. He'd prefer to point, not back, but that's the stuff many good bird dogs are made of.

His bracemate is a pointer. A meat dog with no need for show. Just a bib-overall type, putting in his eight hours, waiting for the whistle to blow so he can go in the crate at the back of the wagon and another pointer can be released to race with Ely.

But what's this? The scout has his hat held high and the long, mellow cry comes across the plowed soybean field, "Point . . .

halooooooo. . . ." The two mules named Kate (that's right, both mules with the same name – regardless of sex – so there's never any confusion over the orders from the driver) head languidly toward the birds. I cozy to the creak of the wagon, the muffled pad of the mules' hooves, the puffs of dust rising about the wagon, the gentle rocking of the seat – and wonder if we were all that blessed when Henry Ford finally decided to go into business. The twentieth century has been that way: the car took away our legs, the microwave our cooking, the TV our conversation, the jet plane our contact with guys along the road.

When we arrive, Ely has catwalked on honor. He's now the pointing dog and the pointer who found the birds is backing. But who's to say the birds haven't walked and the dogs merely kept contact and switched their relative positions?

I drop from the wagon and young Harbert hands me a Franchi over/under 12 gauge, and the gun feels good, fits the hand, is balanced to both carry and point. I walk to Ely and around front, acknowledging his point, then look for quail.

They are there, one standing alert – like a pintail drake caught on a mud bank – his head high, long-necked, fierce-eyed. I look for others. There's another, sitting as though she were on a nest.

Now the sentinel twirls, he's going to lift. "BDBDBDBDBDBD . . ." go his wings. *That noise!* Like a chainsaw hitting a nail in an Osage-orange fence post you thought you'd cut and burn for firewood.

The bird is beating south only to jerk right 30 degrees and head west – straight for the sun. I'm on him. *Bawoom*, goes the Franchi. There's a puff of feathers, and the bird drops its left leg. *Bawoom* goes the second tube. The little bird tumbles in mid-air and strikes the dusty field bouncing.

If it were important to me, I'd be ashamed. You know, if I had to shoot well. Like young Harbert . . . he'd never require two tubes for a pen-raised quail. But then he shoots every day. I wonder if he ever hears that clapping rise? But crack shooting is no longer important to me. I want the bird simply to honor the dog's point and to eat quail for supper.

So I did all right. But not classic. Not like you would want to do. Not you. Where the pressure's on and your friend is rattling you and he's already run five birds with one tube each. I know. I remember the quests and passions of youth. But my purpose now is to keep tuned for bird season. To be credible, not incredible, in harvest. And a shooting preserve lets me maintain that advantage. It will do the same for you.

Oh, you'll hear critics: "A shootin' preserve!" they'll scoff. "I can't believe it . . . you going out there to shoot birds off tree limbs?"

Pen-Raised Birds

Yes, some pen-raised birds do stay domestic. Yes, they do sit on tree limbs. Yes, they do walk on bare ground. Yes, you can pot-shot a barrelful if you've a mind to. But not if they've been seasoned in a tall flight pen. That's the secret. Loft. Where the birds get height. We've just discovered this. No more long flight pens. Instead, tall ones. This helps many things: it gives you a towering bird to duplicate the wild, plus it keeps the pen-raised bird from skimming the grass and possibly pulling your dog into target. And by leaving the birds in the exposed flight pen long enough they oil their feathers: they become ready for the wild. That's the new age of pen-raised birds.

But I forgot to tell you about Ely. He's broken point – a good bird dog doesn't have to be steady to shot and wing – and he's got the bird in his mouth and is heading for young Harbert. I don't think Ely hands up the birds so much as he flips it – like a second baseman beginning a double play. And Ely's on his way, out of the lespedeza, out to the bare ground, off to a row of honeysuckle that arcs across the land: and the bird's not yet in Harbert's pocket.

Ely will be in birds before we get seated in the wagon and the two mules named Kate get a nudge from Fred Walker, our driver, and we clomp along our way – as Fred picks the quail and feathers waft back over us. Then Fred drops the plucked dark-pink body to the footboard.

When the elder Harbert rides close to the mule wagon I tell him how much I admire Ely. He says, "I wouldn't take three dollars for that Brittany."

And I tell him, "Well, that shoots Wilson down . . . he was going to offer you two-fifty."

Harbert says, "That dog's something else. You can put him in your house, and I believe he would bust before he wet the floor. And he likes to be bathed in the tub, and he wants the water to come up on his legs, and he'll pick up a foot and hand it to you, turn his head around to the side for you, and never shake on you. I even put him in the double sink in the kitchen and use the spray thing on him.

"But he does have one problem," admits Harbert. "He should honor a flying bird and not go chasing them. His motto is, 'if that bird can fly ten miles then I can run fifty.'"

The sun sets yonder now, still coming brilliant – all awash with that orange Mom used to put in margarine back when you had to mix it – and the bleached wood of the tenant shacks scattered about the place seems to glow, and an old dead snag oak . . . out there in the pond . . . is the color of hammered lead.

Now the wagon makes those sounds of abandoned windmills . . .

Game preserve hunters seen by camera over mules' backs. There's no better way to prepare for hunting season than shooting a game preserve.

the squeak of metal, the cadence of rusted sucking rod, the haunting rhythm of its going, and Ely pops into a ditch, turns in mid-air, and lands on point. Young Harbert yells to him, "Ely . . . we're out of shells." But Ely won't accept this ruse. "Get on in here and do something," his stone face demands.

So young Harbert dismounts and enters the ditch to grab hold Ely's collar and walk him – protesting – to the wagon. When we get back to the old farm house we'll sit about the great table in the liar's room . . . with cheese and crackers and apples and each man to his own drink. And we'll laugh. And Wilson Dunn will say, "I've got to get me a hand trap and start practicing."

And I will encourage him.

But I'll be thinking of Ely and his nonstop quest for feather. And two mules named Kate. And the glory of a west-Tennessee day. And thinking as well of harried and hurried men who'll enter the bird field come opening day to yell at their dogs, and run all puffing to get themselves over point (for they don't trust Pup to hold), and miss the birds when they flush, and curse, and yell at the dog, and stomp about and cry, "Why can't I ever have any luck? Why do I always get a no-good dog? Why does everybody else get the birds and I work just as hard and get none. . . ."

Well, I can't hear them. Their lamentations fall on deaf ears. There is a way. And it's not their way. Hunting quail is a year-round effort. A year-round enjoyment. The dog deserves this. And the man deserves this.

I've never known the Yankees to stop the ball game and go to the bleachers to find a relief pitcher. If you're going to play the game, you've got to play it all year long. To the dedicated sportsman, opening day merely means you go to a different field today than you did yesterday.

19

Hot Weather Precautions

IT'S CRISP-UP, COLOR-UP, stick-'em-up time in the weed patch. Fall is here. The grasses stiffen, turn gold and wine; the seeds poke whiskers into whatever passes by, hoping—like hippies used to hope—to be transported by their beards to a new life.

Early-bird hunters arrive at stands wearing Banlon, roll-on, and bug spray. No thermos of hot coffee now, it's lemonade they carry. And making their way, or sitting in the shade of a hedgerow, sweat saturates their eyebrows, streaks a line down their back, and sogs their socks.

So it is with early-season teal and dove hunts. The sport beckons, but the heat says, "Whew." And too often such outings end with the gun dog man saying, "I don't know what's wrong with Pup . . . last year he fetched everything I shot . . . but now he won't touch a bird."

The Hot Dog

Avoid such performance by learning to handle a hot dog. Rather, by learning how to handle a cool dog in hot weather. For that's the secret: never let the dog get hot in the first place.

Heading out of town with Pup in the back of the wagon, make sure he has plenty of ventilation. If you're traveling dirt roads and don't want dust in the car, then stow Pup in a kennel crate and toss in a block of ice.

When you get to the bird field, walk slowly to your stand—don't hurry—and force Pup to stay at heel all the way. If you let him tear about the place, sniffing as he wants, casting where he pleases, he'll be stepping on his tongue by the time you're ready to set up.

Once you've arrived at your stand, but before sitting down, give Pup a drink of cold water from *his* canteen (we learned how to do this earlier). Watering finished, tell Pup, "Sit . . . stay." Such commands are all part of basic yard training. Should Pup be afield without such a background, then tie him to your stool or put his leash under your foot—do whatever's necessary to keep him put.

Fifteen minutes after Pup's first drink, give him another. Then in another fifteen minutes, water him again. Keep Pup cool and he can fetch soft-feathered birds all day, but let him get hot and you'll never cool him down. I mean *never*. Once heated he'll start to pant, which will bring slime to his tongue; the slime will turn to paste, and Pup will not retrieve.

For this is the reason dogs refuse to fetch doves or early-season, loose-feathered ducks. The froth of their hot mouth sticks to the feathers, pulls them from the bird, and the dog chokes on them.

Canine saliva is just like glue. Try to pick a glob of it from the kennel floor—it just strings out! Soft feathers adhere to this saliva, and Pup fights to get rid of them. Yet keep the dog cool, keep his mouth water-slick, and he will fetch all day with no grudge.

Also, Pup must be in top physical shape. At least three times a week you've roaded him, right? All year long. And you've kept the weight off him. Kept him lean and hungry. And whenever possible, Pup's taken long swims—when it was too hot to run or road. And he did this in the wake of your boat: the one you were rowing. For you have no business in this heat if you're not in shape, too. Right? And you know this, so there's no need pursuing the matter.

Naturally, you're going to keep Pup in the shade while you hunt teal or dove. Even if you have to build a screen of camo mosquito netting. And on occasion you're going to let Pup go to water—if there's any around—and lie flat on his belly and lounge there, looking foxy and grateful. No, that tepid water isn't going to cool him off, but when he emerges and the water evaporates, he'll feel great: he'll be wearing a swamp cooler.

If there's no water, then carry the block of ice to where Pup will be lying; let it melt there and put Pup on the puddle.

When Pup does make a retrieve and delivers to hand, take the bird, lay it aside, and then dress Pup's muzzle with both hands, wiping away any grass or feathers that might be stuck.

Choking

Should Pup choke on debris, you'll have to decide if the object is in his esophagus or windpipe. Dick Royse, our Wichita, Kansas, vet, once had a guy show up at his clinic with a blue pointer. Yep, the lips were blue – the whole dog looked blue. The pup was choking to death. He'd accidentally swallowed a dove, and it was stuck in his esophagus. Doc was able to push the dove on into the pup's stomach with a probe and everything turned out well.

But what if feathers or straw or a small stick get stuck in Pup's windpipe? There's only one thing you can do. Lay Pup on his side and then come down hard with flat palms on his rib cage. With any luck, the thrust will aspirate the object up and out of Pup's mouth. If not, then get to a vet, fast.

Never try to reach into Pup's throat with your fingers. And don't spend too much time with artificial respiration: if something's stuck, it may refuse to budge.

But this doesn't mean you can't clear debris from Pup's mouth or about his lips. If Pup refuses to open his mouth, you can gain entry by pressing the jaws on each side with thumb and forefinger of one hand – press on the hinges below Pup's eyes. When the lower jaw drops, reach in and pull Pup's tongue to the side with your other hand and hold it there. Pup can't bite; he'd have to sever his tongue to get to you. Now you can clean his inner lips, under his tongue, and the top of his mouth.

Throughout the hunt, keep giving Pup fresh water to drink. Keep him prone. And keep him in the shade. All this will keep the froth from his mouth – will keep the mouth's saliva clear-water slick – so he can fetch featherless.

Remember, too, this is still snake season. If possible, have your dog snake-proofed. There are pros who'll do this for you. They take a defanged rattlesnake, put a remote-controlled shock collar on Pup, have you check-cord him to the snake, and when Pup sticks his nose out to smell, the pro hits the shock button. Never again will Pup go near a rattlesnake. And yes, this is the only time I'll ever put a shock collar on a gun dog. Not only will it save the dog's life, but yours too. For you see, each dog will have a unique reaction to meeting a future rattler, and you'll know what that is. The result? You'll know there's a snake there and avoid it.

Remember, too, always push the bird into Pup's mouth when taking the delivery to hand. Push and twist, never pull.

In all you do, monitor Pup for symptoms of heatstroke, which usually is characterized by rapid, heavy panting; raspy breathing; and acute oxygen deprivation. Heatstroke also can cause Pup to collapse (see the section on first aid).

Teaching Charge

All Pup's life, whenever he's jumped on you, he's been ordered to, "Get down." Which means for him to get away from you or to sit. But now we want him to lie flat in a day's heat. So we need another command beside, "Down," or, "Get down." Sheep dog trainers usually hiss at the dog, saying what sounds like, "Ssssss." That would be good in a duck blind—either floating or earthbound—for it would do away with the spoken word that could spook an incoming flight or a floating raft of ducks.

So let's "ssssss" the dog for a charge command. Or make up whatever command you like. Even say, "Charge." There's fun to be had when going to the blind with a recent acquaintance—you fein instant anger, throw an arm toward the man, and command the dog to, "Charge." The would-be victim gasps and turns to run as he sees the great, wooly beast slowly sink flat to earth.

I like to teach charge on a table. Tell the dog to sit, then pull his feet out to the front of him, breaking the dog down to lie on chest and legs. By using a table I don't have to stoop over.

Or, attach a leash to Pup and run it under your boot, letting it have free play in that void between your heel and sole. Tell Pup, "Ssssss," and pull the lead. Your boot acts as a pulley and Pup is pulled to earth. If he ends up like a praying mantis—with his rump to the sky—then reach over with your free hand and press him down by placing your extended thumb and index finger over his back in front of his hips.

Practice all this in your duck boat in the back yard. If Pup won't charge in the boat's bottom, you can both be dumped to sea.

Remember, Pup will always tell you what he's going to do before he does it. Watch his shoulders. They must move before he can lift his forebody. To short-circuit his thinking, say, "Ssssss." Or watch Pup's ears. He's heard something, the ears cock, and he's going to stand and see what it is. Break his thinking by saying, "Ssssss."

Matter of fact, warm water is the place to introduce Pup to all aspects of boating: boarding, riding, launching. It's amazing what dogs learn. Oh, the first time he may leap over the gunwale, causing the boat to shoot backward, and come down on the rail to smack his chest. But he won't do it again. And he'll learn to come to the exact side of the boat (the widest part) for you to help him board. You lean to the opposite side and reach across the boat to pull Pup aboard by the scruff of his neck, the two of you balancing each other as you go. Why the broadside of the boat? Well, some craft have two pointed ends.

If the craft is very stable (not a pirogue, e.g.), then Pup will learn to put both forepaws on the gunwale, and you can bring him aboard by pressing down on the back of his neck. As the head goes, so goes the body.

In the last analysis, gun dogs learn many things they're never taught. The great water dogs have water sense they seemingly come by on their own. Blessed are the duck hunters who have one. For if nothing else, these hunters can keep a sandwich dry.

20

It's Out There

WELL, IT'S DONE. We've trained Pup with intimacy, not intimidation. We've taken a raw pup and made him into an all-age gun dog with nothing more than a hank of rope, a swivel snap, leather collar, plastic fly swatter, bowline knot, check cord, power bar, training table, nerve hitch, a bunch of other stuff (heavy on the love), and a ton of birds. We have a dog working for us now out of affection, not fear. We've made a lifelong friend.

Like most of you, I have had a typical life. I've been honored and damned, loved and despised, rewarded and denied. There have been sad days, which are never remembered, and great days I'll never forget. Like graduating from school or getting discharged from the service or marrying my wife. But on the long pull, the everyday plugging it out that we all do, there has been nothing more exceptional in my life than going to field with a dog.

There's a strange peace in the bird field, yet at the same time an exultation. A hallelujah and a hush. A breathing and a breathlessness. There is that impetus to get over the next hill, yet a lingering. A hundred steps from your car and nothing you left behind fits. And everything you left behind becomes petty. Though it may be but scrub brush and gravel, still, you walk midst eternal truths. And eternal beauty. And that dog before you has more importance in the world than any one you ever met. He makes more sense, too. And it's his world you want so to enter. Funny, but you made him, took him and raised him, and trained him, and yet – you are not his equal now. That which you begot is more than you. More than you'll ever be. And you don't care if he knows it.

What you groomed through puppyhood now leads you through manhood.

Robert Frost, the poet, taught me the beauty of words. Van Gogh did the same with paint. Michelangelo did it with stone. I can still see his Pieta in that faint light of the Vatican. A hundred philosophers shaped my thinking on country and morality and man and life. But that dog! With one look back over his shoulder he can say more and be more than all those I've mentioned.

A Stranger in a Strange Land

I've never really cared for this century nor the way we live it. I was born too late. I've lived through the low point of man. Life today denies a man privileges, cramps his impulses, and casts him off on corrupt and asinine endeavors. Bill Berlat, to whom this book is dedicated, was for eight years an Arizona Superior Court Judge Pro Tem (juvenile division). He tells me that in a presentencing report the do-gooders at the court house hand judges it is noted whether the accused was breast-fed or not. By My Beloved Jesus Christ, who cares? Did the accused commit the crime or not? We're judging what he did now, not how he supped sixteen years before.

It's that way now. We are all so essentially beside the point. Like that rage this past Christmas where the "animal lovers" were picketing furriers. Yet an old trapper I know, who's spent his life in ice water up to his knees, tells me, "I never saw one of those protesters out here in the winter . . . checking things out." He further said, "I don't know how they can protest what they don't know."

Though we are no longer true to ourselves, and a majority of us no longer know what we're talking about, a day afield with a dog is – to me – a reaffirmation of sanity in an insane world, of beauty midst both squalor and horrid consumption, of meaningful and beautiful purpose when all about me the world's become crippled in thought and petty in pursuit. It may be concrete in the big cities jiggles men's brains loose.

Once, when I was a mighty young man, I failed to pass a saliva test – it was temporary madness – and ended up elected mayor of a rather large city. I'd sit there and listen to the protests, but no one ever submitted a program. I have tried to avoid that in this book. I have

The late John Bailey, greatest bird hunter the world will ever know, shares his noon sandwich with an English setter. John owned his own land, planted and raised his own feed plots and birds, and hunted every legal day. But his joy was the dogs who took him hunting. He and his wife are buried where his horses and dogs lay.

protested beating our dogs to death, but I've also outlined techniques through which you could love the dog to performance. And as for me – after my term ended, I went to the wilderness for the rest of my life.

The future of dog training is our finally understanding the phenomenon of scent and then the subsequent development of the scent collar. If not that, then we'll need to define and develop the nature of ESP in inter-dog and dog-to-human communications.

A Wish

Until then I wish you the scat of the bird, the crack of boot-snapped stubble, the sunrise and sunset, the nibbling of a candy bar beside a flowing stream, the damp earth seeping through your pants, your heels digging furrows, and the dog close to side, eyeing your candy bar, but still forgiving you if you don't share. And your excusing the squirrel his chatter as you thank God you're there.

I wish you that reaching out for a dog to thank. His waiting for you when you tire. His forbearance when you can't hit what he's found. His letting you have your way when you insist the bird fell over here, even though he knows it went over there. His patience in waiting for you to climb through the barbed wire fence. His ignoring you when you belch. His doting on you when you call him in, look into his eyes, and tell him he's a "good boy."

I hope you find all this with your pup.

It's out there.

Index

Page numbers in italics refer to photographs